Lady of the Sea

The Goddess Who Births the New Age

Lady of the Sea

The Goddess Who Births the New Age

Margie McArthur

McArthur Books
Santa Cruz, California

McArthur Books
Santa Cruz, CA, 95062

Copyright © 2004-2014 Margie McArthur, all rights reserved.
www.ladyofthesea.org www.faeryhealing.com
Cover Art by Cassandra Stewart. www.cassandrabeanland.com
Cover Design by Margie McArthur, Abigail McArthur-Jones, and Dream Dancer Design.
Interior Design by Dream Dancer Design. www.dreamdancerdesign.com
Printed in the U.S.A.

No part of this publication may be reproduced or transmitted in any form, or by any means, electric or mechanical, including photocopy, recording, or any information storage and retrieval system now known or to be invented, without permission in writing from the publisher and author, except by a reviewer who wishes to quote brief passages in connection with a review written for inclusion in a magazine, newspaper, or broadcast. Contact **McArthur Books**, faeryhealing@baymoon.com

Library of Congress Cataloging-in-Publication Data
McArthur, Margie
Lady of the Sea – The Goddess Who Births the New Age
ISBN 9780615987071

Also by Margie McArthur
WiccaCraft for Families: The Path of the Hearthfire, Phoenix Publishing, 1994
Wisdom of the Elements: Sacred Wheel of Earth, Water, Fire and Air, Crossing Press, 1998
Faery Healing: The Lore and the Legends, New Brighton Books, 2003

Contents

INTRODUCTION	xi
Mother Night	1
Chapter One - Mother Night	2
Chapter Two - The Starry Milk of the Mother	14
Chapter Three - The White Cow	18
Chapter Four - Mother Dana	28
Chapter Five - Morgen and the Sea Temple	32
Chapter Six - Out of Egypt	38
Chapter Seven - Asherah and Anath	48
Chapter Eight - The Birth of the Universe and the Changing of the Ages	60
Chapter Nine - The Goddess of the Sea and Stars in Our Times	74
Chapter Ten - The Lady Comes to Her Children	86
Chapter Eleven - The Miriam Tradition	102
Chapter Twelve - Medicine Dreams and the Age of Aquarius	114
Chapter Thirteen - The Future and the Art of Navigation	130
Chapter Fourteen - Elements and Temples	136
Chapter Fifteen - The Temple of the Moon, Sea, and Stars	148
Chapter Sixteen - At Work in the Sea Temple	154
Chapter Seventeen - The Themes of the Sea Temple	166
Chapter Eighteen - More Vision Journeys for Sea Temple Work	190
BIBLIOGRAPHY	209
APPENDICES	212
INDEX	222

ACKNOWLEDGMENTS

The work of every author is aided and abetted by other people. I would like to acknowledge some of the many people whose influence, presence in my life, or whose writings have in some way aided me in the writing of this book.

My family – especially David, Nicholas, Abigail, my sweet and supportive sisters, Dodie and Monica, and last but not least, my ancestors.

Dear friends – Josephine McCarthy, Mika and Ishana Ingerman, and especially Gabrielle Laney-Andrews.

Danny & Sara's Rosary Group circa 2002, Resurrection Catholic Community.

Don Cerow – www.athenasweb.com

Tau Rosamonde Miller – www.gnosticsanctuary.org

The Goddess Christians egroup – http://groups.yahoo.com/group/goddesschristians/?yguid=77380035

To these and to many unnamed others I offer my deep thanks and appreciation.

INTRODUCTION

The first thing I want to say in this Introduction is that while this book cites many other works and authors, the thoughts and opinions expressed in it are strictly my own, informed by my research, inspiration, and intuition.

This is a book about the Goddess. It started out being a book about a particular aspect of the Goddess, one which I feel coming into prominence at this moment in time. But it ended up wanting to talk about much more than that. It ended up wanting to speak of many manifestations of the Goddess—the Divine Feminine—her influence on our development as a species, our relationship to her through the ages, and her re-emergence and return to us now as evidenced by dreams, visions, prophecies, and earth changes. It spoke to me, of course, in a language I could understand, that of western culture rather than eastern. And in the end, it did actually get back to the particular aspect about which I had originally felt so impelled to write.

The Goddess is many things. She is the Mother of Form, and as such, is connected to both life and death. We are born from the Spirit World into this wonderful world of Form, and the Goddess is involved and present with us every step of the way. In the end, we die to this world to be reborn into the Spirit World, and she is with us in this as well. She is the creator but she is also the destroyer, because form is finite and she is the Mother of Form: She is the womb and she is the tomb.

The book is organized so that the Inner Work is near the end of the book. I think it's best to read through the book first and savor its contents; to really think about it. Then go back through the book and begin doing the practical work. After working through all the vision journeys, you will probably find some aspect of the work in which you feel called to service. For this book is really about priest/esshood; make no mistake about that—and the path of the priest/esshood is one of service to all beings.

Service is much needed now, as we stand on this cusp, this evolutionary threshold. It is time for the priests and priestesses living in this era to wake up to their vocation….to step forward and be of service.

For this work, in this time, we were born…

Mother Night

*Just as all life on Planet Earth was birthed from Mother Ocean,
So all life in the universe was birthed by the Great Cosmic Mother
Whom we know as the vast dark sea of deep space.
She is the Darkness that gave birth to the Light.
She is the No-Thing which is full of the potential of All Things
Of old she was known by many names:
Dame Night, Dame Dark, Dame Nox,
Dame Hell, Dame Wisdom
Mother Night, Mother Darkness,
Old Fate, Old Veiled One, Old Night,
Nyx*

*She is SHE -
The Great One, Darkness.
And from her emerged HE – the Limitless Light.*

*From their dance of love
Came forth the Many Other Lights -
Elements, Stars, Planets,
Mountains, Plains, Oceans,
Trees, Plants, Animals...*

*She is the Mother, the feminine aspect of divinity.
The one who conceives, gestates, births, nourishes,
And ultimately, takes life back into herself.*

*She is the Birther and yet also the Destroyer.
Queen of Life, Queen of Death,
Queen of Day, Queen of Night
The Great Mother of All*

Chapter One - Mother Night

In the beginning was the Darkness. Limitless Darkness. She was vast and full of potential. No empty darkness here, but rather, fullness, unexpressed. She brooded, like the vast sky over the vast sea. Over time she began to feel, and what she felt was a longing, a pulling, a movement. And as she noticed this, became aware of it, it pulled away from her. It moved outward and came into manifestation as another. It was He, her other self, her Divine Twin.

This first movement of energy, this longing, pulling, as well as her awareness of it, constitute the first manifestation—the Other, the He—coming into being. Light, Limitless Light—the Bright One—born from the Vastness of Dame Dark, the primeval and ever-veiled Chaos or field of possibilities.

As He came into being they became aware of each other, and a longing for reunion occurred. They merged—as separate beings—making love. Their lovemaking created huge waves of energy, from which all life was eventually sparked into being.

Their first children were the clouds of great, beautiful magellanic stardust. These stardust clouds spun and danced with the joy of life—swirling, glowing, spiraling—finally coalescing into Stars Beings. These Star Beings often clustered together in great star-swirls called galaxies, and sometimes many galaxies clustered together as families. The stardust and Star Beings also gave birth: to comets, to solar systems, to planets—including our own dear planet—and other celestial beings.

Some of these Star Beings had special tasks given them by Dame Dark and her consort, the Bright One. These particular Star Beings are those we now sometimes refer to as Angels and Archangels—terms which mean messengers and high messengers. They were messengers because by performing the specific creation tasks assigned to them—in the language of light, sound, and structure—they were carrying forth the message of the Divine Parents. Some call these beings the Lords of Flame and the Lords of Form, though they were, of course, beyond gender, containing both. So perhaps we should call them the Lords and Ladies of Flame and Form. Or perhaps, we should just call them *angels*.

Angels go by many names and have many very specific jobs. It is said that there were several whose particular job was to assist in humankind's evolution into beings who possessed the fire of mind. These angels have, in legend, been referred to by many different names, among them the Watchers, the Grigori, the Sons of God, and the Annunaki, a Sumerian/Babylonian word whose roots mean "heaven and earth."

But...from the One came the Two...and from the Two, the Many. From Dame Dark came the Bright One, the Light—and then, all other manifestations of life.

Our star, the Sun, gave birth to our planet, our planetary system, and all life within it. Reaching out, its long arms streaming forth light and energy, it enveloped and embraced our planet Earth, its star-sparkling arms of light flashing streaks and streams of lightning within Earth's aura/atmosphere. And in a twinkling of stellar time, the body of the Earth responded to this embrace. Microscopic life forms were sparkled into being as beams of starfire touched the Earth's surface and reached down deeply into the heart of the planet. Earth's starry core responded to this touch, reaching upward in mutual embrace.

* * *

Life is everywhere in the universe. Beings floated to Earth on comet tails, they came in on the space winds, on the solar winds. The star-children, tiny living beings of all kinds—water vapors, gaseous vapors, star-sparks—speeding through space in their tiny arks of metallic ore, vapor, and stardust. They met and mingled with the tiny beings which had arisen on and in the Earth. They joined, and became one family.

From the dance of the elements and the streaming of stars came forth many creatures on the Earth, including, eventually, humanity. And humanity, knowing that all life is born from a mother, recognized both Earth and Sky as Mother. And in the night sky's thick band of stars, many saw the nourishing milk of the Sky mother, who is also the Star Mother—the Mother of the Stars—and so it became known as the Milky Way.

* * *

The Oldest Story

The story is told 'round the world and with characters of different names. But the story is remarkably similar in all the places it is told.

We came from the sky—the great vast sky. We came from the depths of space down to this planet we call Earth; from the Otherworld into this one. We came from the No Thing into the Some Thing. Beams of starlight from the vast darkness of space, we came falling from the darkness into the light, from non-being into being, from the sky to the Earth.

There are many versions of this story, many shapes that it takes. The details may differ but the basic story is the same. No matter how strong our love and bond to Mother Earth, the mysterious and beautiful starry night sky is also our home. We gaze up to it in admiration and longing. We make up stories about it, set our heroes and heroines in it, imagine it to be our true home—the place to which we will go after we die.[1]

This great longing for our true origin and home, for the place of beginnings, is, in actuality, a longing for our own source—our God/dess, our Mother-Father, our Divine Source.

The divine energies are androgynous until they polarize in the process of manifestation. For the last two thousand years humanity has had plenty of interaction with God the Father, but not nearly so much with Goddess the Mother. So we begin here our story of the *Mother* of the Universe, the Goddess of Sea and Stars, who, in her most primal form is Mother Night.

The Dark Mother

Who is this Great Dark Mother from whom all else is born?

In ancient Egypt, the vastness of sky was seen as the star-covered body of the Goddess Nuit arching protectively over her husband, Geb, who was the earth. She was the darkness of night, and the stars were born from her body and adorned her gown of sky. Each night she swallowed the sun and each morning gave birth to him again.

Or perhaps she was Neith—great creator goddess who birthed Ra, the sun, from the watery primeval vastness of Nun, and then wove the world into being.

Nun, the great primeval watery abyss itself, was depicted as having both female (Naunet/Nunet) and male (Nu/Nun) aspects, and from Nun arose the Ogdoad—the eight primal forces of creation personified as deities.[2] Mut, whose very name means "mother," was a title sometimes used for Naunet/Nu, she who later was perceived a deity in her own right.

In ancient Greece the primordial Sea of Nothingness was called Chaos. From Chaos arose Nyx–the goddess and embodiment of the darkness of night, and Erebus–the god and embodiment of the darkness of the Underworld. From these two came forth Brightness of both sky and day, and many other offspring as well—the rest of creation. From Chaos (the nothingness which is full of everything) comes Cosmos—the disorganized "everything" now woven into harmonious, well ordered form. The act of creation was seen as organizing and structuring the primal Chaos, bringing it into a useful order.

In ancient India she was called Aditi, which means unfettered, limitless, boundless, and she was goddess of the unlimited vastness of space. She was the mother of Agni, god of fire, the sun god Mitra, and Varuna, the god in charge of celestial order and lord of the sea. Aditi was also mother of the twelve Adityas, divine beings who were connected with the months of the year—thus bringing in the element of measurement, or Time. Aditi was sometimes depicted as a cow. Cows were, of course, highly important in India, signifying nourishment and wealth in a very real way. This reference to Aditi as a cow is important and we will return to it later.

In Norse mythology the great void was known as Ginnugagap (which means "gaping gap," or "seeming emptiness") and the first being to emerge was the primeval cow mother, Audumla, whose milk nourished the first of the giants, Ymir, from whose body the rest of the world was eventually constructed.

Mother Ocean

The earthly equivalent of the Great Sea of Space is the watery deep of the sea which covers the great majority of our planet's surface. It is Mother Ocean who is the source of all life and all beings on this planet. Fertilized by the divine fires of sun, lightning, and volcanic magma, life came forth from her great watery womb; it grew, transformed, evolved, and after aeons, found its way ashore. Life, in all its complexity, is born of Mother Ocean's bounty, and carries within it the Star Ancestry of the planet.

That is important to remember. We are children of both earth and sky, and both fire and water. All life comes from the stars of the great sea of space. In a very real way, "we are all made of stardust."

In his seminal work, *The Lost Language of Symbolism*, Harold Bayley tells us that the "conception of the Sea as the Great Mother of all creation is common to ancient cosmogonies. Whether this universal belief arose because physical life was known to have originated in water, or whether the sea was symbolically employed because of innumerable analogies between Water and Wisdom, is a point that it would be futile to discuss: it cannot, however, be questioned that from the remotest ages the Spirit of Truth or Wisdom has been typified by Water and the Sea."[3]

Goddesses and Gods of the sea are found in many cultures, and the great watery abyss is found in many creation stories.

In the early Sumerian culture it was Nammu, the primeval sea, who was the Primal Mother of all, giving birth to heaven, earth, and the first gods. In the later Babylonian, Akkadian and Assyrian traditions of Mesopotamia, Tiamat was the Primordial Sea Mother Goddess who, through mingling her salt waters with the sweet waters of her mate Apsu (the abyss), brought forth the earliest and most chaotic form of the world. Their early intermingling then separation brought forth Mummu, the mist between the waters above and the waters below. The legends tell us that Tiamat's grandson, Marduk, battled with her and killed her, creating the earth from the parts of her body—a form of a mythological motif that speaks of the "pieces" of creation arising from the breaking apart of an original wholeness.

There are echoes of Tiamat in the Hebrew creation story found in Genesis, which begins with the primordial waters of "the Deep" over which the Ruach Elohim, or spirit/breath of God, moved to initiate the process of creation. The Hebrew word for this watery Deep is Tehom, which is etymologically related to the Babylonian word Tiamat and means the same thing—the deep watery abyss, the original sea of chaos. And just as Marduk in killing Tiamat created the earth from her body parts—bringing order out of chaos—so did the unnamed Hebrew God (although elohim is plural, so the word gods might be more accurate) begin "his" creation of the world by dividing the waters to create sea and sky. The Bible says, "He separated the waters that were above from the waters that were below." The breath of God, the Ruach Elohim, seems roughly equivalent to Mummu of the Babylonian tale. [4]

According to Homer, in ancient Greece Tethys and her husband Oceanos were the elder deities of the ancient primal sea. He was the ocean that encircled earth's lands, and she was the fertile surface waters of the ocean, and, as well, the deep, Underworld waters that flowed upward to become rivers and springs. Their many children were the rivers, streams and springs of the world known to the Greeks. Tethys and Oceanos might be the same deities as the two known as Thalassa, whose name means fish mother, and Pontus, whose name means deep (i.e. very dark) sea. [5]

Domnu was the mother goddess of the Fomorians in the Ireland of long-ago, and goddess, as well, of the great deep sea. Her name means Deep Sea or Abyss. Her counterpart in Wales was the mysterious Don, mother of the Gods–a dim and shadowy figure about whom not much is revealed in the old writings. The constellation known to us as Cassiopeia was the Llys Don, or "Court of Don" in early Welsh lore; the constellation being her royal court and starry abode. It is thought that Don may be the same Goddess that both the Insular and Continental Celts knew as Dana, Danu, Ana, and Anu. Dana will be further discussed in a later chapter.

In African-based spiritual traditions the goddess of the sea is Yemaya, (also spelled Yemoja, Yemonja, Yemanya, Iemonja). She is still widely loved, revered, and honored today in areas influenced by African culture and spirituality. She is considered a very motherly type of goddess. Indeed, her name, similar to the Greek Thalassa, means "Mother Whose Children are the Fish," implying that she is a fertile and bountiful mother whose children are as numerous as the fish in the sea, and perhaps also reminding us that all life on earth came from the sea. She is considered to be the source of all the waters, including the rivers. Like the Egyptian goddess Isis, she assists fishermen, grants safe passage on the sea, protects mothers and children, and is linked with the moon. Her male counterpart is Olokun, who rules the treasures of the deep.

Earth's Dark Goddess

The Great Dark Mother from which all is birthed has purely terrestrial aspects as well as celestial and oceanic ones. The Dark Goddess is found on earth as well as in the sky, and *within* the earth as well.

In her earthly aspect she is referred to as the Dark Goddess, the Black Goddess and/or the Underworld [6] Goddess. Thus, her earthly, dark, Underworld Goddess form is inextricably linked with her celestial and oceanic ones—linking the starry abyss, the seas, caves, and even the dark meteoric stones that occasionally fall to earth.

In the Underworld she is the Dark Goddess of death and rebirth, of destruction and regeneration. She weaves the fate of all beings. She—sometimes wearing her guise of the Three Norns or Fates—weaves life then unravels it, only to weave it yet again in new forms, using threads both old and new. She is Life and Death. She is the wisdom found in darkness and silence. She is the tomb that receives the dead, as well as the dark womb of the earth, which cradles and nourishes the seed.

In all of this, she is the darkness who gives birth to the light, the primal state of No Thing from which All Things arise.

The Vast and the Vessel - A Mystery of the Goddess

The primary difference between the Dark Goddess of the great vastness of space and the Dark Goddess in the earth is the issue of vast openness versus seeming confinement. Dame Night is the vast, dark, limitless expanse of the heavens who creates and populates the universe, while her earthly counterpart represents similar energies *within* the planet. In addition to the life-giving cauldron of the ocean's waters, life seems to spring forth from the powers within the planet, and ancient humanity thought of the Underworld as not just a dwelling place of the dead, but also as a source of regeneration and life—a vast watery cauldron itself, essentially. There are, in fact, tales and legends which refer to vessels and cauldrons originating in the Underworld and full of the stuff of life—sustenance and regeneration—an abundance of the powers of life and death, powers and treasures that accompanied these cauldrons when they were brought up to our earthly realm.

Interestingly, the realm of the Dark Goddess of the Earth is frequently depicted as defined space—caves, caverns, cauldrons, cubes, containers. This is what happens when unlimited "space" falls into manifestation, into form. For there to be space, it must now be defined, boundaried, circumscribed. It is still "space," but now a hollow—a defined but receptive space, to be acted upon and filled with something, perhaps a new manifestation or form.

As that first movement sparked into being in the Void of infinite potentialities—Limitless Space—a spinning began, a spinning that spiraled outward as it moved around its center axis, creating depth and dimension in the figure of a torus—a round, donut-shaped form that continued to evolve and enlarge. Tori are "containers." Scientists now speculate the universe may be toroid in shape. It is certain that the recently-discovered axis of the universe [7] and earth's electromagnetic grid are toroidal in shape, as are the electromagnetic fields of the black holes, the human aura, and the energy field of the human heart. Therefore, as both Limitless Space and Limitless Light begin to manifest into form, they become Limited Space and Limited Light. That is the nature of physically manifest reality on this plane of being, and is how the Vast becomes a Vessel.

As manifestation/limitation occurs, the energies descend down the planes of existence, shaping the physical world—creating worlds, realities, and orders of beings on their descent into the final physical form of being.

The Dark Goddess

This androgynous God/dess of the depths of earth has been called by many names. Widely venerated in the Germanic lands she was the goddess known as Hella/Holle/Holda/Hulda, goddess of the Underworld—the land of spirits and death. All variations of this name come from the proto-IndoEuropean root word *Kel"* or *Kolyo*, which means "covered" or "the veiled one." [8] In this veiling she is similar to the Celtic goddess referred to as the Cailleach, the "Old Veiled One."

The word "Kolyo" is related to the Hindu Kali; the word "Cailleach" may be as well. [9]

The Egyptian goddess Isis is referred to as being veiled. An inscription in her temple at Sais read: "I am that which is, which hath been, and which shall be; and no man has ever lifted the veil that hides my Divinity from mortal eyes." This is reminiscent of the Hindu goddess (and concept of) Maya, whose name also has to do with the "veil of illusion" which covers and conceals a greater reality.

The Hindu word Maya actually means "illusion." The word can refer, on one level, to a confusing, deceptive, and negative form of illusion. But on another level, it's possible that a deeper meaning is that of the illusion of matter that covers the spiritual reality of pure formless beingness. As such, Maya would not be a negative term in and of itself, but rather, would refer to that which prevents us from seeing something in its complete and true reality.

It is interesting to find references to these goddesses who were referred to as *The Veiled One*. Whenever we see reference to an archaic, mysterious, veiled goddess, we may suspect we are looking at some form of the Primal Goddess, who usually has a terrifying aspect of some kind, and often has both terrifying and beneficent aspects. [10]

Mother Holda

The Teutonic goddess known as Holle/Holda was the goddess within the earth, and yet she was also the goddess beyond the earth—the great Dark Mother who was the source of all things, though a distinction was not always made between these two realms of within and beyond. Holda's runic symbol, Hagall, was the hexagonal snowflake shape, the points of which indicated the four directions/elements, and the above and below. Mother Holle's lore shows her to be associated with winter and snow. As her story tells us, when she shook her featherbed it caused the snow to fly on the earth. But she is also associated with life and growth. She possessed an oven and an apple orchard—both indications of her powers of creation, life, and death. [11] Her association with the

Underworld is shown by the fact that access to her realm was gained by falling down a well.

Teutonic lore associates Holle/Holda with the elder tree, whose German name, *holdre,* means "hollow." Elder was thought to be a powerfully magical tree and home to the Elder Mother, whose permission must be asked before cutting the tree for use. Magically, the wood was used as protection against evil sorcery and magic, and to drive away evil spirits. While the "hollow" meaning is thought to refer to the easily removable inner pith of the tree's branches that allowed it to be used for pipes and whistles, the name is also an interesting reflection of the veiled and "hollow space" nature of the goddess associated with the tree.

Baba Yaga

Baba Yaga is a similarly primal Russian Goddess. Fierce and terrifying, she was said to live deep in a dark forest. Her round hut was made of body parts and had bird feet. Like the earth and the night sky, the hut turned around and around. A fence surrounded her home, a fence made of bones and skulls. Baba Yaga flew about in a mortar and pestle, sweeping her tracks away with her birch broom. She was a spinner and a weaver and had power over sun and moon, both of which seem to rise and set from her hut. But the central feature of Baba Yaga's hut was her stove, or pech, whose fire both created and consumed, clearly representative of the power that governs both life and death—a power that perhaps we may name *wisdom*.

To Baba Yaga's hut, the stories tell us, came the young maiden Vasilisa. Because the fire in her family's hearth had gone out, Vasilisa had been sent to fetch fire from Baba Yaga's stove. But just as in the Mother Holda story where the good daughter had to work for Mother Holda before she was sent back to middle earth showered with gold, Baba Yaga made Vasilisa work hard to earn this gift of fire. [12]

Kybele

It is thought that Baba Yaga's origins lie in the ancient goddess Kubaba, who was later known as the Anatolian Kybele and the Greek Cybele. She may be the oldest known named goddess, preceding even those of Egypt and Sumeria, though her name is found in the 4500 year old "Sumerian King List" as the only female monarch listed. Her true origins are lost in the mists of time and Middle Eastern history, but her worship spread far and wide.

There was a sacred black stone, said to be meteoric in origin, associated with her worship at her cult center of Pessinos, in Phrygia (modern day west-central Turkey). This stone was taken to Rome in 200 BC on the advice of Rome's Sibylline oracles, in order to bring the Great Mother's protection to that city. Once there her cult grew, as it merged with the preexisting cults of the Greek Mother Goddess, Rhea.

It is thought that her name, which is said to mean hollow vessel, cave, and/or cube, is cognate with Kaaba—the sacred cube-shaped building at Mecca, the holy center of Islam. The Kaaba is said to have been built by Adam and later restored by Abraham. In pre-Islamic times the Kaaba was surrounded by 360 "idols" and was clearly a site of worship.

Within the outer wall of the Kaaba rests the *Hajar al-Aswad*, the sacred black meteoric stone, similar to other black meteoric stones found in the Middle East. Black meteoric stones were often used to represent the divine or deity, particularly the Goddess, and it is very likely that the black stone at the Kaaba is one of these. This understanding of the stone is obviously not found in Islamic belief, but the Kaaba and the stone predate Islam. [13] Both the blackness and the stellar origin of the stones link them with the Great Dark Sky Mother who birthed the Cosmos. About 65 feet east of the Kaaba lies the famous well of Zamzam, which was said to have provided water to Abraham's concubine Hagar and their son Ishmael.

The Sacred Shapes of Life

Esoterically, the cube shape is often used as a symbol for the earth. When unfolded, a cube becomes a cross—the "cross of matter," that is, the material realm with its center and four directions and elements. Because it represents the material realm, the cube may be seen as the receptive, feminine aspect of the Divine, that of *form*. Thus, the cube represents the Goddess, who unfolds herself simultaneously into the four directions that define space, and the four primal elements—air, fire, water, and earth—of which the material world is composed.

Energy, as pure force, may be seen as the active, masculine aspect. It is sometimes depicted as a straight line, though it can also be depicted as an S-shape, or spiral. The spiral is another very significant shape. The spiral represents movement, including that first movement of energy coming forth from the Void. Spirals are not flat, except in one-dimensional drawings; rather, they have dimension and depth. The spiral moves in a corkscrew fashion (see torus, above) and has been mythologically symbolized as a whirlpool, a serpent, and a whirlwind.

Kabbalah and the Veils

Another way of explaining this Divine Feminine Source power comes from the Kabbalistic concept of the *Ain Soph*. What does this Kabbalistic concept mean? It is the great veiled Void that exists beyond/prior to manifestation. In Hermetic Kabbalistic thought this Void is considered to have three veils; they are called the Three Veils of Negative Existence—the Ain, the Ain Soph, and the Ain Soph Aur. These are beyond manifestation and therefore beyond description, but their action has been imagined, and it results in the first manifestation—Kether, the Crown.

The movement of these veils toward the manifestation of Kether has been poetically described in the first verses of Genesis:

> *And the Earth was void and without form, and darkness was upon the face of the deep. And the Spirit of God moved upon the face of the waters. And God said, "Let there be light," and there was light. And God saw the light that it was good; and God divided the light from the darkness. And God called the light Day and the darkness he called Night.*

Kabbalistic scholar Gareth Knight suggests that the dark Void can be equated with Ain, or Nothingness. He suggests that the Spirit of God moving upon the face of the waters can be equated with *Ain Soph*, the Limitless; and the light created by this divine movement as the Ain Soph Aur, or "Limitless Light." (14)

Dame Dark/Darkness/the Void, then, is seen to be the state of Ain, or Nothingness, in which movement—the Ain Soph—arises, and which, through the agency of the movement of Spirit, eventually gives birth to Light—the *Ain Soph Aur*.

But before the Light is the Dark, which holds within it, or veils, the potential for the light and life that are to follow.

What Science Says

Science refers to a unitary field that connects and unites all matter. Upon reception of the Nobel Prize for Physics in 1919, physicist Max Planck said, "...All matter originates and exists only by virtue of a force which brings the particle of an atom to vibration and holds this most minute solar system of the atom together. *We must assume behind this force the existence of a conscious and intelligent mind*. This mind is the matrix of all matter." *(italics mine)* (15)

This field was generated at the moment of the Big Bang, or whatever event originated the universe. From a spiritual perspective, this conscious field itself is the Mother of Form, whom I will call Mari (i.e. Mary), from mare, the Latin word for "sea." The matrix/mind behind it is also Mari in her form of the Great Conscious Void—both unmanifest and manifest reality. Form was birthed by the Mother at the moment of the Big Bang. Mari/Mary is the force field of energy whose web gives structure and form to the universe. This matrix is perceived by magical workers as both Mother and Web of Life.

It is said that this matrix is all pervasive throughout the universe. It is like a vessel—a cauldron made of etheric-webbing, perhaps—which holds all material form; it contains, connects and unites all parts of the universe. It is the web on which the material universe is woven, and we, being part of the universe, are all part of this web; we live *on* the web as well as *in* the web. Because it is an all-encompassing field, it is also the bridge between the outer realities and our inner ones. (16)

So it would seem that science has finally found its way to what spiritual traditions have been, in essence, teaching us for many years: we are all connected, we are all related.

Notes:

1) As an ancient initiation ritual from the Orphic Mysteries states, "I am a child of earth and starry heaven but my race is of heaven alone."

2) The Ogdoad deities date from the Old Kingdom, Egypt's 3rd-6th dynasties (circa 2686 - 2134 BC), and are four male-female balanced pairs—Naunet and Nu (primordial waters), Amaunet and Amun (air and invisibility), Kauket and Kuk (darkness), Hauhet and Huh (infinite space, infinity, eternity).
http://en.wikipedia.org/wiki/Ogdoad

3) Bayley, Harold; *The Lost Language of Symbolism*, Dover Publications, Inc., NY, 2006, p 197; Williams & Norgate, London, 1912

4) It should be noted that the *Ruach Elohim* is also referred to as the *Ruach HaKodesh*, a term that also is used to refer to the Holy Spirit. *Ruach* is a feminine word and *Elohim* is masculine but with a feminine plural ending.

5) It should be remembered that these stories were based on the prevailing myths of both the authors' locale and whatever knowledge the author may have had of the wider world. Thus the word "sea" often meant a large local body of water and/or the Mediterranean Sea, rather than the Atlantic Ocean.

6) See Appendix D for an explanation of Underworld, Middleworld and Upperworld.

7) www.news.ku.edu/1997/97N/AprNews/Apr17/ralston.html
physicsworld.com/cws/article/news/2011/jul/25/was-the-universe-born-spinning

8) Jackson, Nigel A., *Call of the Horned Piper*, p 18; also, *Arcade Dictionary of Word Origins*.

9) The Hindu word Kali means "time." The rather fierce Hindu goddess Kali is a goddess of death, among other things, because time consumes all things, bringing them to their ultimate end—death. The Irish word Cailleach means "old woman," the adjective "old" implying a state near in time to death. But cailleach is also used to refer to veiled women (such as nuns, though not all nuns are elderly), because it is related to the word caille, which means "veil." Thus the link between Kolyo, Kali, and Cailleach is through both the veil and time. A veil "covers and conceals," just as the earth covers and conceals the bodies of the dead after time/death has consumed them.

10) When we speak of dark and light we are actually speaking of the Divine Progenitor prior to it polarizing into gender. But I use the term Goddess to describe the birth-giving function, and the term God to describe both the energy which engenders life and the "child" that it engenders. There have been cultures that have ascribed their beginnings to a Mother Goddess, and those who have ascribed their beginnings to a Father God. Some cultures see the Earth & Moon as Feminine and the Sun as Masculine, while others see the Earth as Masculine and the Sky as Feminine. Often this depends on which divine function is defined as primary.

11) The story of Mother Holle is found here: www.sacred-texts.com/neu/grimm/ht11.htm

12) An echo of what must have been a tale of initiation, in which the young innocent seeker is sent to the Underworld to see the Primal or Dark Goddess to earn the gift of renewed life.

13) Ancient Arabians worshipped three major goddesses— Al Manat, goddess of fate, or time; Allat, who was the mother of the gods and called "The Lady," and Al Uzzah, who was associated with the planet Venus and was most likely the same deity as Allat. Prior to Islam, the Kaaba, with its 360 idols, was a pagan shrine, and it is likely that Allah (whose name means "the god") , who was the principal god of Mecca, was one of the many gods worshipped there. Later in time the three goddesses were said to have been the daughters of Allah.

14) Knight, Gareth; *Practical Guide to Qabalistic Symbolism*, Red Wheel/Weiser LLC, Boston, MA, 2001

15) Planke, Max; "Das Wesen der Materie" (The Nature of Matter), speech at Florence, Italy, 1944 (from Archiv zur Geschichte der Max-Planck-Gesellschaft, Abt. Va, Rep. 11 Planck, Nr. 1797)

16) Braden, Gregg; *The Divine Matrix*, Hay House, Inc, 2007.

Chapter Two - The Starry Milk of the Mother

The Milky Way

The most prominent feature in the dark skies of night is the river of stars we call the Milky Way. It is our home galaxy; our sun is a member of this particular cluster of stars. As it flows from Northeast to Southwest across our night sky, the Milky Way looks very much like a river—a white river against the cobalt darkness of the night. To some early sky watchers this celestial river was mirrored by the life-giving waters of a terrestrial river running through their own landscape. To others, such a white flow across the sky seemed like milk, and the Milky Way was to them the milk of the Mother Goddess.

So it would seem that in several cultures the white stream of stars of the night sky was looked upon as the milk of the great Mother Goddess—Night. Our name for our home galaxy, the Milky Way, comes from Greece, where this spray of white stars against the dark sky, called *Galaxia Kuklos (Milky Way)*, was thought to be the milk of the great mother goddess Rhea. She was one of the Titans, her parents being the primal divine couple, Uranus (Sky) and Gaea (Earth). She was wife of Cronos (Time), and mother of Zeus. In a later version of the story it is the milk of Hera, wife of Zeus, which is said to have created the Milky Way, and the suckling child was Heracles.

The very word *galaxy* is from the Greek words, gala and *galaktos*, which mean "milk." In Rome our galaxy's name was the same as it was in Greece: the Milky Way. In Latin this is *Via Lactea*—*Via* meaning "way" or "road," and *Lactea* from *lactos*, which refers to milk.

In western Estonia it was sometimes referred to as the *Piimatee*, or Milkpath.

In East Asia the Milky Way was sometimes known as the *Silvery River*, while in India it was known as *Akashaganga*, which means "River of the Sky," *ganga* meaning river, and *akasha* referring to the sky, but also to that invisible spiritual "fifth element" which is also called ether, pneuma, and deep outer space. So *Akashaganga* can also mean River of Space, or River of the Spirit Realm, the spirit realm being the place (outer space) from which the material realms originated.

In Ireland the name for the Milky Way Galaxy is *"Bealach na bÃ finne,"* which means "The Way of the White Cow." In Scotland it was called the "White Stream of Heaven," the white stream referring to milk.

The Pathway in the Sky

As can be seen from some of the names above, sometimes the *way* or *path* part of the name was given as much, and occasionally more, emphasis as the "milk" part.

The Middle Dutch term for the Milky Way was *Vroneldenstraet*, which means the street or highway of the Lady Holda (referred to in the preceding chapter). It was also referred to as the *Road of Souls*. This refers to Holda in her role as leader of the Wild Hunt, in which she sweeps through the night skies during winter, gathering up and taking the souls of the dead to her realm while sweeping out the old tide of life so the new may come in. Not surprisingly, much of Holda's lore is connected with winter, and some of it with death.

It was also known as the *Road of Souls* in Peru, and in the Mayan lands is known as Xibalba Be, or Road to the Underworld. It is interesting how a spot in the Upperworld of the sky was known to be the entrance to the Underworld. Once again, the meaning pertains to a passageway between the realms of spirit and matter, life and death.

In the Mayan tradition of the *Xibalba Be*, there is a very specific part of the Milky Way's path across the sky that is considered the actual entrance to the Underworld – an area of interstellar dust known as the Dark Rift (also called the Cygnus Rift) of the Milky Way. This area is near the constellation of Sagittarius. This part of the *Xibalba Be* forks in a way that gives the appearance of its two parts surrounding an opening—the actual entrance to the Underworld.

Interestingly, in some cultures of the Baltic area, the Milky Way was known as the Bird Way or Bird Path. While this may have been a reference to the path of migratory birds, spirits were often thought to travel in the shape of birds.

It may be inferred from all of the above that our home galaxy, the Milky Way, was perceived mytho-poetically by our ancestors in terms of liquidity—a stream of mother's milk, a river of spirit substance in the sky, *and* as a way of travel from one end of the sky to the other, and from one realm to the other. This *Way* must be traveled—the celestial crossed or sailed upon—to make the transition to the other realms.

Behind this—River of Stars, the Bird Way, the Silvery River, the Way of the White Cow, the Milky Way—behind all these stories and images, we find the source of the River and the Way—the shadowy figure of the Dark Primal Mother, the dark Void of the Night Sky, the womb from which the light of the stars, and all creation, is born.

The Sacred Waters of Life

With a constant need for fresh water, humans have traditionally made their homes near fresh water sources such as ponds, streams, lakes, and especially rivers. Rivers have been held sacred, seen as divine beings or gifts from a divine being. Many precious objects have been found in rivers, giving mute testimony that offerings were made to these bodies of water or to the deity they embodied and represented. Rivers were, and are, used for transportation, thus enabling the growth of human community, commerce and civilization. In a very real way, rivers sustain life.

It is an interesting fact that there are many rivers in Eurasia that are named after Goddesses. A few examples that spring quickly to mind are the Braint and Brent in Britain, which are named after Brigid/Brigantia, and the Danube, the Don, Dneiper, Dneister, and Donets in Eastern Europe, which are named after Danu/Dana. These rivers flow through territories once inhabited by Celtic tribes.

The much beloved African goddess Yemaya was originally a river goddess; it was said that she became an ocean goddess as her people traveled across the wide waters, taken into slavery. Perhaps Yemaya's sweet waters became salty from the tears of her people as they were stolen from their homes. Her male counterpart Olokun is thought to be the depths of the ocean, while Yemaya is the rich surface level, teeming with life. Yemaya's daughter, Oshun, is a river goddess and associated with love and fertility.

The Nile River in Egypt has also been associated with the Milky Way and thus with the goddess Nuit, whose arched body was the starry sky.

Milk and Water

There is a link between milk and water. Milk is our first food. It is the first food of all mammalian creatures and thus essential to our life, while water is essential to *all* life. Plants, animals, and the soil all need water in order to survive and prosper. Water is the mother substance of the planet. Oceans occupy 70% of the globe's surface and are home to 90% of earth's life forms; while civilization itself began and grew up along the banks of rivers, lakes, streams and springs.

Just as Mother Earth supplies the water that nurtures land and people, so do mother mammals supply the fluid of life to their offspring. Milk is an extremely nutritious food, capable of supplying all the nutritional needs of the baby animal for several months.

Both milk and water were seen in the ancient world as gifts of divine beings.

All of which leads us to the subject of Cow Goddesses, and their relationship to River Goddesses, a subject that we will treat in the next chapter.

Chapter Three - The White Cow

The White Cow

From Lady Wilde's book, *Ancient Legends, Mystic Charms & Superstitions of Ireland*, we have the legend of the White Cow. This tale starts with a wise maiden who came from the sea to prophesy to the people of Ireland of the coming of the three sacred cows, the Bo Finn (white cow), the *Bo Ruadh* (red cow), and the *Bo Dhu* (dark or black cow). These cows and their descendants, she said, would assure that the people would never know want. The cows arrived, just as the sea maiden had predicted. They were washed up onto the shore by a mighty wave on the day which had been foretold. The people were waiting there to greet them, lining the shore, and rejoiced greatly to see them. It was said that the cows:

> ...stood upon the shore for a while, looking around them. Then each one went in a different direction, by three roads; the black went south, the red went north, and the milk white heifer—the Bo Finn—crossed the plain of Ireland to the very center, where stood the king's palace. And every place she passed was named after her, and every well she drank at was called the Lough-na Bo (Lake of the White Cow), or Tobar Bo Finn (Well of the White Cow,) so her memory remains to this day.[1]

After some time had passed the white cow gave birth to twins—male and female—and from them descended a great race of cattle. Then the white cow disappeared into a cave by the sea, the entrance to which no one knows, and it was said that there she will stay, in an enchanted sleep, until the true king of Ireland awakens her.

* * *

It is interesting to note that in this story there are three cows which come from the sea. References to things triple are frequent in Celtic lore. The colors of these cows—white, red and black—are colors traditionally sacred to and representative of the threefold goddess: White for the maiden aspect, red for the mother aspect, and black for the crone aspect. These colors may also be looked at as being representative of the three traditional realms of Upperworld (the sky world with its bright sun, moon, and stars), Middleworld (our earth and its red blooded creatures), and UnderWorld (the blackness of the deep inner earth). In Celtic goddess lore there are many threefold goddesses, but they are not so tidily divided into maiden, mother and crone. These aspects are in actuality correlative to functions. Many of the threefold goddesses perform more than one of these functions, and are also known to shapeshift from beautiful maiden to hideous hag.

In this story it is the white cow that is the most famous. The other cows disappear from the story, but it is the white cow whose story is told, thus alerting us to her importance. Many places are named after her. In Celtic lore, white animals—particularly if they have red eyes or ears—are often creatures from the Otherworlds, the spirit or faery realms, and they frequently come bearing special gifts for the people. In this story, the white (faery) cow goes to the "center" of Ireland, represented by the king's palace. Traditionally, a "center" is the place from which all things begin and end. By the simple fact of her journey, she spreads her Otherwordly blessings on the land she treads and the wells from which she drinks. From this Center she goes out again when her work is done. She travels to the sea from whence she came, but rather than going back into the sea, she sleeps in a sea cave till the true king comes to awaken her. In other words, she does not really leave the physical world, but sleeps in that "borderland" place between the spirit world and physical.

That this prolific white cow, mother of a great race of cattle in Ireland, now sleeps in a sea cave till the true king one day awakens her gives us a clue to her actual identity. She is, in reality, the Cow Goddess, the Mother Goddess who provides for the people, sustaining them with the gifts of her body, and whose fecundity is awakened by the fertile male power of the True King. He is "true" because he can enliven the gifts of life she holds, gifts that slumber in potentia in the womb-cave until he awakens them with his activating, fertilizing power.

The Sacred Cow

In ancient times the Goddess was seen as the giver of life and death and as the provider of sustenance, fertility, abundance and wealth. Societies that kept cattle could not fail to notice that the cow exemplified these exact virtues, and thus we find the emergence of cow goddess, or goddesses associated with cows. While this focus on cattle was confined to areas where there was sufficient pasturage for these animals to live, if one looks at the historical time period at which this was occurring, it is found to be during the Age of Taurus, the bull (approximately 4200 BC - 2000 BC), whose female counterpart is the cow.

This period of time saw the rise of many of the important civilizations and cultures of the ancient world, among which may be counted the Egyptian, Indian, Mesopotamian, Minoan and Mycenaean cultures.

Cattle were wealth in many parts of the world, just as other milk producing animals—such as sheep, horses, camels, yaks, llamas and the like—were wealth in other areas. The Celts had a respectful and loving relationship with their cattle, as did the Vedic culture of India, where cattle are sacred to this day. Not only were cattle an important source of wealth and nourishment, but cattle—and their many gifts—were spiritually revered in many parts of the world. Evidence of this is found in the lore, legends, and myths of not only those cultures but those they influenced, as well. And while this spiritual manifestation is usually referred to as the "Bull Cult," with emphasis on the powerful, virile, fertilizing male aspect, cows and cow goddesses obviously played a very significant role in it as well.

The Milk of the Mother

The subject of cows leads inevitably to that of milk. Milk is the first food of all mammals, including humans, and humans have long augmented their diet by making use of the bounty from milk-producing animals.

Long ago humans noticed that milk-giving animals are capable of producing much more milk than needed by their offspring, and realized that by domesticating these creatures they could have this wonderful nutritious gift in their lives for longer than just the period of the animal's offspring's infancy. It was discovered that the lactation period could be extended for many months, even into the animal's next pregnancy. Because of this, many cultures have, at some point in their history, domesticated milk-giving animals.

Milk products have been a vitally important food throughout history. Milk was known to be a very concentrated and nourishing food. It was often fermented to increase its nutritional value and longevity. The butter made from its cream was not only delicious but strengthening (and important source of essentially fatty acids), and in Indian tradition was seen as a *Sattvic* or spiritually pure substance, the consumption of which, in its clarified form called *ghee*, was held to bring clarity, calmness, and spiritual illumination.

From this it can be seen that it was believed that milk—as a special gift of the Mother Goddess—had benefits which transcended the merely physical.

The Cow Goddesses

The archetype of the Cow Goddess was one of the most prominent, ancient, transcultural deity forms. She is found in ancient Egypt. She is found in India, and throughout the areas where Indo-Europeans migrated, dwelt, and spread their culture. The Cow Goddess, wherever we find her, is representative of motherhood—fertility, nourishment, sustenance, care and comfort of the young, and often love and beauty as well.

Wherever she is found, she is associated with the nourishing and sustaining value of milk and/or water—and quite often the two merged as in Egypt, where the Milky Way was seen as both the milk of the Celestial Cow Mother Goddess as well as the heavenly counterpart of the life-sustaining Nile River.

In addition, these motherly cow goddesses are quite often linked with the moon. Perhaps the waxing and waning horns of the moon reminded people of cow horns, or perhaps the round white full moon reminded them of a pail of milk. But cow goddesses and the moon are linked in legend and lore from Ireland, to Egypt, to India, and beyond. And since the moon's travels through the night sky mark the passage of time, it may be said that these moon/cow goddesses are Goddesses of Time.

We have mentioned some of the Cow Goddesses in the previous chapter, but now we will look at a few more.

EGYPT
Hathor, Mehet-Weret, and Bata

The Cow Goddess is found in Egypt as Hathor, whose name means "house of Horus." As mother of Horus, her body, her womb, was his "house." Also referred to as the Mistress of Heaven, she was frequently depicted as a golden cow, sometimes covered in stars, and was called the Cow of Gold. She is also depicted with a woman's face and cow's ears. Hathor was the embodiment of the Celestial Cow Goddess, and one of Egypt's very early goddesses.

Sometimes she is pictured as a cow standing in a boat, surrounded by papyrus reeds, with a calf standing next to her. The cow/calf scenes show her as mother. The boat is that of Ra, in which he daily crosses the sky, and shows her celestial connection. The reeds, which are abundant in the Nile Delta, are also representative of the boundary between realms, and the fertility that emerges from those boundary areas.

Similar enough to Hathor early on to have been the same entity at one time was Bata, who was honored in Upper Egypt in the time before the Middle Kingdom (2000 BC). Sometimes referred to as Bat, her name includes the syllable "ba" which, in Egyptian religion, was one of the parts of the tri-part soul. Depicted with human face and bovine features, she was referred to as the "Great Wild Cow," and "She Who Lows," and was considered to be, early on, a deification of the Milky Way, as well as the essence of the soul, thus showing a link between the starry realms and the soul.[2]

An even earlier form of the Cow Goddess was known as Mehet-Weret, whose name means "Great Flood." She was seen as the great flood of the primal waters from which creation emerged. She was also seen as a cow goddess, and Hathor, who seems to have taken over many of her attributes, may well be a later version of both Bata and Mehet-Weret.[3] [4]

INDIA
Aditi

Aditi, as previously mentioned, is a very archaic Indian mother goddess who most likely predates Hinduism. She was referred to as the Cosmic Cow—nourisher, source of prosperity—and is seen as the mother of the gods and of time. Her name means "unfettered, unbounded, limitless," thus suggesting the sky, space, consciousness, and all time and eternity itself, all of with which she was associated.

GREECE
Hera and Io

The Greek goddess Hera was the spouse of Zeus and the mother of many of the other gods. She was referred to as "cow eyed," and it was the spurting of her milk that was said to have created the Milky Way.

Also from Greece is Io, who was the daughter of a river god. Io caught the eye of the ever-amorous Zeus. He transformed her into a white cow to avoid the jealous rage of his wife, Hera. Later, in flight from Hera's anger, Io traveled down the western coast of Asia Minor (later named the Ionian coast), and crossed the bodies of water later named after her—the Ionian Sea and the Straits of the Bosphorus (which means the" Ford of the Cow"). Io eventually ended up in Egypt, where she became a devotee of Isis, and was later known as Io-Isis.[5]

This is, of course, only one version of a very complex story that may, in actuality, refer to the spread of people, as well as their ideas, and godforms, into new areas.

SCANDINAVIA
Audhumla

We have already mentioned the figure of the primeval creative cow of Norse mythology, Audhumla, whose rich milk, flowing in four streams from her four udders, nourished Ymir the giant at the very beginning of the cycle of life, before earth's creation.

Audhumla herself was created from the melting ice of the Ginnungagap when ice met fire at the beginning of the world. She sustained herself by licking the salty ice blocks around her. As she licked one of these, the figure of a man began to emerge from it, bit by bit, and thus Buri, oldest of gods and men, came into being.

In this story we see the Void, the two polarities of water (in the form of ice) and fire, and the primal cow mother goddess—her milk flowing in four streams (perhaps referring to the four directions)—from whom the rest of creation emerges and is nourished.

IRELAND
Boann

The important ancient Irish Goddess Boann is easily seen to be a water goddess as she was associated with the River Boyne, which, along with its two major tributaries, is named for her. She is also associated with the sacred Well of Segais—the well of inspiration and wisdom whose official keeper was Boann's husband, Nechtan. This sacred well was surrounded by nine hazel trees that bore crimson colored nuts that contained all the wisdom of the world. Within its waters swam salmon who feasted on the hazelnuts, and thus, imbibed the wisdom.

According to one legend, the Boyne was formed when Boann approached the sacred well in disobedience of the proper protocols for doing so and its waters rose up to drown her. The waters flowed forth and became the river now named after her.

But Boann's very name translates to "she of the white cattle." In Irish *Bó* means cow, and *fhionn* (or *finn*) means white; thus "white cow." These two words make up the name of the River Boyne, which in the original Irish was *Abhainn na Bóinne*. The Boyne is, therefore, the *River of the White Cow*, and we may consider Boann to be a cow goddess as well, and quite likely, the White Cow of the legend recounted at the beginning of this chapter. The Milky Way is her road, or way, as reflected in the heavens.

Interestingly, the word *Bó fhionn* sounds remarkably similar to that of the Indian deity *Govinda* (an epithet of Krishna) whose name means "protector of cows" or "friend of cows," referring to his position as Divine Herdsman. The Indian word for cow is *Go*, and is from the same Indo-European root word that gives us *Bó*, while *fhionn* and *vin* are essentially the same word, and mean "fair" or "white."

In support of this we find that an earlier form of Boann's name was *Bovinda*, which also means "the white cow."

Given her association with cows, water in general and the River Boyne and Well of Segais in particular, Boann's true nature would seem to be that of a Goddess of nurture and sustenance—be it the physical sustenance of the sacred substances milk and/or water, or the spiritual sustenance of wisdom and inspiration from the Otherworldly Waters of the Sacred Well or the nourishing starry milk of the Milky Way.

As we have noted previously, these names in all likelihood date back to the Age of Taurus—4000 to 6000 years ago—a time when cattle were an essential and important part of the people's lives, wealth and livelihood.

The white cow mentioned in the Irish legend given at the beginning of this chapter seems to represent an almost archetypal rather than location-specific version of the Cow Goddess, since it is emphasized that she went to the Center of Ireland rather than a specific location or direction, bestowing her blessings upon the entire island as she made her way. The geographical aspect may be represented by the black cow and the red cow, who went to the south and north respectively, but more than this is hard to ascertain since they disappear from the story at this point.

But since the white cow went to the Center of Ireland, we may presume she went to the ancient province of Meath (which means "middle"), which represented the center of Ireland both politically and spiritually, and contained the ancient political center of Tara as well as, a bit to the west, the ancient spiritual center called Uisneach. This is not far from the location of the Boyne River valley and its complex of archaic stone structures. So the legend may well refer to the coming of Boann, as the primal White Cow Goddess, to the people of Ireland, and perhaps, as well the precession of the Vernal Equinox into the sign of Taurus.

Boann may well have been the preeminent great mother cow goddess of Ireland. Her cult was prominent in the Boyne Valley 5500 years ago (structures in the Boyne Valley predate the Egyptian pyramids). Boann's legends tell us that she bore to the Dagda (All-father god of the ancient Irish) a love child called Aenghus Mac Og (which means "young son"). Aenghus was born at the winter solstice and thus represents the reborn light of the sun. He is a god of light, but also of love.

I must emphasize again that the white cow in the legend came from the sea—the ultimate source of all life and sustenance on the planet. Given the connection between the watery ocean and the great sea of sky, this legend of the white cow takes on a cosmic meaning as well: the source of life is from the depths of sea/starry sky. The white cow's path through the heavens was the Milky Way. Was its Dark Rift, perhaps, the Well of Segais?

Interestingly, the average human gestation period and the bovine gestation period are very close to the same: 279/280 days for humans, and 285 for cows–a fact which our ancient cattle-keeping ancestors could scarcely have failed to notice.

Brigid

The Celtic Goddess Brigid is not intrinsically a Cow Goddess, but her legends and lore associate her with cows, along with her more usual associations with sacred fire and sacred wells.

In the Celtic legends, the lore of the Catholic Saint Brigid and the Celtic Goddess Brigid are so mixed as to be well nigh inseparable at this point in time. Many of the things said about the saint are so very magical it is certain they must derive from her earlier form as the goddess.

Brigid was said to have been raised on the milk of an Otherworldly (i.e. white hide, red-eared) cow, such milk being her preferred form of sustenance. In addition, Brigid was said to have been a milkmaid. She is sometimes portrayed as such and is shown milking her cow into a great cauldron-like pail. She traveled with a white cow who supplied her with milk as she needed it. Such was her association with milk and nourishment that she was also said to be the wet-nurse and foster mother of the Christ Child.

Brigid, both goddess and saint, is very much associated with sustenance and nurture, and indeed, with the forces that bring about and sustain life—fire and water. Her feast day, Imbolc, occurs during the lambing season, a time of new milk.

Like Boann, Brigid was associated with rivers—the Braint on the Isle of Anglesey and the River Brent in Middlesex, England.

NORTH AMERICA
White Buffalo Calf Woman

Biologically related to cattle, the buffalo was the North American continent's equivalent in terms of its importance to the people as a source of fertility, nurture and sustenance. Although she does not date back very far in time (insofar as I know), I sense a connection between these archaic cow goddesses of the old world and White Buffalo Calf Woman—she, the beloved woman of the Sioux who brought them the Sacred Pipe and their seven sacred spiritual rites, which are forms of spiritual sustenance.

After instructing the people in the seven sacred rites and the use of the pipe, White Buffalo Calf Woman told the people she had four ages within her and that she would look back upon the people in each age. But at the end of the fourth age, she told them, she would return to the people to help restore balance and harmony. Then she walked away, and the people watched her go. A little way off she laid down and when she arose she was a black buffalo. She did this three more times, and the people watched her lay down and then arise as a yellow buffalo, a red buffalo, and finally, as a white buffalo calf.

It would seem that these four buffalo signify the four ages she mentioned, which may quite possibly be connected with the four quarters of the astrological "Great Year"—Taurus, Leo, Scorpio and Aquarius. They may also signify the four races of humankind, the four seasons of the year, and the four directions of the sacred circle of the earth, as represented by the Medicine Wheel.

White Buffalo Calf woman may also be a link to Taurus (the constellation rather than the Age), since the Lakota Sioux saw their beloved buffalo in the star grouping that we call Taurus the Bull.

It is interesting to note that on August 20, 1994, a female white buffalo calf was born on a farm in Wisconsin, the first such calf born since 1933. Many Native Americans considered the calf, who was named Miracle, to be the fulfillment of prophecy, and traveled in pilgrimage to visit and honor her.

Summary

What we have looked at in this chapter is the relationship between milk and water, between cows and rivers, between Cow Mother Goddesses and River Mother Goddesses, between rivers of water and rivers of milk.

Continuing with this line of thought, we have included in this comparison the river of stars known as the Milky Way. We have mentioned the connection of the Cow Goddess with the River Boyne; now we can include the Goddess Brigid's bovine connections, and in the chapter which follows, we will expand on the Goddess Dana's river and bovine connections.

In yet another sense, rivers, especially the starry ones, are connected with the flow of time. Time is a factor of form; in the spirit world time does not exist. Time flows through our lives like a river, bringing things in on its currents and sweeping them away again. We travel the river of time, with its many twists and curves, as we move through our lives.

Once again....it's all about "flow."

Notes

1) *Wilde, Lady Jane Francesca, Ancient Legends, Mystic Charms & Superstitions of Ireland*, Ward & Downe; London, 1887, p169
2) en.wikipedia.org/wiki/Bata_(goddess)
3) en.wikipedia.org/wiki/Mehet-weret
4) www.thekeep.org/~kunoichi/kunoichi/themestream/mehetweret.html
5) Graves, Robert, *The Greek Myths, Volumes 1 & 2*, Penguin Group, Canada, 1955

Chapter Four - Mother Dana

The early Irish honored a mother goddess who was called Dana, or sometimes, Ana/Anu.

These names and their variations crop up in other mythologies as well, from Vedic to Sumerian. While the Sumerian Anu was male (and seen as a sky god and father of many gods), in other mythologies Anu/Ana/Danu/Dana is decidedly female. In actuality, the original deity form in all these cultures may well have been androgynous—containing both male and female qualities. What is clear is that the syllable "An" seems to be associated with the sky—the heavens—in many ancient mythologies.

Dana is an important figure in Eurasian religious consciousness and is important to the story being told here.

Dana

In researching the Irish Dana, one inevitably comes upon the fact that this same goddess is found on the European continent as Danu. In addition, she is very likely the same goddess that is mentioned in Ireland as Anu, and the twin hills near Killarney called the Paps (breasts) of Anu, are named after her.

The root of the word *dana* is translated variously to mean *to flow*, (PIE *dhen-,) or *gift*—both of which are appropriate to rivers.

The Danube, from whose headwaters the Celtic tribes are said to have spread outward into Europe, is the great mother of many European rivers. It is named after Dana/Danu, as are several other European rivers, most notably the Don, Dneiper, and Dneister in Russia, the Don in Scotland, and the Don in Yorkshire. The modern Irish form of the word includes the meaning "swift flowing."

According to Peter Ellis's book, The *Druids*, Dana/Danu means "waters of heaven" (i.e. heavenly waters, or waters from heaven). Although "waters of heaven" sounds as if it might refer only to rain, it may also refer to earth's rivers, as well as referring to, in a larger sense, the heavenly river of stars which was seen as the source realm of things on earth. What is on earth mirrors what is in heaven—As Above, So Below. Therefore, the "waters of heaven" become the life-giving waters of earth—in the form of the rain, but also, and especially, the great rivers, since so many rivers on the Eurasian continent have some form of Dana/Danu/Don in their names.

Thus it would appear that Dana/Danu/Anu is a Celtic Goddess who encompasses the life-giving "flow" on earth and in heaven. In addition, she may be seen as the stellar, watery abyss of sky from which life emerges.

Dana also occurs in Vedic and Greek cosmologies. In both she is associated with water. The Vedic/Hindu Dana was the goddess (or personification) of the primordial waters of creation, which may be likened to both the great sea of being and, in human terms, amniotic fluids—the vast deep.

In Greek myth Danae was the mother of the great hero Perseus, who was fathered by Zeus in the form of a shower of gold. After Perseus was born, Danae's father, afraid he would be killed by his grandchild, set Danae adrift in a wooden cask with the baby—a theme typical of stories where a god is fearful of being supplanted by a younger version of himself. And so Danae drifted with her child of light—who would grow up to be a famous hero—in her tiny vessel on the great sea till the vessel was washed ashore. It could be said that this tale provides another mythological instance of the mother emerging from the darkness of the sea with her child of light.

In Vedic culture the word *dana* implies "distributing, giving," and a river certainly distributes its life-giving essence to all that lives along its banks. Rivers *are* gifts which allow life, and also, *give* gifts (water, fish, plants) that allow life to continue, just as do the heavenly waters of rainfall.

Dhenu is a Sanskrit word meaning milk cow. Although it may or may not be related etymologically, it would appear that the sound is similar to *dana/danu*. The term *Kama Dhenu* means "heavenly milk-giving cow," and refers, mythologically, to a mythical, milk-giving, wish-granting cow (also called *Surabhi*) formed at the beginning of time when the gods churned the milky waters of the primordial ocean of space in order to create the worlds.

The milk of the Heavenly Cow is the nourishing, pleasurable, wish granting, and material substance for life—all very Venusian themes, and not surprising since the planet Venus rules the sign/constellation of Taurus, the Bull/Cow of the starry heavens. Also of interest is the fact that the boundary area that bridges the constellation signs of Taurus and Gemini was anciently known as the Gateway of Life, the place from which the powers of life flowed forth. But more of this in subsequent chapters.

Don and Domnu

Dana's Welsh equivalent, Don, is a dim and mysterious figure, mentioned only occasionally in the Mabinogion as the mother of the gods. Not much is known about her beyond the fact that she bore at least five children—Gwydion, Arianrhod, Gilfaethwy,

Gofannon and Amaethon—and was the sister of the wizard, Math ap Mathonwy, and wife of the god Beli.

As a mother goddess, it is likely she was thought to have power over fertility. Her name, Don, is said to mean the *Watery Abyss*—a reference to the sea. But interestingly, Don was also linked to the sky in the form of the constellation *Llys Don*, or "Court of Don," known to us today by its Greek name of Cassiopeia, which is located near the constellation of watery Pisces.

In Ireland the goddess Domnu was the even more obscure and shadowy mother goddess of the Fomorians, that strange race of misshapen beings whose stories connect them to the vast deeps of the sea.

It would appear that the life giving and life sustaining powers of water in continental Celtic culture was represented by Dana/Danu as river, with Don/Domnu as her oceanic equivalent in the insular Celtic culture.

Aine

The Irish Goddess Aine was extremely popular in the Irish province of Munster, where she was considered to be the Queen of the Faeries. She is thought to be a regional version of Anu, whom some scholars think is quite likely to be the same being as the great Celtic Mother Goddess Danu/Dana.

Aine has associations with all the elements. The mountains known as the Paps of Anu were thought to be her breasts, her home was in a hill (Cnoc Aine); she was thought to have created the lake Lough Gur, and she sometimes appeared in the shape of a "faery whirlwind" over that lake. One of her primary associations was with the sun. She was known as the wife of the sea god Manannan MacLir (although sometimes she was said to be his daughter), from whose bed she arose every morning. She was worshiped at the Summer Solstice, when people lit torches in her honor and carried them in procession from her sacred hill to their fields and crops. She was also linked with the fertility of the land.

With attributes encompassing all of these elements of life, Aine is most certainly a version of the Great Goddess, the Mother Goddess of life who encompasses both the fiery and watery aspects of creation and who, indeed, contains all things within herself.

There are undoubtedly several other goddesses from various spiritual traditions of the world who could be included here, but space constraints preclude discussing any more of them.

Life Givers, Life Sustainers

When we focus on the connections of Dana/Danu/Ana/Anu to the great watery and starry abyss of space, we see her aspect as the birthing mother. When we take note of the many rivers named after her, we are seeing her in her aspect of the sustaining mother—the Mother River, she who nourishes and sustains her children with her sweet waters, which allows them to live.

Rivers originate from either glacial water or water sources deep within the land. Many of them flow to the sea. This is true of the Danube, the Volga, the Mississippi/Missouri, the Nile, the Ganges, the Yangtze, and the Amazon—the world's longest, most important, and culturally significant rivers.

Riverbanks, like seashores, are places of liminality. As boundaries between two differing environments, they are also seen as boundaries between worlds and states of consciousness. Wisdom and inspiration, which nourish us, arise at the boundary of the seen and unseen, of normal consciousness and altered consciousness.

In his book *The Druids*, Peter Berresford Ellis tells us that "the ancient Irish bards deemed that the river's edge, the brink of the water, was always that place where *eicse*—which means wisdom, knowledge and poetry—was revealed. *Eicse* also meant divination," and is possibly related to *esca*, a word which referred to both the moon and water. [1]

Ellis reminds us also about the very early Hindu creation myths which refer to Aditya (Aditi) as the mother of the Gods. Aditya was also the name of a mythical river which was the source of all the waters of the world. One of the meanings of Aditya/Aditi is, of course, space, and it is the Vedic element of *Space* from which, in this early Vedic story, the sky, earth and all the rest were formed.

In this we see a correspondence made between the Mother Goddess, the depths of space that gave birth to the rest of creation, and a primeval divine river that is the source of all the waters—and therefore all of water's life-giving/life-sustaining powers—of the world.

As is evident, links are being drawn here between the original "Void of All Potentialities," the Great Mother Goddess, the stars, the earth's waters (especially rivers), liminality, and the feminine power of inspiration—which lead to knowledge, poetry, and eventually, wisdom.

Notes
1) Ellis, Peter Berresford; *The Druids*; Wm B Eerdmans Publishing, MI; p 239

Chapter Five - Morgen and the Sea Temple

Morgan and Morgen

One of the most important Sea Temple [1] figures in the Western Mystery Tradition is undoubtedly the mysterious British goddess Morgen. Called Morgan le Fey in the Arthurian tales, she is often portrayed as the evil, self-serving enchantress with whom we are all too familiar.

But a different image of her is to be found in the 12th century *Vita Merlini* (Life of Merlin) of Geoffrey of Monmouth, who drew upon yet earlier sources in his writing.

Morgen

The *Vita Merlini* portrays Morgen as a skillful healer, who, with her eight sisters, lived on a holy isle reached only by traveling on the Otherworld Sea. This island may well have been the prototype for the legend of the mystic Otherworld Isle of Apples known as Avalon. Apples were the Celtic fruit of life, death, and immortality. Morgen dwelt on this Isle with her sisters, it was said, practicing the arts of healing. She was the ruler of Avalon, which was also known as the "Fortunate Isle."

It was said that Morgen and her sisters were daughters of the island's king, *Avallach*, whose name is derived from the Celtic word *Abal*, which means apple, from whence comes Avalon, "Isle of Apples." Mythically, the apple—whose seeds form a pentacle in the fruit's center—is the fruit of both life and death. Avalon, Isle of Apples, the Fortunate Isle, was the Celtic paradise, linked with the Otherworld/Underworld realm of faery, and Avallach (or Afallach) was sometimes referred to as the King of Faery.

Morgen and her sisters may well be the nine sisters associated with the Cauldron of Annwn (Annwn was the Welsh name for the Underworld), as mentioned in the *Preiddeu Annwn*, or Spoils of Annwn, one of the earliest stories of the Arthuriad. This pearl-rimmed cauldron, the chief treasure of Annwn, was kept in a cave deep in the Underworld where the maidens were said to heat it with their breath.

This cauldron, which was associated with inspiration and was said to never boil the food of a coward, is thought by some to be the archetype of the grail of all subsequent grail legends. But the presence of the cauldron's nine caretaking guardians link this story to Morgen and her sisters, showing us that Avalon, Morgen's Fortunate Isle, and the Welsh Underworld of Annwn are one and the same place. Arthur's attempt to steal the cauldron was an attempt to wrest the spiritual powers of the Underworld and by force transport them to the mundane world.

According to the *Vita*, King Arthur was taken to Morgen's isle to be healed after his last battle. In other accounts, Morgen was one of the three queens who came in a barge to fetch him to her isle of healing. [2] Thus the isle is once again shown to be a place of healing, which is in accord with its association with the cauldron, Morgen, and her sisters.

There are other accounts in European lore about islands of magical women. First century Roman geographer Pomponius Mela wrote of an island of women off the coast of Brittany; the women were priestesses of an unnamed Gaulish god and maintained his oracle. Mela lists shapeshifting, weather-working, healing, and divination among their powers. Another geographer of the same era, Strabo, mentions this isle as well.

Morgan le Fey

The Morgan le Fay of the Arthurian tales is a complex character with a complex history. In *Le Morte D'Arthur*, Thomas Malory's popular 14th century version of the stories, Morgan is the youngest of the three daughters of Gorlois and his queen Igraine (Ygerna), the other daughters being Elaine and Morgause. Upon Gorlois's death, Igraine married Uther Pendragon and gave birth to Arthur. Morgan was, therefore, in Malory's telling, Arthur's half sister.

In Geoffrey of Monmouth's earlier version of the story, [3] Igraine and Uther have two children, Arthur and a daughter named Anna.

Malory indicates that Morgause married King Lot of Lothian and the Orcades (i.e. Orkney Isles), while Morgan is unhappily married off to King Urien of Rheged and bears him a son named Owain/Ywain. Yet Morgause is a later name for Lot's queen; in the earliest mentions she was called Anna. Geoffrey's *Vita Merlini* tells us that Arthur's sister Anna was given to Lot in marriage.

As the tales evolved, the characters of Anna, Morgause, and Morgan were confused and conflated, and some of Morgause's stories—such as Malory's account of her inadvertent incest with her half-brother—were transferred to Morgan.

So it is very likely that Morgause and Anna were, in actuality, the same person, and that the Arthur of Geoffrey's story may have had only one sister, Anna, and that Elaine, the other sister mentioned by Malory, was a later addition. This means, quite simply, that in the earliest versions, Arthur did not have a sister named Morgan.

Yet what of Morgan, daughter of Gorlois, who, Malory tells us, was found to be so skillful and bright that she was "put to school in a nunnery where she became a great clerk of necromancy," and was thereafter called "le Fay," meaning "the faery," which refers to a woman of the Otherworld? ⁽⁴⁾ From whence did she arise and find a place in Mallory's telling of the tale?

If you will remember from *Chapter Four*, the "an" syllable in divine names is significant as it refers to the heavens.

Morgan's true origins lie further back in time. In order to discover them we must look at the mythology of Wales. In the Welsh stories we find mention of a character called *Mabon ap Modron*. The mention is brief: Mabon is stolen from his mother three days after birth, and much later, King Arthur and his companions launched a search and finally found him.

Because the kidnapping of Mabon had happened so long ago, Arthur and his fellow searchers are guided by the oldest animals in the world, each animal passing them on to another, even older animal. It is eventually a salmon, the oldest of all and associated with wisdom in the Celtic tradition, who leads them upriver to the walls of *Caer Loyw* where Mabon, now a young man, is found imprisoned in a dungeon referred to as a "house of stone," having not seen the light of day for a very long time. Caer Loyw means "Castle of Gloyw"—a place now called Gloucester—from the Celtic word *Glevo*, meaning bright place, and perhaps the Old English *Gleaw* meaning wise, prudent.⁽⁵⁾ It is strange that Mabon is in a dark prison in a place whose name means "bright" place.

But the interesting thing about Mabon, for our purposes at least, is his name, which means, roughly, "Son, son of the Mother."

The Welsh word for mother was Modron. Mabon's name indicates he is *the* Son of *the* Mother—not just any son of any mother. His mother/modron is the Mother Goddess, known on the continent as Matrona but more often in the usual Celtic triple form as the Matronae (Latin), or the Mothers. Modron derives from Matrona. The Romano-Celtic version of Mabon is Maponos, which means "Great Son" or "Divine Son," and further underlines his divine status. Maponos was associated with music and poetry, much like the Greek Apollo.

Please note Mabon's association with darkness: he was stolen from "between his mother and the wall"—presumably a dark cozy, and perhaps even womblike, place—and was imprisoned for years in a dark stone dungeon. This mythic motif would seem to link the story to the similar motif of the Middle Eastern Kybele/cave—the enclosed but hollow space that is the terrestrial manifestation of the divine Primal Mother—mentioned in *Chapter One*. This may indicate that Mabon is an initiation story—he is light born of darkness, having gained wisdom during his many years in the dark stone prison. Indeed, this myth might be telling us that the stone prison itself—that dark and hollow place—might be his Mother, the mother of his newfound wisdom.

The Modron and her Son are both shadowy figures in British myth; they are mentioned only a few times. More is known of the Matronae. Carvings of them are found in France/Gaul, showing them to be nourishers, healers, and goddesses of plenty.

They are, as are all other mother goddesses, life givers and life sustainers, and are often associated with healing wells and springs, showing us, once again, the association of the goddess with water.

Which brings us back around to again Morgen/Morgan… and how the Modron is related to her.

* * *

As we have mentioned before, the earliest descriptions of Morgen describe her as a healer, wise in the ways of herbs, and able to fly with wings like the Greek Daedalus. She is said to live on an island with her eight sisters, to whom she teaches these arts. No mention is made of the treacheries of the later Morgan le Fay, arch-villainess of the Arthurian tales; and indeed, these came later as Morgen—clearly a woman with powers the Church deemed appropriate only to men—was demonized.

An interesting fact links the figures of Modron and Morgan. They are both said to be the mother of Owain, son of King Urien of Rheged. In *Welsh Triad 70* Modron is said to be the mother by Urien of Rheged of Owain, whose name means "nobly born youth" and his twin sister Morvydd. In Malory's story, Owain is said to be the son of Urien and Morgan. This would seem to link Modron, Morgan, and Anna; perhaps they are one instead of three? Or perhaps the other sisters represent the other realms, and we are looking at another example of the ancient three-fold goddess whose realms encompass earth, sea, and sky.

There is a folktale which corroborates Modron's maternity of Owain. In this tale Urien mates with a mysterious washerwoman he meets at the ford of a river [6] and she bears him twins—a son Owain, and a daughter Morvydd.[7] The woman, unnamed in the story, says she is the daughter of Annwn (the Welsh Otherworld/Underworld). [8] Clearly she is a divine being, and the Triads tell us she is the Modron. [9]

So it would seem that Morgan's maternity of Owain in Malory's tale might be a memory of her origins as the Modron, who is the Welsh form of the old primal mother goddess who gives birth to the (Son of) Light, wisdom from the dark.

Therefore, it looks as if Malory's figure of Morgan le Fay, the angry, vengeful sorceress sister of Arthur has its roots in the figures of both Modron, the ancient mother, and of Morgen, healing goddess and ruler of the Fortunate Isles, who by fourteenth century was seen as wicked, and indeed, as the embodiment of at least five of the seven deadly sins. [10]

The name Morgen itself means *sea-borne*, "borne of/by the sea," as in one who comes *from* the sea (or perhaps even born from the sea), is carried by the sea. In Irish the name Morgan means "sea dweller" or "lives by the sea." In Welsh it refers to the edge of the sea. Stories that form the foundation of what came to be called the Western Mystery Tradition relate that Morgen came from ancient Atlantis, borne upon the waves of the

Atlantic from one of Atlantis's large islands to the much smaller one of Britain during the final days of the Atlantean civilization.

Morgen's association with the sea links her to the sphere of Binah on the Kabbalistic Tree of Life. Binah is the great astral sea, the beginning of all "forms" that will later come into manifestation. *The Western Mystery Tradition* by Christine Hartley, the great 20th century initiate and student of Dion Fortune, describes Morgen thus:

Of her there is little that we can say, for she is ever the hidden one, the shadowy woman who stands behind, giving of her power from the inner planes. She is the feminine principle of the great Triangle of King, Priest and Priestess; she is the Word, the life-giving Force. She is the Spirit of God, the third person of the Trinity who is or should always be feminine—the Ruach of the Hebrew, the Sophia of Greece, Wisdom that sits up on her seven hills. Morgan is she who teaches men to work with power; she is Binah on the Tree of Life; the great Mother of Form through whom is the manifestation of Force. She is also Isis of the Moon, and her place on the Tree of Life can be Yesod, for in the later pantheon she is changed into Arianrhod. Like all women, she is all things, and her aspects are infinite. The Church was afraid of Morgan and left her alone, contenting itself with calling her the Witch-woman. But always she draws us back to the primordial sea from which she came, to the old mysteries of Atlantis, whence our own have derived their life; she is that strange and lovely lady whom we can sometimes glimpse on a rocky seashore, rising out of the water, shadowy in the sea mist and foam. She has all wisdom and knowledge." **(11)**

Ms. Hartley also tell us that Morgan (and Merlin and Arthur as well) was a generic name and that there had been many cycles of them throughout the ages; which suggests that these names were more of a job title than a personal name. This sheds light on the name confusion—Morgan or Anna—of Arthur's sister.

It is interesting that Christine Hartley links the figure of Morgen with Isis, the Hebrew *Ruach* (the Holy Spirit), Wisdom, Sophia, and the much later Welsh goddess Arianrhod, in addition to Binah. Binah is "Understanding" **(12)** on the Tree of Life, while Chokmah is "Wisdom." Chokmah is usually considered male in the Kabbalah but is represented as female, Wisdom, in the Book of Proverbs where she is God's first creation and the helper who assisted him in creating/forming all else. Wisdom can also be understood as the divine order, the harmonious pattern of the cosmos, and as the embodiment of that divine order.

In conclusion, it can be seen that the figure of Morgan le Fey is most likely a late-in-time representation of the Great Goddess. The powers attributed to her show that she is otherworldly; Kabbalistically, they relate to the creative and formative powers of Binah, Chokmah, and Yesod. Her reputation for healing and her ability to fly inform us that before she was seen as human she was mostly likely seen as a being of the Otherworld, with powers that extended over the realms of both life and death.

Her name, Morgan/Morgen, may well have been her title; "le Fey" links her with the Otherworld, which is often referred to as the realm of faery or "fey." Her original name, Anna, links her with the heavenly realm. Her link with the Welsh Modron confirms that she was originally seen as a deity. Her name, Morgen, means "sea-borne." Her island home also links her with the sea, and the very name of that island links her with the apple, fruit of life, death, and immortality.

Notes:

1) The Sea Temple will be discussed in depth in Chapter Eleven and Chapter Fifteen.
2) Geoffrey of Monmouth, *Viti Merlini* , Latin text by Geoffrey of Monmouth, Translated by John Jay Parry [1889-1954], University of Illinois, Urbana, IL. 1925

In the Vita Merlini, Taliesin speaks to Merlin, saying,
"The island of apples which men call "The Fortunate Isle" gets its name from the fact that it produces all things of itself; the fields there have no need of the ploughs of the farmers and all cultivation is lacking except what nature provides. Of its own accord it produces grain and grapes, and apple trees grow in its woods from the close-clipped grass. The ground of its own accord produces everything instead of merely grass, and people live there a hundred years or more.
There nine sisters rule by a pleasing set of laws those who come to them from our country. She who is first of them is more skilled in the healing art, and excels her sisters in the beauty of her person. Morgen is her name, and she has learned what useful properties all the herbs contain, so that she can cure sick bodies. She also knows an art by which to change her shape, and to cleave the air on new wings like Daedalus; when she wishes she is at Brest, Chartres, or Pavia, and when she will she slips down from the air onto your shores. And men say that she has taught mathematics to her sisters, Moronoe, Mazoe, Gliten, Glitonea, Gliton, Tyronoe, Thitis; Thitis best known for her cither.
Thither after the battle of Camlan we took the wounded Arthur, guided by Barinthus to whom the waters and the stars of heaven were well known. With him steering the ship we arrived there with the prince, and Morgen received us with fitting honour, and in her chamber she placed the king on a golden bed and with er own hand she uncovered his honourable wound and gazed at it for a long time. At length she said that health could be restored to him if he stayed with her for a long time and made use of her healing art. Rejoicing, therefore, we entrusted the king to her and returning spread our sails to the favouring winds."
3) Geoffrey of Monmouth, *Histories of the Kings of Britain,* translated by Sebastian Evans, LL.D; J.M. Dent & Co: Aldine House, London, W.C.; 1904
4) Sir Thomas Malory, *Le Morte D'Arthur,* New York, University Books, 1961
5) www.etymonline.com/index.php?term=Gloucester
6) An echo of the earlier Irish tale of the Dagda's mating with the Morrigan (whose name means Great Queen or Shadow [i.e. shades, ghosts] Queen) as she straddled the River Unius in the province of Connacht the night before the Second Battle of Magh Turedh, washing the bloody clothes of those who were to die in battle the next day. Riverbanks are, in myth, "in-between places;" boundaries between this world and the Otherworld.
7) Morvvyn is sometimes rendered as Morfudd.
8) MacKillopAD, James, *Oxford Dictionary of Celtic Mythology,* Oxford University Press, 1998
9) en.wikipedia.org/wiki/Morgan_le_Fay
10) The seven deadly sins are Wrath, Greed, Lust, Pride, Envy, Laziness and Gluttony
11) Hartley, Christine, *The Western Mystery Tradition,* The Aquarian Press, Thorsen's Publishing Group, Wellingborough, North Hamptonshire; 1986, p 63
12) "Understanding" in the sense of contemplation, discernment, and deductive reasoning that give the ability to process the Wisdom that is Chokmah.

Chapter Six - Out of Egypt

THE NILE, THE MILKY WAY, AND THE EGYPTIAN MOTHERS

Hathor

There are several different Egyptian creation stories—a fact unsurprising for a civilization that encompassed such a large geographic area, evolved over so many years, and lasted for such a long period of time. As a result, it is difficult to arrive at a straightforward Egyptian cosmology and unravel the complex and frequently conflicting relationships among the various deities. The confusion is increased because often it can be seen that deity forms may have merged or that new deities have taken over the roles and functions of older ones.

Nonetheless, the image of the celestial goddess, often depicted in the form of a celestial cow—her milk as the river of stars in the night sky—is found as one of the earliest deity forms.

Hathor's origins go far back in time—further back than we can accurately ascertain—to a time before she was known as Hathor, the mother of Horus. She is one of the earliest Egyptian deity forms, predating the Dynastic periods of Egyptian history, and most likely comes to us from the Nile Valley people of the time before kings and pharoahs ruled.

Hathor means "House of Horus," Horus being the sun (in later Egyptian mythology), and Hathor being his "house"—the mother/womb that gave birth to him each morning and received him back again at night. Since the sun transits the sky it would seem that Hathor is linked to the sky.

She was a goddess of love, beauty, music, dance, women, fertility, children—very much a joyous, sensual, nurturing, loving mother goddess. And yet she had another side as well. She was a goddess of destruction, having once—as Sekmet—been Ra's vengeful and destructive eye. She was, as well, a goddess of the dead, in which capacity she was known as the Lady of the West since west was the direction of the Land of Death. There are definite crossovers in her role as goddess of the dead with that of Neith, although Hathor was the Lady of the West, and Neith was said to guard the east.

Whether depicted as a cow, or simply as a nurturing mother, she was always associated with the sky and stars, and was known as the Mistress of the Heavens, the celestial realms. And always present in Hathor's lore was a relationship with life-giving waters from the sky. It is quite likely she is related to other early Egyptian sky goddesses, such as Nuit, Mut, Meret-Wehet. It is certain that the later figure of Isis assumed some of Hathor's attributes and functions.

She was also known as the "Mother of Mothers," a clue to her antiquity as a Mother Goddess.

The goddess Hesat (or Hesahet) was the another manifestation of Hathor, the divine celestial cow mother. Her very name means "milk," and she was said to be the wet-nurse of the other deities. Interestingly, she was also said to be the mother of the jackal-headed god of death, Anubis.

Nuit

Another Egyptian goddess associated with the sky was Nuit. Although originally linked with the daytime sky and the clouds, she was later associated with the sky in general. She was depicted as a beautiful dark lady who stretched across the sky, facing downwards, her body covered in stars and her arms and legs touching the four cardinal points and serving as the pillars of the sky. Thus, she *was* the sky, and the earth, Geb, was her brother-spouse. She gave birth to five divine children, the major deities of a later version of Egyptian religion—Osiris, Horus the elder, Isis, Set, and Nephthys.

Because Nuit, like Hathor, was seen to give birth to the sun god, Ra, everyday, and swallow him up again at night, she was also associated with death as well as birth, and with the Underworld and the Land of Death.

Neith

Neith (also called Nit) was the goddess of Sais, in the Nile Delta, but was worshipped throughout Egypt. An ancient goddess known in predynastic times (c. 3000 BC), she may have originated further to the west, in Libya.

Neith was depicted as wearing the red crown of lower Egypt and holding two arrows crossed over a shield or bow. She was considered a goddess of hunting and of war. It was said that she made warriors' weapons and guarded their bodies after death. [1] But although she was held to be a war goddess, she was considerably more complex than that.

She was one of the four Egyptian Goddesses (the others being Isis, Nephthys, and Selket) who watched over the dead. Among her titles were "mother goddess, mother of the gods, queen of the gods, lady of heaven, and the great lady."

Perhaps because her symbol resembled a weaving shuttle, she came to be seen to be a weaver goddess. Her very name was linked to the root of the word for "weave," *ntt,* which, interestingly, is also the root for the word *"being."* Over time she came to be considered the creator goddess, she who wove the world into being.

Her role as weaver goddess fused with her role as guardian of the dead and it was thought that she wove the wrappings and shrouds placed upon mummies.

Her name could also be interpreted as water; in some stories it was said that she was the mother of the sun god, Ra (Re) and had given birth to him in the primeval waters known as Nun. Thus she was known as the protectress of women, particularly as they gave birth. In this birth-giving role, she was also sometimes depicted as a sky cow goddess.

In late dynastic times there is no doubt that Neith was regarded as nothing but a form of Hathor, but at an earlier period she was certainly a personification of a form of the great, inert, primeval watery mass out of which sprang the sun god Ra. [2]

But Neith/Nit as related to the primeval waters of Nun is herself linked back to another early goddess, Mut, whose name means "mother." Mut was originally a title for the waters of Nun but was later perceived as a creator goddess. The word Mut also means "white vulture" a bird which the Egyptians thought to be very maternal as well as able to give birth without fertilization by a male. After the two kingdoms of upper and lower Egypt had united, Mut was depicted as a woman with the wings of a white vulture, holding an ankh, Ma'at's feather at her feet, and wearing the crown of the united kingdom.

In some of the earliest references to Neith as creator, her gender is not made clear, implying that she was neither male nor female but contained both. This marks Neith as an ancient and very primal power.

In *The Greek Myths* Robert Graves tells us that the Greeks equated their goddess Athena with Neith, saying that Athena had come originally from the North African province of Libya; he mentions that pottery finds in Crete suggests a large Libyan influx there early as 4000 BC as well as a larger one by 3000 BC when Upper and Lower Egypt were united into one kingdom. [3]

In her birth-giving role especially, we can see in the figure of Neith the great deity of the deep and water-like void of space—she, the source of all and who wove the world into being.

Tanit

Tanit was a Carthaginian goddess, rather than an Egyptian goddess. But she must be mentioned here since her name, in Egyptian, means "Land of Neith." Tanit was actually the Phoenician/Canannite goddess Anat/Anath, who had been brought to Africa in the 9th century BC by seafaring Phoenician traders who established a colony in the form of the city of Carthage on the North African coast. Carthage became a major power, conquering nearby lands, until by the 6th century BC it controlled the North African coast as far east as the border of Egypt. (4)

Anat/Anath was a very significant goddess whose worship was widespread in the Middle East; her roots lead back to the Sumerian Inanna. (5)

The Nile Goddesses—Anuket and her mother, Satis

The Nile was the river on which Egypt's civilization depended, as its yearly inundation was what granted fertility to the otherwise dry land. Khnum and Satis (also known as Satet) were the deities of the source of the Nile, and their daughter, Anuket (also Anqet) was originally seen as the goddess of the Nile itself. Her name meant *She who embraces*, as the Nile's flooding embraced the fields and rendered them fertile. Because of her connections with fertility and nourishment, she had a motherly aspect, and was, as was Hathor, occasionally depicted as suckling the young pharoah.

Her mother, Satis, whose name means "to pour out," was also connected with the yearly inundation of the land by the Nile, and according to Lewis Spence, "She carries in her hands a bow and arrows, as did Neith, typical of the rain or thunderbolt." (6)

The Nile was seen as the terrestrial counterpart to the Milky Way. Life came from the waters in the sky and the waters of the Nile. Deities associated with water were therefore usually associated with both birth and death and also the Land of Death. This is true of Satet, one of whose functions was to wash and purify the dead so that they might enter the gates of the heavenly otherworld.

Many of Satis's attributes link her with both Hathor and Isis, while Anuket was eventually linked to Nephthys.

Isis

The Egyptian goddess Isis was one of the most beloved goddesses of the ancient world. Her worship spread very far indeed. But if we trace the figure of Isis far back into time we discover some very interesting things in her history.

Isis is the Greek rendering of the Egyptian name *Auset*, which is said to mean "throne." Yet the name *Auset* most likely comes from *UaZit*, who was the primary goddess of Upper Egypt in the time before the two Kingdoms—Upper and Lower—were united into one. UaZit was a snake goddess; she was a cobra. The primary goddess of the Lower Kingdom was Nekhebet, who was a vulture goddess. When the two kingdoms were merged, the two goddesses worked together for the good of the whole kingdom. After a while the figure of Auset/Isis began to emerge from these two. She was seen as a winged goddess, often wearing the uraeus, or cobra crown. Alongside this, the figure of Isis's sister Nephthys (who may be an earlier development of Nekhebet) took on a more defined role, as did the figure of another of her sisters, Hathor, who was often seen as a cow goddess.

Isis-as-throne may be looked at in another way as well. The motherly Isis is often pictured with the infant Horus on her lap. Thus, she is the "throne" for Horus, the child who will be king. She is the throne not only because he sits upon her lap, but because hers is the divine womb from which this god-king springs. She is the root and *seat* of his power, and as such, she represents the sovereignty of the land of Egypt itself. As the two lands of Upper and Lower Egypt merged into one nation, the goddesses representing each of them (cobra and vulture) merged over time into the form that we now know as the mighty and beloved Isis.

Some early creation myths involve the idea of the universe hatching from an egg. In the Pelasgian creation story from ancient pre-Hellenic Greece (as reconstructed by scholar/author Robert Graves), things began with a cloud of chaos, from which arose Eurynome, goddess of all things. She created the first duality by separating sea from sky so she could dance upon the waves. As she danced she stirred the north wind, Boreas, into existence. She was enchanted with this new thing, the wind, and caught it and playfully rolled it between her hands. Boreas, the wind, then turned into a serpent, Ophion, who looked upon Eurynome with desire and mated with her. She turned herself into a dove and laid the universal cosmic egg, around which he coiled his body seven times. The egg hatched, splitting in two, and released all of creation—including sun, moon, and stars—into being.

As with the cobra and vulture of Egypt's original two kingdoms, we see again in this story both serpent and bird, each of them egg-laying creatures, reminding us of the primal cosmic egg, from which, in these early stories, the universe was said to be hatched.

Cobras are poisonous and vultures are known to be carrion eaters. Thus, both snakes and vultures are connected with life and death. It would appear that roles and characteristics of both Nekhebet and UaZit merged in the figure of Auset/Isis, with some of the roles and characteristics lapping over into the goddesses Nephthys and Hathor.

As previously noted, the image of Hathor as our now-familiar motherly cow goddess would seem to date from the time when cattle and milk were a primary part of the food sources of the Egyptian people. Some sources say that earlier on, Hathor, similar to UaZit, was seen as the Primal Serpent Goddess who created all life. This illustrates the overlapping of roles and characteristics of these ancient deities. The imagery may, in addition, be linked to the astrological age: Taurus imagery is cow/bull, while Gemini imagery often shows up in the form of eggs or an egg-laying creatures. When the cosmic egg is cracked open (its two pieces demonstrating the duality of Gemini) the world and all its creatures flow forth from it.

Hathor is often depicted with cow ears. And Isis herself is quite often represented wearing a horned headdress or crown that holds a solar disc between the horns. The horns may represent the horns of a bull/cow, and this image of the sun between the horns may be representative of the Age of Taurus, the time during which the spring equinox sun rose between the horns of the Taurean bull.

As time passed the imagery of Isis and her sister Hathor merged and mixed. Both are shown with horns that might be interpreted as cow horns or lunar horns (i.e. the waxing and waning crescents), and a disk between them. This disk is often the sun, although in some cases may represent the moon.

It would seem that quite early on after the two kingdoms were united and the persona of Isis expanded, she assumed the roles of many other of the earlier, more primitive goddesses, becoming thereby a sort of "All Mother." Thus she became the quintessential Egyptian Goddess whose sphere of influence included earth, sky, magic, nature, motherhood, and even the land of death— encompassing, therefore, all realms of being and life. She was thought to provide food for both the living and the dead.

The appearance in July of her star, Sirius/Sothis, marked the imminent inundation of Egypt by the Nile. This annual inundation indicated the abundance, fertility, and prosperity to come, as well as the start of the new year. This time also marked the time when the birthdays of Isis and her sibling deities—Osiris, Horus the Elder, Set, Nepthys—were celebrated. So in addition to being the beginning of the new year, this time was, in a sense, representative of the beginning, or at least the renewal, of both time and life. This time period, roughly July 14-19 by our calendar reckoning and at the very end of the sign of Cancer, is very close to the later-in-time July 22nd Christian feast day of St. Mary Magdalene, whose cult in France was located in regions where the Isis cults had previously flourished.

One of Isis's many titles was that of the *Star of the Sea*. In ancient Egypt, Greece, and Rome, devotees of Isis gathered in early March, when the storms of winter had passes, to celebrate the feast of *Ploiaphesia* or the "Launching of the Ships." This Isian festival, which included dancing, music, feasting and processions, was centered upon on asking for the blessings of Isis on ships and those who traveled on them.

As the quintessential Mother Goddess, Isis was the *Star of the Sea* of Space, in a way that the others deities with stellar aspects were not.

The Isis Temple at Philae, which was built during the 30th Dynasty (380-343 BC) on an island in the Nile River, originally faced another island called Biga. The use of this island was reserved solely for the priesthood of Osiris, who was supposedly buried there. Biga was believed to be the first land to have emerged from the primordial chaos.

The curtain-enclosed sanctuary, or Holy of Holies, of the Isis Temple was said to be the place where the goddess resided, and was also thought to be the source of the waters of life. The base stones of the first wall surrounding the entrance to the temple were thought to represent the stones that appeared as the waters of life receded at the beginning of the world. In the west section of this thick wall—called a pylon—was a small door that led to a place called the Birth House. (7)

These features indicate how closely Isis was connected with life's beginnings, from the very origins of physical life emerging from the water, to the birth of all creatures.

The influence of Egypt upon the surrounding areas was great, and eventually it spread to all the Mediterranean countries and even beyond. From her beginnings as a Goddess beloved by Egyptians, Isis was eventually adopted by other peoples and cultures and her worship and rites spread to many places in the ancient world. She was well known in Greece, Rome, Spain, southern France, and traces of her cult have been found even in Ireland. It reached a peak in the 3rd century BC but began to die out in Rome after the introduction of Christianity. By 550 A.D. the last of the Isian Egyptian temples had been closed down.

The cult of Isis may well have even traveled with the East African ancestors of the Yoruban people to the Niger area of west Africa, where she became associated with the Ogun River, just as Isis was associated with the life-giving waters of the Nile and became known as the great mother goddess Yemaya. Later, when the people were taken as slaves and made the great passage over the waters of the Atlantic Ocean to the Americas, Yemaya became associated with the ocean.

The actual rites of Isis were part of the ancient secret mystery traditions, and thus were never written down. Traces of them may be found, however, in a late 2nd century A.D. book called *The Golden Ass*, written by Apuleius, an initiate of the Isian Mysteries.

In this book, which describes his experiences leading up to and including his initiation into the Isian mysteries, Apuleius describes a vision of Isis he experienced.

As he rested on the seashore by the light of the full moon, Apuleius fell asleep. He awoke in terror in the silence of the night, to find the moon rising over the sea in "unusual splendor." He felt the mystery of night and silence all around him, and realized that "this was the hour when the goddess [Isis] exercised her greatest power and governed all things by her providence—not only animals, wild and tame, but even inanimate things were renewed by her divine illumination and might; even the heavenly bodies, the whole earth, and the vast sea waxed or waned in accordance with her will."

He prayed to Isis, pouring out his supplications, then once again fell asleep on the sandy shore. But he awoke quite soon thereafter, because...

> "... lo! from the midst of the deep there arose that face divine to which even the gods must do reverence. Then a little at a time, slowly, her whole shining body emerged from the sea and came into full view. I would like to tell you all the wonder of this vision, if the poverty of human speech does not prevent, or if the divine power dwelling within that form supplies a rich enough store of eloquence.

First, the tresses of her hair were long and thick, and streamed down softly, flowing and curling about her divine neck. On her head she wore as a crown many garlands of flowers, and in the middle of her forehead shone white and glowing a round disc like a mirror, or rather like the moon; on its right and left it was bound about with the furrowed coils of rising vipers, and above it were stalks of grain. Her tunic was of many colours, woven of the finest linen, now gleaming with snowy whiteness, now yellow like the crocus, now rosy-red like a flame. But what dazzled my eyes more than anything else was her cloak, for it was a deep black, glistening with sable sheen; it was cast about her, passing under her right arm and brought together on her left shoulder. Part of it hung down like a shield and drooped in many a fold, the whole reaching to the lower edge of her garment with tasseled fringe. All along the border of that gorgeous robe there was an unbroken garland of all kinds of flowers and fruits.

In her hands she held emblems of various kinds. In her right hand she carried a bronze rattle [the sistrum] made of a thin piece of metal curved like a belt, through which were passed a few small rods; this gave out a tinkling sound whenever she shook it three times with a quivering pulsation. In her left hand was a golden cup, from the top of whose slender handle rose an asp, towering with head erect and its throat distended on both sides. Her perfumed feet were shod with sandals woven of the palm of victory.

Such was the vision, and of such majesty. Then, breathing forth all the blessed fragrance of happy Arabia, she deigned to address me with voice divine:

Behold, Lucius, I have come, moved by thy prayers! I, nature's mother, mistress of all the elements, earliest offspring of the ages, mightiest of the divine powers, Queen of the dead, chief of them that dwell in the heavens, in whose features are combined those of all the gods and goddesses. By my nod I rule the shining heights of heaven, the wholesome winds of the sea, and the mournful silences of the underworld. The whole world honors my sole deity under various forms, with varied rites, and by many names . . . and the Egyptians, mighty in ancient lore, honoring me with my peculiar rites, call me by my true name, Isis the Queen.

I have come in pity for thy woes. I have come, propitious and ready to aid. Cease from thy weeping and lamentation, and lay aside thy grief. For thee, by my providence, the day of salvation is dawning! Therefore turn thy afflicted spirit, and give heed to what I command. The day, even the very day that follows this night, is dedicated to me by an everlasting dedication, for on this day, after I have laid to rest the storms of winter and stilled the tempestuous waves of the sea, my priests shall dedicate to the deep, which is now navigable once more, a new boat, and offer it in my honour as the first fruits of the year's seafaring. Thou must await this festival with untroubled heart and with no profane thoughts."[8]

Isis instructed Lucius Apuleius to find a priest the next day, and obtain initiation into her mysteries, after which, she said, he would be healed.

Isis was a major force in the ancient world and as we have stated, her worship spread throughout the known world and was found in many places. So, also, did the spirituality of Egypt find its way into many other parts of the ancient world, as had that of Sumeria and Babylonia before it. These spiritual traditions most assuredly influenced others in the area, including the new and still evolving religion of Judaism.

As can be seen, there are many overlaps in function and form with the goddesses given above, which is due, I believe, to the evolution of the basic form of the All-Mother type goddess over time as well as due to regional differences.

Notes:
1) en.wikipedia.org/wiki/Neith
2) Budge, E. A. Wallis, *The Gods of the Egyptians*, Gilbert & Rivington, London, 1903
3) Graves, Robert, *The Greek Myths, Volumes 1 & 2*, Penguin Books, Canada, 1955
4) http://lexicorient.com/e.o/carthage.htm
5) The Sumerian goddess Inanna grew to be the most important of the Sumerian goddesses. She was associated with the planet Venus, as were her successors Ishtar, Astarte, Anath, Atargatis, Aphrodite, and Venus. By some sources she is considered to be the daughter of the moon god, Nanna, and his wife Ningal (daughter of Enki/granddaughter of Nammu), and granddaughter of the air/storm god, Enlil, and his wife Ninlil. Since Enlil was the son of Anu, the heavens, and Ki, the earth, this made Inanna their great-granddaughter, and the great-great-granddaughter of Nammu/Namma, the primordial sea from which Anu & Ki first emerged, though she is seen as more closely related to Nammu through her mother, Ningal, and grandmother, Ninlil. Over time she assumed increasingly greater importance (which may explain the closer relationship to Nammu and Anu) and during the reign of Sargon her status was exalted to that of Anu.
6) Spence, Lewis, *Myths and Legends of Ancient Egypt,* George G. Harrap & Co, London, 1915
7) www.crystalinks.com/isis.html
8) Apuleius, *The Golden Ass*, William Heineman, London, MCMXV

Chapter Seven - Asherah and Anath

GODDESSES OF THE LAND FLOWING WITH MILK AND HONEY

The Promised Land

As many of us learned in bible study, Canaan was the "land flowing with milk and honey," the land to which the God of the Bible sent the children of Israel, telling them it was to be their homeland and directing them to conquer the inhabitants and take possession of the land.

But before the children of Israel became rulers of the land, with their embryonic monotheism and jealous god, the people of Canaan worshiped, among other deities, two important goddesses, Asherah and Anath. Having come from Egypt, and with ancestors who had lived in Canaan, the people were not unfamiliar with the concept of a goddess, or with either of these goddesses. [1] In fact, at this point in time they were not really monotheistic, despite Moses's conversations with Yahweh and Yahweh's insistence on being their special god.

According to the Bible, as the Hebrews settled into the land of Canaan both Asherah and Anath became dear to their hearts. So much so, in fact, over time, their prophets began to fulminate against them in ongoing attempts to enforce the newly emerging monotheism. As the centuries went by, it seemed that whenever things went wrong, and especially when the kingdom was threatened or under attack by a foreign power, the prophets would lay the blame on the peoples' continuing devotion to deities other than Yahweh, who was, as he himself had admitted, " a jealous god."[2]

The prophet Jeremiah said,

> *"Seest thou not what they do in the cities of Judah and in the streets of Jerusalem? The children gather wood, and the fathers kindle the fire, and the women knead their dough, to make cakes to the queen of heaven, and to pour out drink offerings unto other gods, that they may provoke me to anger."*
>
> —Jeremiah 7:17–18

But the people defended their worship of her, saying,

> *"But we will certainly do whatsoever thing goeth forth out of our own mouth, to burn incense unto the queen of heaven, and to pour out drink offerings unto her, as we have done, we, and our fathers, our kings, and our princes, in the cities of Judah, and in the streets of Jerusalem, for then we had plenty of victuals and were well and saw no evil..."*

—Jeremiah 44:17 [3]

The setting for Jeremiah's rebuke was the Hebrew settlement in Egypt, to which many of the Hebrews had fled after the Babylonians attacked and conquered Jerusalem in 586 BC

In Old Testament mentions of the goddess, especially as queen of heaven, it is not easy to tell whether the reference is to Asherah, mother of the gods (i.e. mother of the angels, that is, mother of the stars) or to her daughter, Anath, who was also called Ashtart, an epithet for Anath, according to scholar Raphael Patai. [4] In the Canaanite stories, Anath was the daughter of Asherah and El. She was associated with the planet Venus, and had been known in Sumeria as Inanna, in Babylonia as Ishtar.

In the Hebrew Temple in Elephantine, Egypt, Anath was worshipped as the consort of Yahweh, just as in other places, Asherah was so honored.

The queen of heaven referred to in the above passage was most likely Anath, though it may have been Asherah. However, I feel a case may be made for Asherah as a queen of heaven, based on what has been discovered about her pre-Judaic history.

Asherah

Who was Asherah and why was she so dear to the people? Asherah was the pre-Canaanite Ugaritic form of an important northwest Semitic goddess. The Ugaritic people of what is now Syria knew her as Athirat, the Akkadians as Ashratu, the Hittites called her Asherdu(s), and in Southern Arabia she was known as Asharath. The earliest reference to her is around 1750 BC, when she is mentioned on a Sumerian monument as Ashratum, wife of Anu, the Sumerian (and later Akkadian) god who corresponds to the great Canaanite father and sky god El.

She was related to, and often conflated with, her daughter Anath, who was known to the Greeks as Astarte.[5] Asherah's worship made its way to Egypt where she was sometimes known as Qudshu or Qedesh (again, a possible conflation with Astarte), a title that means "Holiness." With many similarities to Hathor/Isis, she may have been the same goddess, many of the functions and attributes being the same. At the least, the two were often combined.

As the primary goddess of the northwest Semitic tribes, Asherah was part of the official religion of the Hebrews before she was banished by the later Hebrew prophets and kings who desperately sought to make Judaism monotheistic.

Asherah, in her many forms and names, was known to be a fertility goddess, connected with desire, love and sexuality, as was her daughter Anath. Sometimes Asherah was seen as a goddess of both war and love, since, like many other early goddesses, she seemed to exhibit opposing characteristics—love and war, chastity and promiscuity, motherliness and blood-thirstiness, life and death. [6]

But it was her connections to fertility, love, human sexuality, and children that made her such a strong mother figure and such an important goddess to the people. In Canaanite religion her mate was the god El, by whom she was the mother of 70 sons. [7] El means, simply, *god*. Asherah was also known as *Elat*, (sometimes rendered *Elath*) which is the feminine form of El and means, simply, *goddess*. The southern Semitic equivalent of Asherah may have been the Arabian goddess Al-lat, later considered to be, along with her sisters Al-Mana't and Al-Uzza, one of the daughters of the god Allah (perhaps the Arabian equivalent of El). Al-lat seems to have been associated with the moon, while Al-Uzza was associated with the planet Venus, as were Inanna, Ishtar, Anath, and several similar goddesses.

Asherah was associated with water and the sea. Raphael Patai tells us that "…apparently, her proper domain was the sea, just as that of her husband El was heaven." [8] Her name, Asherah, means, quite literally, "She who treads on the sea," and she was known to be the protectress of ships at sea—very similar to Isis and Mary as the Star of the Sea. In Phoenicia (adjacent to Canaan) she was known as Tanith (Tanit), and was shown pictured with fish and dolphins. She was the Lady of the Sea—which was the Mediterranean Sea since the earliest traces of her worship were found on the Mediterranean coast at Sidon (now in Syria) but also quite possibly the Sea of Galilee, later famous for its New Testament associations with Jesus and on which he himself is said to have trod. I consider Asherah's realm of sea to include the "Sea of Space" as well those of earth. She was also associated with the moon, and some depictions of her show her with lunar "horns."

Asherah was also very much associated with trees. Her iconic image was a wooden pole or pillar, and her worship was often carried out in sacred groves or near trees. The original version of the pillar was itself quite likely to have been a tree. An image atop an ivory box found at the Ugaritic settlement of Minet el-Beida (the White Harbor) and dating to roughly 1500-1150 BC seems to depict Asherah as a tree. She is in the center of the image, with an animal to either side of her. In each hand she holds a short leafy branch; the animals are upright, reaching up to nibble the branches. The Old Testament books of Deuteronomy, Jeremiah, and Kings all mention that worship of the old gods took place, "on every high hill and under every green tree."

Asherah is also associated with snakes. Since one of her epithets was "Lady of the Serpent" and since she was sometimes represented in the form of a bronze serpent, the Biblical tale of the Garden of Eden becomes more interesting, particularly when one realizes that one of Asherah's epithets, *Chawat*, rendered *Chawa* or *Hawah* in Hebrew, translates in English to *Eve*. It could just be that Eve, whose name means *life* or *mother of all life*, the Tree, and the Serpent were originally manifestations of one and the same entity. Indeed, the case for the divine mother Asherah being the Tree of Life is very strong, as the Tree of Life represents the physically manifest world—divinely ordered "spirit in substance."

One representation of Asherah in her form of Tanit (and yes, there is a connection here between this Tanit and the Carthaginian Tanit mentioned in the previous chapter), depicts her as a pole around which two ribbon-like objects appear to be wrapped. This is very reminiscent of a caduceus, which is an ancient symbol of healing arts. Since Asherah is associated with snakes, this might explain why, in the Exodus story of the Old Testament, God instructed Moses to create a bronze serpent and mount it on a pole so that the desert-wandering Hebrews might be cured of venomous snakebites. This object was called the *Nehushtan*, which means "brass (i.e. bronze) serpent." Although not referred to as such in the Bible, the healing *Nehushtan* clearly seems to be a symbol of Asherah, whose iconic imagery includes both snakes and poles. It resided for years in the temple but was destroyed during the reign of Hezekiah, one of Israel's first monotheizing kings.

It should be noted that a pole or staff with one or two snakes circling it has been the symbol of the healing arts for a very long time. In ancient Sumeria a staff with two serpents on it was associated with the healing deity Ningishita (whose name means "lord of the good tree"), who was, perhaps, the precursor or prototype of the Greek healer Aesclepius, whose staff had a single serpent circling it. The staff with two serpents, the caduceus, was also associated with the Egyptian Thoth, the Phoenician Taaut, the Greek Hermes, and the Roman Mercury—all of whom are deities of wisdom, communication, and alchemy. This should alert us to the fact that wisdom and healing, in the ancient world, were seen to be related.

The serpent has long been a symbol of the body's inherent power of cosmic wisdom and expanded consciousness, which in India is called the *kundalini*. Sleeping, it lies coiled at the base of the spine. But upon awakening it rises up, winding its way around the spine through the body Ida (feminine) and Pingala (masculine) energy channels and chakras, and uniting these two energies as it journeys up the spine to the crown chakra —where it awakens consciousness, awareness, and brings a recognition of our oneness with the divine. Sometimes this process is depicted with two serpents (rather than one), the Ida and the Pingala, whose union opens the portal to this expanded consciousness.

Since, according to author Raphael Patai, a representation of Asherah stood within the Jerusalem Temple of Solomon for nearly two-thirds of its existence, it seems clear that she was an integral and accepted part of early Judaism. In addition, archeologists have discovered small "house shrines" (called *naos* (singular), *naoi* (plural), which means *temple, inner sanctum*) containing double thrones. The two thrones would seem to indicate that more than one deity was honored, and that Yahweh did indeed have a

ASHERAH AND ANATH

consort. That this consort was Asherah, or sometimes Anath/Ashtart, is made clear by the fact that her symbols and sacred animals adorn these house shrines.

Asherah was associated with lions; at least one image found by archeologists depicts her in the form of a tree or "asherah pillar," standing on the back of a striding lion. In another image she was depicted in the form of a tree, or pole, standing atop a lion with an ibex on either side of her. In the Sinai, images of her have been found which show her as lion-headed. In some of the pre-Canaanite Ugaritic texts, her sons are referred to as her lions. Among the many images of Asherah (and Anath as well) found in the area comprising modern day Syria, Lebanon, Israel, and even down into Egypt, several contain lions—Asherah is shown either with a lion, standing on a lion, or as a human woman with a lion head.

The lore of Asherah also associates her with doves. Doves, long a symbol of the Goddess in the Middle East, were frequently associated with goddesses of fertility and love and in the bible are associated with the spirit of God, the Holy Spirit, whose Old Testament equivalent is the Book of Proverbs figure of *Wisdom*, who was the "Presence" of God in the world, and was later referred to as the *Shekhinah*. [9] As noted in the previous chapter, the Pelasgian Eurynome was in the form of a dove when she laid the cosmic egg from which the entire universe came forth.

Later, in Christianity, the dove was symbolic of the Holy Spirit. This is found in the story of Jesus's baptism at the River Jordan, when it was said that the Holy Spirit descended upon him in the form of a dove. The Aramaic word for spirit is a feminine one—*ruach*, meaning breath—and for centuries there have been those who held that the Holy Spirit, rather than being part of an all male trinity, is actually feminine, as was the Shekhinah, the feminine "Presence of God" as found in Judaism.

There is a definite link between Asherah and the Egyptian Goddess Hathor. Both Asherah and Hathor were known to be nurturing mothers, while at the same time connected with war. Asherah was the Lady of the Sea, while Hathor was the Lady of the West, which was, in Egypt, the direction of the Land of the Dead. In esoteric lore, the direction of West is associated with sunset, endings, and the sea. Some images of Asherah show her wearing a horned headdress, similar to the cow-eared one associated with Hathor. Hathor, like Asherah, was frequently portrayed in the form of a pillar.

The pillar association is one Asherah shares with the Egyptian god Osiris. In the story of Osiris's murder by his jealous brother Set, the coffin of Osiris is thrown into the Nile, and drifts upriver. It drifts from the mouth of the Nile across the Mediterranean Sea to Byblos, in Phoenicia (the coastal area of Canaan), where it becomes tangled into a tree. The tree grows around it, but is eventually cut down and a pillar is made from it. Isis finds Osiris within this pillar, removes his body, and tells the people to worship this pillar for it once contained a god within it. [10]

It is tempting to see these wooden pillars as representative of an ancient Tree of Life. In a mystical sense, they certainly are just that. The Kabbalistic Tree of Life is a glyph or symbol that depicts the unfolding of the life force into material form. Osiris in the tree (or Hathor and Asherah, for that matter) represents the power of divinity within form, bringing to mind the much later *Gospel of Thomas*, wherein Jesus, referring to the presence of the divine spirit in all things says, "Cleave the wood and I am there; lift the stone and there you'll find me."

Anath, Ashtart, Astarte

In the Canaanite stories Asherah had a daughter named Anath. While Canaanite myth records stories about Anath, over time her stories and those of her mother began to merge, making it hard for us to effectively separate them.

Anath is known primarily as a goddess of love, fertility, and war. She seems to have been much more bloodthirsty than Asherah, but shared many of her mother's other characteristics and symbolism. The most significant difference between the character of the two goddesses being that Asherah was widely acknowledged as a mother while Anath was primarily seen as a maiden—a warlike, bloodthirsty maiden, but a maiden nonetheless. Like Asherah, Anath was associated with doves, lions, and serpents.

Just as there was a link between Hathor and Asherah, a link exists between Hathor and Anath as well; stylistic similarities in their appearance are found in some of the statues, they shared certain characteristics, and both were seen as Mistress or Queen of the Heavens.

In the story of Isis finding the body of Osiris in the pillar in Byblos, later versions of the story said that the pillar was located at the Temple of Anath at Byblos.

Probably the most famous of Anath's stories concerns her participation in the death/resurrection story of her brother-consort, Baal, wherein she travels to the land of death to rescue Baal, defeats and destroys Mot, the god of death, and restores Baal to the land of the living.

Anath is also referred to as Anatu, Anata, Anthat, Ashtart, Astarte and, in the Old Testament, as Ashtoreth, which means "womb," or "that which issues from the womb," or "she of the womb," an appropriate title for a goddess of fertility. In Canaanite mythology her brother-consort, Baal (which means "lord"), was the "inducer and symbol of male fertility." [11] The mentions of Anath/Asthoreth in the Old Testament are very negative, of course, since the writers were intent on implementing monotheism in accord with Hezekiah's and Josiah's purge of all deities but Yahweh.

Over time, Anath's worship became predominant over Asherah's. By the 4th century BC her worship had almost completely eclipsed Asherah's in Sidon, which had previously been one of Asherah's major cult centers.[12] From this point on the conflation of Anath and Asherah often makes it harder to determine which goddess is being referred to.

Like Inanna, Ishtar, Isis, Hathor, Neith, Aphrodite, the Virgin Mary, and many others, Anath was called the Queen of Heaven.

As we can see from the Book of Jeremiah verses given at the beginning of this chapter, in honor of the Queen of Heaven men built fires and women baked special cakes that they offered as sacrifices to her. The bible also mentions that, before Josiah's purge, the women wove "houses" for her, the nature of which are not described. This may well be related to a custom in Sumeria, from whence much of Canaan's religious ideas and practices derived, of the temple priestesses weaving reed huts, or tents, as residences (called *gagum*) of the priestesses and sanctuaries (called *giguna*) for the Goddess, places where her rites, including the Hieros Gamos, were enacted. In Mesopotamia the huts were woven from the ever plentiful reeds, while in the much dryer land of Canaan, yarn made from goat hair was used. (13)

Exploring the origins of the figures of Asherah and Anath leads us directly back to some of the oldest known goddesses, namely, the Sumerian goddesses Nammu and Inanna. It is very likely that Asherah, Anath, Astarte, Ishtar, Hathor, Isis, and even the much later Aphrodite and Venus are simply evolutions and regional variations of Nammu and Inanna—Nammu, the great primordial sea of being, and Inanna, who was, quite plainly put, an embodiment of the force of desire/attraction that allows for the continuation of life. (14) As time went on and the stories evolved (and perhaps the deity herself evolved) the inevitable next stage occurred, in which the goddess acquired motherly characteristics, though not every such goddess was said to have given birth even if linked with love, sexuality, and fertility.(15) And of course humans being what they are, she inevitably acquired warlike characteristics as well.

The association of love and fertility goddesses with "desire" is quite interesting as desire is an emotion—a movement of energy—which precedes creation. Desire sets up a magnetic attraction to bring the object of desire closer, so that union of some kind can occur. This is quite appropriate for goddesses connected with love—which leads to creation in the form of mating and motherhood. Deities of desire represent a very primal force of the universe, as is indicated in *Chapter One*.(16)

Although scholars have not reached decisive conclusions on the exact meaning of Inanna's name, it is worth noting that it contains the syllable "an," which, as we have seen, is associated with the heavens. Some scholars contend that it means "Great Lady of An." Others note that since *in* means queen and *anna* refers to the heavens, her name means simply "queen of heaven." (17) In addition, it should be noted that the name of her later Babylonian equivalent, Ishtar, means "star," and that she has been associated with the planet Venus (both stars and planets being referred to as stars at that time). It would seem that the Babylonians considered the planet itself to be the body of Ishtar in the heavens.[18] A prayer to Inanna from 2000 BC suggests this: "I say "Hail!" to the Holy One who appears in the heavens!" [19]

The word *Ishtar* is related to Ashtart, Astarte, and Esther (of biblical fame). Each of these good ladies has an association with the planet Venus as the "Morning Star," either etymologically or mythologically.

The mythologies of both Inanna and Ishtar show links to the Underworld in the form of journeys they made to that dark realm. Ishtar's sister (and possibly 'other self'), Ereshkigal, was ruler of this realm, the Queen of the Underworld. There was antipathy on the part of Ereshkigal toward Ishtar, which may be representative of death being jealous of life, or winter of spring. But the journey of Life/Ishtar into the Underworld may also be interpreted as the quest of the *expression* of life going in search of the *source* of life, which is found, as always, in the dark places of both Underworld and the vast sky.[20]

So with Asherah and her daughter Anath, we find that ancient Canaan and later Israel had goddesses whose realms encompass land, sea, and sky. Asherah, goddess of the Land Flowing with Milk and Honey, Lady of the Sea, Lady of the Serpent, Lady of the Lions, and her daughter, Anath, who shared these attributes and in addition was called the Queen of Heaven, are, in my opinion, most definitely representative of the Divine Feminine who is both sea and stars and who births all life.

Atargatis

In ancient times, the land of Canaan encompassed what is now modern day Israel, the Palestinian territories, Lebanon, and extended southward to the coastal areas of modern day Jordan and northeastern Egypt, as well as northward to parts of Syria.[21]

So before we leave this Land Flowing with Milk and Honey, it is important to note a later Lady of the Sea who was the pre-eminent goddess of Syria, particularly northern Syria from at least the 3rd and 4th centuries BC. She was also venerated as far south as the coastal city of Ascalon (i.e. Ashkelon), in what is now Israel, a place known as a center of worship of Astarte.

Her name was Atargatis and she was often depicted as a mermaid. She was also known as Atarath, Athart, and to the Greeks as Atargatis, Ataratha, and later as Derketo. Many of her characteristics and much of her imagery are directly related to Asherah, Astarte, Anat, Ishtar and Inanna and link her with the sea, fertility, and motherhood. The figure of Atargatis may well be a conflation of all of these goddesses.

As scholars Garstang and Strong say about the Great Mother in their 1913 translation of Lucian's famous "De Dea Syria,"

> *Among the Babylonians and northern Semites she was called Ishtar: she is the Ashtoreth of the Bible, and the Astarte of Phœnicia. In Syria her name was 'Athar, and in Cilicia it had the form of 'Ate ('Atheh). At Hierapolis, with which we are*

primarily concerned, it appears in later Aramaic as Atargatis, a compound of the Syrian and Cilician form. [22]

She was the primary goddess of the area comprising northern Syria. The first evidence of her is found on coins dating back to the 3rd and 4th century BC Her main center was Hieropolis but her worship was spread throughout the Mediterranean area by Syrian traders and slaves.

Atargatis was associated with springs, rivers, and the sea. She was linked with lions, doves, and fish, which are often pictured nearby or on her. In some places she was pictured with dolphins, and in others is shown with the eight-pointed star of Ishtar/Venus nearby. She is shown riding on a lion or walking with a lion on either side of her.

Wisdom

In *Chapter One* we spoke of the Great Primeval Sea—the Primal Mother—who was known to Sumerians as Nammu (also Namma), to Egyptians as Nun, to Babylonians as Tiamat, and to the Hebrews as the Tehom, or The Deep—the great abyss, or void, from which life originated. In Babylonian cosmogony, Wisdom was thought to dwell in the depths of that great primeval sea. Nammu's son, Enki (also known as Ea), was called the Lord of Unfathomable Wisdom.

Therefore, it was the depths of the great primeval sea itself—the Deep, the Tehom, the Abyss—that was considered Wisdom, and her son Enki/Ea, the "Lord of the sweet waters," was the god of wisdom who organized and managed it. [23] So when we see a reference to the Deep, the Tehom, the Abyss, or the Void, we are seeing a reference to the great primeval sea, the source of all Wisdom.

Before concluding this section of the book we need to take a look at an interesting figure whose roots go back to that great primeval sea, but are also to be found within the goddesses Asherah, Anath, and their predecessors—as well as within various Egyptian, Persian, and even Sumerian deities—and that is the Biblical figure of Wisdom.

The figure of Wisdom in the Old Testament seems to be a personification of the spirits of truth, justice, righteousness, cosmic order, and harmony. All of which—particularly cosmic order and harmony—are what give "form" to pure spirit. [24]

In the Book of Proverbs, it is Wisdom who is God's first creation/emanation. It is Wisdom who helps him create the rest of the universe—giving form and life to all things. Wisdom speaks, in the Book of Proverbs, expressing her delight in assisting God as a master craftswoman, an artisan, in the work of the creation. She also expresses her delight in humans, with whom, it seems, she had a particular relationship. This lets us know that in the Hebrew religious tradition, the divine creative power was seen as both masculine and feminine; God had a partner in creation—it was not a purely masculine affair—and that the partner, Wisdom, is quite friendly and accessible to humans.[25]

Given the presence of the above-mentioned *naos* shrines uncovered in Israel, it becomes clear that Asherah was seen to be the feminine aspect of God: she was God's "Presence," God's Holy Spirit. She was Wisdom, the first emanation of the Divine; the maternal power who formed and fashioned the world and gave it life.

From the earliest days, when the Spirit of God dwelt or came into manifestation for the people or the high priests, it was often referred to as God's "Glory," and was perceived as a cloud, a pillar of fire, or a brilliant radiance. After the first Jerusalem temple had been constructed, the Glory was said to dwell within the Holy of Holies in the temple. The Hebrew word meaning "to dwell within" was *shakan*, from which the feminine word *Shekhinah* derives. It comes from the same Sanskrit root word as do the Hindu words *shakti* and *shaktipat*. [26]

The Shekhinah, then, was the *presence* of God/Wisdom/Asherah, as that presence manifested from the world of spirit into the physical human realm. She was seen as the Presence of God in the physical realm, just as was the Tree of Life. She was, in essence, the *soul* of the world—the individual divine spark of spirit of the planet and its lifestream. But more than that, she was the soul/spirit infused physical substance of the planet.

Wisdom/Shekhinah is closely linked with the Christian concept of the Holy Spirit and the Sophia of the Orthodox Church, but a thorough detailing of these interconnections is beyond the scope of this book.[27] However, it is worth noting that in the Gnostic Gospel of Thomas, Jesus says that the Holy Spirit is his mother (meaning his "spirit mother."). Therefore, when at the end of the Gospel of John as Jesus is preparing to ascend to heaven and says he will send the Holy Spirit, who is the comforter and consoler, to be with the apostles, he is really saying he will send his mother.[28] Christianity holds that the descent of the Holy Spirit at Pentecost—in the form of tongues of fire and a rush of wind—fulfilled this promise.

The Egyptian goddess Ma'at was seen as a personification of divine cosmic order and harmony and fulfilled a similar function as the Biblical figure of Wisdom. Later in time Ma'at was paired with the god Thoth, who had the same attributes. In addition, the Egyptian goddess Sia (who may have been the same as either Ma'at or Thoth) personified the Divine Mind, which included the qualities of perception and understanding. Her consort was Hu, who personified the Divine Word, the power and authority of the spoken word. The God Heka personified the Divine Power, thus completing the Divine Trinity that represented the creative power of the gods—creating the world anew with every sunrise. [29]

The mind, the word, and the power—working as one to create the "form." This is the power of Wisdom, the Divine Pattern which gives Form to "spirit manifesting" into the physical dimension—very similar to the Mother of Form about whom we have been speaking in these chapters. [30]

ASHERAH AND ANATH

* * *

We have now looked at many facets of the Divine Mother who birthed and nourished the world. But there is another facet we must consider—that of the Galactic Mother who moves, changes, evolves, turns the wheel of life, and governs the cosmic tides of life. This will be taken up in the following chapters.

Notes
1) Some scholars have come to the conclusion that there was probably not much of a difference between Hebrew beliefs and the native Canaanite beliefs at that point in time. It is becoming clear that the Hebrews already worshipped a goddess before Moses and Joshua led them into Canaan—if, indeed, the Exodus ever did occur in the way it is described in the Bible. Some theories hold that the people who later became called Hebrews were already dwellers in Canaan, but began using somewhat different religious beliefs and practices to separate themselves from the rest of the pagan population. To put this in an historical timeline, the Hebrew religion's rejection of the Goddess began with King Hezekiah (circa 715-686 BC) and was completed by King Josiah (circa 621 BC) just 30-40 years before the Babylonians conquered Jerusalem and carried many of the inhabitants into captivity. When the Babylonian captives were released years later and returned to their homeland, the priesthood rebuilt the temple and resumed their previous monotheistic, anti-goddess version of the religion, causing many people to migrate elsewhere (including Egypt) in protest.
2) The Holy Bible, King James Version, *Exodus 20: 5*
3) The Holy Bible, King James Version, *Book of Jeremiah*
4) Patai, Raphael, *The Hebrew Goddess*, Avon Books, NY, 1967, 1978, p 55
5) Astarte, like Ishtar, did not share some of Asherah's most important roles: wife/consort of the chief deity, mother of the lesser gods, and goddess of the sea.
6) Patai, Raphael, *The Hebrew Goddess*, Avon Books, NY, 1967, 1978, p 154
7) There is quite likely a connection between the 70 sons of Asherah and the much later 72 angels of Hebrew tradition, who were said to have been appointed by God as "princes" of the 72 nations of the world—*Israel* being the name of both the foremost nation and the greatest of the angels. (Barker, Margaret; *Temple Themes in Christian Worship*; T & T Clark, Int., London & NY; p 83) It should also be noted that Jesus was said to have had 72 disciples.
8) Patai, Raphael, *The Hebrew Goddess*, Avon Books, NY, 1967, 1978; p 19
9) It is very likely that Wisdom and the Shekhinah are the same being, with the Shekhinah being a later version of Wisdom. References are often found to a Heavenly Shekhinah and an Earthly Shekhinah. These are actually references to the Spirit/Presence of God---the Divine Feminine---in both of her forms, heavenly and earthly. The Earthly Shekhinah is the Divine Presence/Holy Spirit/Mother, who chooses to remain on earth with her children rather than remain in the heavenly realm of non-material bliss.
10) Saying, in essence, that the tree was the womb which held and birthed him. This, in turn, relates back to the concept of the Goddess as the Tree of Life.
11) Patai, Raphael, *The Hebrew Goddess*, Avon Books, NY, 1967, p 57
12) _____p 56
13) Teubal, Sabina, *Sarah the Priestess: The First Matriarch of Genesis*; Swallow Press, Athens, OH, Chicago, London; 1984; pp 100-102
14) And the continuation of life, it must be said, involves both creation and destruction. The new creation must be protected, and old unusable forms must go, in order for the new to flourish.
15) Though Inanna herself was not a mother.
16) Thus both the Mother and her Daughter are linked with the Sea Temple.
17) Wolkstein and Kramer, *Inanna Queen of Heaven*, Harper & Row Publishers, NY, Cambridge, Philadelphia, San Francisco, London, Mexico City, Sao Paolo, Sydney; 1983)
18) Related to this is the fact that the shape that Venus traces in the sky over an 8 year period of time is that of a pentagram. This is essentially the shape of the old varieties of the rose, a flower associated with Inanna,

Ishtar, Anath-Astarte, Isis, Aphrodite, Venus, and several others, as well as with the Virgin Mary, and Mary Magdalene.

19) Wolkstein and Kramer, *Inanna Queen of Heaven*, Harper & Row Publishers, NY, Cambridge, Philadelphia, San Francisco, London, Mexico City, Sao Paolo, Sydney; 1983)

20) From a strictly astronomical point of view, it might also be interpreted as the period of time when Venus disappears from the evening sky before reappearing several days later as the Morning Star.

21) http://en.wikipedia.org/wiki/Canaan

22) Armstrong, Herbert A & Garstang, John, *De Dea Syria*, Constable & Co, LTD, London, 1913; p 1

23) Mead, G.R.S., *The Wedding Song of Wisdom*, p 52; The Theosophical Publishing Society, London and Benares, 1908

24) Breck, John, *The Spirit of Truth*, St Vladimir's Seminary Press, Crestwood, NY, 1991

25) This version, wherein the Tehom, or source of all being, seems to be neutral, the creator male (God the Father), and his helper female (Wisdom), seems to demonstrate somewhat of a gender reversal from the Sumerian/Babylonian stories where the Deep/Tiamat/Tehom is female, wise, and creates from within her own wise being, though later "managed" by her son.

26) Shakti is defined as the female principle of divine energy, especially when this energy is personified as the supreme deity; in other words, the Goddess. Shaktipat is defined as defined as the transmission of the Shakti energy.

27) See Appendix A for more on these connections

28) Though the translations that have come down to us have used the male pronoun.

29) Breck, John, *The Spirit of Truth*, St Vladimir's Seminary Press, Crestwood, NY, 1991

30) Both Wisdom/Chokmah and Understanding/Binah are the Divine Feminine. Wisdom/Chokmah is the Bride/Partner of God in creation, at which point she becomes Binah, the Mother of Form.

Chapter Eight - The Birth of the Universe and the Changing of Ages

A Stream of Stars

The first children of the Dark Mother and the Bright One were the great magellanic clouds of stardust which spiraled, swirled, and coalesced into the very first stars, star clusters, and galaxies. These were followed, vast eons of time later, by the formation and evolution of planets, upon which life forms evolved.

A spiral represents movement and is the shape of the initial movement of the "fluctuation in the void" that sparked the universe into being, as well as being the shape that energy takes in its movement. Be it the unfurling of a flower or of a galaxy, the spiral shape movement is prominent in life's unfolding. The significance of the spiral was noted by the ancients and is found represented in myth as the whirlpool, the serpent-dragon, the caduceus, and other symbols that are used to illustrate the life force as it moves and fertilizes creation.

Scientists tell us that the shape of the universe may well be toroidal. A toroid is formed when energy spirals outward, corkscrew-fashion, in two directions from a center point, forming an ever widening double funnel shape, and eventually curves around to meet itself. The recent discovery that the universe appears to revolve around a central axis (determined by and related to how light travels through space), has given weight to the toroid-shape universe theory.[1]

But it all started with the Dark Mother, the Bright One, and the stardust. We are made from stardust; *everything* is made from stardust.

Creation begins at the center and spirals outward. Dissolution causes forms to dissolve, disperse, and in some cases, to eventually spiral inward, back toward the center—all of this over unimaginably vast expanses of time. Of course, along the way many other things occur—quasars, comets, black holes, and the like. But all follow the pattern described above, which is essentially one of an initial movement (often explosive) outward, a spiraling expansion, and an eventual contraction.

So it comes back to the stardust, streaming and spiraling through space—coalescing, clumping, warming, cooling, creating. One might say that creation was carried on a stream of stardust....

The Spinner-Weaver Goddess spins the threads of creation into being, and weaves them into the tapestry of life.

The Gates of Life and Death

We have spoken much of the great silvery-white river of stars that streams across our night sky and is known as the Milky Way, and its importance to many cultures. Within that great starry milky river is a dark rift that was known as the womb of creation by some cultures. The Mayan culture, in particular, paid great attention to this part of the sky, seeing the dark rift as well as the central bulge of the galaxy as the womb, birth canal, and yoni of the Great Mother, as well as the heart of the Sacred Tree that marked the road to the mysterious Underworld where creation began and ended. This dark rift is located in the constellation of Sagittarius and is quite near the Galactic Center.

In old European cosmology, the area of the sky at the end of the constellation of Taurus and the beginning of the constellation of Gemini was known as the Gate of Birth (i.e. life), while the area between the constellations of Scorpio and Sagittarius was known as the Gate of Death. These are the two main points in the sky where the zodiacal ecliptic and the Milky Way intersect.

In the night sky, the Galactic Center is in the direction of the constellation Sagittarius. The Galactic Anti-Center is in the direction of Gemini. When we look at the Milky Way in the summer sky, we are looking through the Gate of Birth/Gate of Life—the last degrees of the constellation Taurus and the first degrees of the constellation of Gemini—and toward the Galactic Center. When we look at the Milky Way in the winter sky, we are looking through the Gate of Death, also known as the Gate of the Ancestors—the last degrees of Sagittarius and the first degrees of Capricorn—and out into deep space.

For our Celtic ancestors these Gates were also marked by the star grouping known as the Pleiades, whose midnight culmination around the time of All Hallows Eve (November 1st) marked the start of winter and the opening of the Gate of Death in the Celtic calendar, and whose heliacal rising around the beginning of May marked the start of summer, and the opening of the Gate of Life.[2]

While this is clearly tied to the solar-dictated seasonal tides of the northern hemisphere of Planet Earth, it's interesting that the parts of the sky considered to be the Gates pointed toward and also directly away from the Galactic Center. Since summer is the time of life's growth, and winter the time of decay and death, it is likely, although impossible to prove, that our ancestors believed that some galactic life-giving or life-destroying energies emanated from these two parts of the sky during these times of the year.

Creation's Story

Many creation myths describe creation as coming from the sky or the sea, though the life-forms that inhabit the world are often seen as coming from out of the earth or the sea.

In the Irish legend mentioned in earlier chapters, the cows came out of the sea, as did the maiden who announced their impending arrival. The Watery Abyss births earthly life, just as the Starry Abyss, the Sea of Sky, births all life.

In her magical novel, *Sea Priestess*, esoteric author and magician Dion Fortune tells us that life emerges from the starry abyss of space, and that from that beginning the polarities—darkness and light, movement and stillness, feminine and masculine—arise.

> *"I looked out into the measureless depths of interstellar space and saw arise a fountain out of which water like liquid moonlight poured in boundless abundance. This, I thought, is the First Begetting. I watched the liquid light gather into a great pool in the deeps of space. I saw currents arise in the pool, and presently it began to swirl, and out of its swirling motion arose the suns. And I knew that water had two moods - the flowing and the still, and not until it is still can life arise in it."* (3)

Insofar as the pan-Celtic traditions go, it might be said that in her earliest forms the Goddess Dana (Danu/Don/Ana/Anu) is the watery abyss from which existence and form is birthed. She is therefore equivalent to Mother Night/Dame Dark/Nyx—the great abyss of space who birthed the stars and thus all life—and to the Egyptian *Nun*, the primordial waters.

To summarize briefly the essentials of the first few chapters, the milk of this mother is the great starry river we call the Milky Way, which spans the heavens from horizon to horizon like a great sky-bridge arching over the earth. Its counterparts on earth are the many great rivers which sustain her earth's creatures and which are inextricably linked with the Mother in her role as the Cow Goddess.

Thus, Dana (as well as Boann, as previously noted) might be seen as the Heavenly Cow, the Mother who births and nourishes life. And in Egyptian mythology, as we have seen, it was primarily Hathor and Isis who were seen in this role of Heavenly Cow, sustainers of the people.

Dion Fortune continues, her novel's heroine, Morgan, speaking of her vision of the beginnings of the sea as the source of life on earth:

> *"'And there came to me a vision of the sea as the source of all things, I saw her lay down the sedimentary rocks and withdraw and leave them land; I saw the slow process of the lichens and the weather that broke down the rocks into soil; I saw the sea rise and take them again as primordial slime; and in that slime arose the first life. And I saw life come ashore from the slime and grow feet and wings.'*

> *Then I knew why Morgan worshiped the sea, for it is the first of created things, and nearer to the Primordial than anything else."* (4)

There are many levels at which this creation might be viewed. From the cosmic perspective, life and manifestation are birthed from the Great Void.

From a galactic perspective, life and manifestation are birthed from our Galactic Center, which, interestingly, contains a black hole in its center. Black holes are locations in space where the gravitational pull is so great that the surrounding matter and anti-matter are eventually pulled inside and disappear. Black holes literally absorb what is close enough around them to be caught in their gravitational pull. And yet, our galactic family of stars and planets was spun out from the galaxy's earliest form, so even galaxies with black holes give forth as well as take in—exactly as does the Great Goddess who is the Mother of all Form, she who births all life and takes it back to herself when its time is done.

Interestingly, almost all galaxies have been found to contain black holes in their center. Physicists working in the field of general relativity theory have postulated the possibility of corresponding white holes—hypothetical regions of "spacetime" that are the reverse of black holes: nothing can enter them but they emit light and matter.

From an earthly perspective, life was birthed from the Primordial Sea, and thence evolved into its many forms—a process which is still underway, whether or not we are aware of it.

What activated the conception and generation of life in the skies and on the planet? In a poetic and elemental way of speaking we might say that within the original Void (Space), an energy (Fire) arose, causing a movement (Air). These together kindled and sparked something new, which formed, coalesced, and gestated (Water) as it condensed into the solidity of substance and structure that is form (Earth). These were the first movements of energy; and from these all else came into being.

Scientists have estimated the "Big Bang" and that which followed immediately thereafter occurred approximately 13.7 billion years ago.

Oneness, separation, differentiation—these are the themes of the old story that are played out over and over again on levels ranging from cosmic to human. Light separates itself from the darkness so that it can become light. Male separates itself from the primordial birthing-female oneness so that it can become male. Life evolves in as many forms as planetary habitats demand. This is the pattern of life as it develops and evolves. I believe it is also the pattern of consciousness as it develops and evolves. And as humans with the gift of imagination, we are constantly creating stories to describe this process and our place in it.

All religion is really "nature religion," having both a cosmic dimension and a terrestrial one. All religions, at their most primal level, actually have their origins in the sky—the movements of the sun, moon, stars and planets, which were seen by most cultures as divine beings whose influence extended to life on earth—and the earth, upon whose beneficent abundance, in the form of water, vegetation, wildlife, and good weather, all life depends.

The Precession of the Equinox

From our viewing perspective on earth we watch the eternal wheeling of the stars of the night sky. Thousands of years ago our ancestors discovered the phenomenon we now call the Precession of the Equinoxes.

"Due to the gravitational pull of the sun and moon on the earth's equatorial bulge, the earth's spinning motion is subject to a slow wobble. Through the course of time this wobble changes the appearance of the stars in the night sky. The earth's north-south axis (the imaginary line that extends north-south through the body of the planet and infinitely beyond in both directions) appears—over the course of approximately 26,000 years—to perform a slow circle dance through the sky, returning at the end to the point where the dance began. This circle dance is called the Precession of the Equinoxes.

It is this circle dance that creates the Zodiacal Ages, as the sun appears to rise within a different constellation (of the twelve well known, irregularly sized and shaped constellations positioned around the earth's ecliptic plane) every 2,160 years. With twelve constellations, each 2,160 year period is like a "month" in the 26,000 year "Great Year." The direction of this motion through our twelve constellations is opposite that of the sun. Thus, while the Sun appears to move from Aries to Taurus, to Gemini, the precessional movement is from Aries, to Pisces, to Aquarius—counterclockwise." (5)

Below you will find a chart containing very rough and rounded off approximations of the dates of the Zodiacal Ages.

Astrological Age	Began	Ended	Opposite Sign
Aquarius	2012 AD	4172 AD	Leo
Pisces	148 BC	2012 AD	Virgo
Aries	2308 BC	148 BC	Libra
Taurus	4320 BC	2308 BC	Scorpio
Gemini	6480 BC	4320 BC	Sagittarius
Cancer	8640 BC	6480 BC	Capricorn
Leo	10,800 BC	8640 BC	Aquarius
Virgo	12,960 BC	10,800 BC	Pisces
Libra	15,120 BC	12,960 BC	Aries
Scorpio	17,280 BC	15,120 BC	Taurus

A Short Primer on the Last Several Astrological Ages

Looking backwards from our perspective in time, it becomes apparent how these astrological themes have played out in culture and history, and quite often in the life of an "Avatar" whose life seemed to embody the themes of the age. Without getting into a long essay on how, when, where, and why astrology developed, I'd like to present just a few examples which show how the themes of the most recent Astrological Ages have manifested in culture, societal development, and religion.

Pisces, the Fishes - We are living in the last years of the Piscean Age. Pisces means "fishes," and the fish was an early symbol of Christianity. Jesus told his disciples, most of whom started out as fishermen on the Sea of Galilee, that they would become "fishers of men."

There are those who take this symbology a bit further and say that the almond-like fish shape that currently finds its way onto bumper stickers was originally without the lines that comprise the tail, thus making it truly almond shaped. This almond shape has another name. It is called the mandorla and is created when two circles of the same size are drawn so that the outer edge of each is placed in the exact center of the other. Some say that this convergence of the two circles represents the union of complementary opposites. The mandorla thus created represents not just the combined energies of the two, but the offspring of their union. In medieval Christianity it was widely used artistically to indicate a halo or radiance around a being of great holiness, the Virgin Mary and Christ in particular. But prior to Christianity, this shape was held to represent the yoni of the goddess, the divine source from which all life emerged.

The shape has mathematical significance and was of great interest to the early Greeks. It is also reminiscent of the shape of the human eye.

Watery and very changeable, Pisces, which is said to be a higher vibration of Venus, is ruled by Neptune—the planet of idealism, receptivity, compassion and empathy, mysticism and spiritual strength, yet also of impressionability, impracticality, irresponsibility, escapism, deceit and delusion.

Just above is the astrological glyph for Pisces. It represents two fish swimming in opposite directions. This indicates the dual nature of Pisces, which is often at war with itself. There is no doubt that the last 2000 years have served up generous helpings of both sides of this dual nature.

♈ Aries - the Ram - Prior to the Piscean Age, which began shortly before the birth of Jesus, was the Age of Aries the Ram, during which sheep were an important theme.

Indications of this are found in the symbol systems of Middle Eastern religions, including Judaism, where lambs were among the most important sacrificial animals at the Jerusalem Temple, and in the Egyptian religion, where the solar creator god, Amun-Ra, was often pictured as having the head of a ram. Of course, in the pastoral cultures of that era sheep were a big part of everyday life so it's not surprising to find such references.

One might say that the beginning of the Age of Aries is signaled in the Old Testament by the story of God's demand that Abraham slay his son, Isaac, as a sacrifice, with a last minute reprieve granted by an angel who instructs Abraham to sacrifice a lamb in Isaac's stead.

The symbolism of lambs as a sacrificial offering was carried forward into Christianity (which began as an offshoot of Judaism) with Jesus being referred to as the sacrificial *Lamb of God*. Implicit in the concept of sacrifice is that of the scapegoat, or substitute, who takes on the weight of a culture's collective ills and wickedness, and by whose death such ills are expiated and erased.

Aries is a fiery and individualistic sign, full of courage, initiative, and new ideas. The Age of Aries was an age of warriors, rugged individuals, and empire expansion. In terms of religion, it was, as stated above, the time of the birth and growth of Judaism (Aries's fiery nature showing itself in the Moses story with its burning bush and pillar of fire), and indeed, of monotheism itself—which began not as the idea that there was only one god (an abstraction which developed over time), but that a particular god would covenant with a particular person or group, and become their special god.

Judaism, which has had an indisputable influence on western civilization and culture, began with such a covenant between a man, Abraham, and a god who became known as Yahweh. Years later, when the Ten Commandments were given to Moses, the first commandment stated, "I am the Lord thy God, who brought thee out of the land of Egypt, out of the house of bondage. Thou shalt have no other gods before me." Note that this commandment does not state that other gods are nonexistent, only that Yahweh is to be first, and to be "their" god because he's done them a big favor.

Further verses go on to expressly prohibit the use or veneration of any images or natural objects as representations of the divine, thus clearly drawing a line in the sand between the older pagan religions which did these things, and the new religion the god of Moses was starting. The Hebrew people were, in fact, given a tremendous amount of instruction in ways to differentiate themselves from those "other people," who were not in covenant with Yahweh—things including specific bodily mutilation (i.e. circumcision) and dietary laws (i.e. which led to the Kosher laws), and other forms of ritual cleanliness. All of this was done to create something new, something individual, something separate and very different from religions of the past. Yahweh even promised his people a land of their own. It was an unfortunate inconvenience that this land was already populated and that for Yahweh's promise to be fulfilled, the residents had to be disposed of by warfare and slaughter, as the bible so dramatically recounts. But all of these—the separation from past and moving into newness and the future, the new land, the new religion, the new relationship with the divine and the new way of being, even the warfare—are quite Arian themes.

♉ **Taurus, the Bull** - This era was focused on the Taurean themes of nurture, sustenance, growth, expansion, sensuality, beauty, love, prosperity, strength, and stability. Evidence of these themes is found in the ancient cultures of Sumeria, India, Ireland, and Egypt, with their beautiful structures and abundance of bovine themes and references. It is likely that the pyramids—beautiful to behold and solid enough to last millennia—were built during this era. We have spoken much of this era in previous chapters so will not elaborate further here. The religion of this era had deities that personified these themes, in particular, the cow and bull deities.

♊ **Gemini, the Twins** - Pictured in the heavens as two young men seated side by side holding hands, the divine twins show up in the artwork and legends of many lands. In Greece they were known as the Dioscori—Castor and Polydeuces, the twin sons of the goddess Leda and the great god Zeus. Twin brothers as incarnations of Rama, himself an incarnation of the god Vishnu, figure heavily in Hindu legends.

The twins represent not just identical brothers, but significant related twosomes: siblings or sibling-couples of same or different genders. In Egypt we find Geb and his sister-wife Nuit, Shu and his sister-wife Tefnut, Osiris and his sister-wife Isis. In Greece we find Cronos and his sister-wife Rhea; Zeus and his sister-wife Hera. Bible stories are full of them too: Adam and Eve, Cain and Abel, Sarah and Abraham, Jacob and Esau, and Leah and Rachel, for example.

Ruled by Mercury, Gemini is also about ideas as well as communication and transportation, and archeological evidence suggests that there were significant advances in both during this time. Travel increased and trade grew, leading to an exchange of ideas, as well. With regard to communications and travel, the story of the Tower of Babel and the subsequent dispersal of the people comes to mind.

♋ **Cancer, the Crab** - Today this part of the sky is symbolized by Cancer, the crab, whose sturdy shell protects its tender body. But earlier this sign was symbolized by the ark, or ship. The ark is a vessel that contains and carries life. Thus it is symbolic of the womb, and *is*, ultimately, the womb of the Mother. Awareness and worship of the Great Mother Goddess grew during this time, and to this day the sign of Cancer is associated with gestation, protectiveness, motherhood, nourishment, and sustenance. In addition, agriculture and the domestication of animals may have begun during this time, leading to a more settled and stable way of life.

In the sky we have the constellation of Argo Navis, the great starry ship which sails the deeps of the sky. It was originally the ship of the handsome and princely Jason, who, with his skilled crew of childhood friends—which included the hero Heracles, the Gemini twins Castor and Polydeuces, and the musician Orpheus—sailed off to obtain the Golden Fleece that would help Jason regain his kingdom, which had been usurped by his uncle.

The ship had been built by the carpenter Argus, and Athena, goddess of wisdom and reason, had placed in the ship's beam a piece of Greece's oracle oak tree, Dodona, so the travelers would be prophetically guided. The gaining of the Golden Fleece was inextricably bound up with Medea, daughter of the king of Colchis, who fell in love with Jason and helped him to gain it by intrigue. After this they escaped with the golden fleece, and eventually married. The dark side of motherhood is shown near the end of the story when, in a jealous rage, Medea kills her own children.

♌ **Leo, the Lion** - The Age of Leo was a regal age, and perhaps the time when monarchies and dynasties were first formally established. Astrologically, Leo is ruled by our bright golden sun, and the Age of Leo was most likely a time of sun worship, or rather, a time when the solar disc was seen as the most appropriate symbol or embodiment of the divine.

The importance of the lion—traditionally known as King of the Beasts—in parts of the Middle East, particularly Egypt, is well attested by the number of important lion headed deities. Sekmet, Tefnut, and others come to mind. Such deities are found also in Tibet, India, Pakistan and were often related to the strong, regal power of the sun. One is reminded, as well, of the lion-headed Egyptian sphinx. Although it is said to be 4500 years old, there are some researchers who say that the weathering on it is due to water rather than wind, and that this could have only occurred during a period of greater moisture. This pushes the date back to roughly 10,000 years ago, a time not far past the end of the last ice age, a time when increasing warmth had caused glacial ice sheets to melt and sea levels to rise.

♍ **Virgo, the Virgin** - Astrologically, the primary characteristics of the sign of Virgo are purity, perfection, and parthenogenesis—which is the female power to conceive, gestate, and birth offspring without fertilization from male power. Thus the Virgin, always pictured as female, actually contains both polarities within: the female aspect births the male aspect. Therefore, Virgo is the sign that represents the Cosmic, Galactic, and Terrestrial Mother who births all life from within herself.

Gestation involves sustenance, so Virgo is also about sustenance; Virgo literally builds and sustains life. In earthly terms this sustenance is about food, especially grain. It is possible that agriculture began in a serious way at this time, first, as the harvesting of wild grain, and later, the cultivation of grain, and is what allowed humans to truly move from hunter-gatherer societies into settled agricultural societies, allowing civilizations to develop. Virgo is also about work, labor, service, and careful and critical attention to detail, all of which are necessary to good agriculture and long-term survival.

Virgo is said to be the source archetype of every virgin mother goddess.

The Age of Virgo began at roughly the same time as the last glaciation period was ending. Ice sheets were retreating and the land beneath them was coming back to life. With new land opening up, and all the new life springing forth, the great Earth Mother was providing a new beginning and fresh opportunities for her children.

The time prior to the Age of Virgo moves us back into the last Ice Age; so we will stop here as there are really no records beyond this point from which to draw conclusions about the Ages of Libra, Scorpio, Sagittarius and Capricorn.

Now

We are now poised to move into the Age of Aquarius, about which we will speak more in subsequent chapters.

What the Ages Mean For Us

As Precession occurs and the Ages change, earth's wobbling axis points to different points of the sky, creating for us a different view of the zodiac throughout time, and sometimes even a new north star. As has been mentioned above, during the different Ages, changes occur which reflect the different themes that seem to be played out during that period of time. It is quite intriguing how widespread these changes manifest, as documented in the mythologies of the time.

Metaphysically speaking, this is because different influences or frequencies are being emitted from the galactic core during these different ages. The frequencies flow out to us—filtered by the zodiacal sign rising on earth's eastern horizon on the morning of the spring equinox—and influence life on earth.

The way I choose to think of this—from a mythopoetic rather than scientific perspective—is that just as the milk of a human mother changes as her child grows and develops, to better suit the child's developmental needs, so too does the "milk" (to use a mammalian analogy) of the Divine Mother change as the life on our planet evolves, grows and changes. The milk we need now is not the milk we needed when we were sea-swimming protozoans or primates stalking through primeval jungles. We've changed as we've evolved and traveled the evolutionary time spiral. We've developed, we've grown in consciousness and awareness, and different sustenance is needed to aid this growth, which continues over time as we explore what it means to be truly human.

We may gain insight into the type of nourishment needed and the type of development expected by a look at the astrological themes associated with the particular sign of the zodiac—which was developed over thousands and thousands of years of sky-watching and philosophizing by cultures of the ancient world. These themes and developments are embodied in human cultures and consciousness. Yet each astrological sign has its positive and negative aspects, and the potential for both of these to manifest is always present.

Despite the hopes and wishes of many New Age folk, moving into the Age of Aquarius is not going to be an automatic "cure-all" for the ills of the present world situation. The possibility for great progress is there, and right beside it the possibility for a very negative outcome, with the worst aspects of Aquarius being embodied in addition to, or instead of, the positive ones featured in story, song and wishful dreaming.

The fact of the matter is that the energies of the various ages are about inner transformation and growth as well as outer manifestations of a particular age. We are evolving in consciousness, striving and reaching to grow into the wisdom of our most divine self. The Age of Aquarius brings us particularly powerful energies to work with in this regard since the sign itself is about higher consciousness, intelligence, and lightning speed communication.

While my description of the evolution of life and consciousness may sound like it's a linear thing, I don't think it really is. I think that in actuality it is more of a cyclic and spiraling process, and thus just one of many paradoxes the universe presents to us.

This line of thinking leads inevitably to the question of "What's next and what can we do about it?" We will address these questions in the chapters that follow.

The Mayan Calendar and the New Age

One of the most interesting anthropological discoveries of the last few centuries has been the discovery of the Mayan time reckoning system, often referred to as the "Mayan Calendar." While too complex to explain here, this calendar has proven to be a sophisticated, elaborate, and accurate calendrical device, covering a span of many centuries. This system was created several centuries ago by ancestors of the modern day Mayan people, and points backward in time to the beginning of an age and forward to that age's ending.

A few clarifications are in order we proceed any further. An astrological age is generally considered to be about 2160 years in length—that being 1/12th of the 25,920 year length of the Great Year of the Precession. Similar to our calendar year, the Great Year can also be divided into four "seasons," each of which would be roughly 6450-6500 years in length. Keep these figures in mind when reading what follows.

In the many years since I began studying it, the Mayan calendar has become quite the popular topic, particularly as a vehicle for the inevitable and endless number of sensationalistic doomsday predictions that seem to arise whenever any astronomical phenomena is popularized. As I write this, a new movie has just been released in which the calendar's end date is being said to be the end of the world! In actuality, the calendar points to the end of one World Age and the beginning of another, as we have noted above.

Work on decoding this calendar has been done by several scholars (most notably John Major Jenkins and the late Jose Arguelles), but the one whose theories are most applicable to this book is John Major Jenkins. In particular, his hypothesis about the meaning of the calendar's end date of December 21, 2012, is of special interest.

According to Jenkins, the Mayan calendar's end date represents, astronomically, the conjunction of the Mayan constellation of the Sacred Tree (the Milky Way's dark rift area) with the plane of the ecliptic and the winter solstice sunrise point. Jenkins says that according to the calendar, this conjunction represents the end of one age and the start of another. The dark rift is located within the Sacred Tree constellation, which is also the direction of the galactic center. The dark rift is also considered the road to the Underworld, as well as the birth canal of the Mother Goddess. Both of these images suggest a place, or portal, for the emergence of a new lifestream or current of stellar energies. (6) And since the galactic center contains a black hole, this Sacred Tree/ecliptic conjunction is also a conjunction to that black hole.

Jenkins tells us that the Maya saw this alignment as Father Sun uniting with the Great Mother's womb—the dark rift. The new age that is conceived comes into form through the transforming and renewing power of the Great Mother.

This tells us that the Mayan calendar end date is the apex of the actual moment of the end of one age and the birth of the energies of the incoming new age. Thus, although the Maya people used different terminology, the end date is most likely related to the arrival of the Age of Aquarius. But I think it's more than that. Since the start date of the Mayan calendar was 3114 BC I would suggest that the calendar's end date and the World Age it represents is not just an astrological age but perhaps the beginning of an astrological season.

These things having been said, these conjunctions happen over a span of time, during which their energies are perceived and experienced, before coming to this moment of exactness. Thus the actual birth is not really one moment in time, but, as with human birth, the "baby" emerges slowly, and only after several pushes on the part of the mother. Over the last 20+ years there have been several other significant astronomical transits and alignments that, from an astrological point of view, might be said to be "pushes" which are opening the way or setting the stage for the 2012 event.

December 21, 2012 may just have been the moment in time when the new stellar energies from this galactic center's black hole came pouring out the strongest in our direction, although it will take a while for these to be embodied and manifested here on earth; perhaps hundreds of years.

Birth requires a mother, so it is interesting to find that there is a very significant astrological feature to the sun's rebirth at all winter solstices, including the one of 2012. At midnight on solstice night, the zodiacal sign rising on the eastern horizon is that of Virgo, the Virgin Mother who births the divine Sun-child—the light born from the time of deepest darkness.

The manner in which the Mother Goddess is currently manifesting and bringing through this new age will be the subject of our next few chapters.

Notes

1) "A Twist of Time and Space,"
www.rochester.edu/pr/Review/V60N1/feature5.html
www.trumpetuniverse.org/universalaxis.html
2) Stewart, R. J.; *The Prophetic Vision of Merlin*; Arkana, Routledge & Kegan Paul, London, 1986; pg 143
3) Fortune, Dion; *The Sea Priestess*, Samuel Weiser, Inc. NY, NY; pp 186-87
4) ___, p 186
5) McArthur, Margie; *Wisdom of the Elements*, Crossing Press, Freedom, CA; p 64
6) Jenkins, John Major; "The How and Why of the Mayan End Date in 2012 A.D." The Mountain Astrologer, Dec. 1994

Chapter Nine - The Goddess of the Sea and Stars in Our Times

The Goddess of Many Names

She has many names, yet she is always the one who is, who has been, and who will be. She is Life Manifesting, and therefore, she is change—the cycle of change, the great wheel of change in the universe.

Although she never really went away, the Goddess has been ignored and suppressed in the western world for much of the last 1500 years. When the tide of Christianity flooded over the western world, she was swept away in all save her Virgin Mother aspect. As this tide has continued beyond the western world and into Africa, Asia, and the Middle East, the same has been largely true in many of these places. In general, as the tide of monotheistic religions—Judaism, Christianity and Islam—has washed through the world, the stature of the Great Goddess of many aspects has been reduced more and more as these religions attempted to obliterate goddess worship wherever they found it. And as the tide of fundamentalist Protestantism continues to sweep the modern world, there is active opposition to any suggestion that the Mother of Jesus might be important in and of herself, beyond her role as simply the Vessel of the Incarnation.

But they cannot obliterate her. She is the Matrix, the source from which all else springs. She is that which brings forth her Other. She is both Mother and Daughter, and Mother and Son. She is the great sea of space which birthed all life, as well as the great salty sea on earth from which all earthy life came forth. She cannot be driven away by dogma and doctrine, wars and decrees.

She has been denied, and knowledge of her mysteries have been suppressed or driven underground over the centuries. But she always reemerges, and has been doing so again, strongly, for the last 40 or 50 years, although her tide has been rising for a time before that. How can she not? She is at the root of everything.

In her current re-emergence, she has shown us many of her thousand-fold aspects and names. This chapter addresses certain aspects of her current re-emergence—specifically, those as Mother of Form and Lady of Life and Death—and what that might mean for us and our world. But first, some history....

The Star of the Sea

> "Then she sang, and I knew that this was Isis, unveiled and dynamic...
>
> I am the star that rises from the sea – the twilight sea."[1]

Colonel C.R.F. Seymour, a powerful magician of the early 20th century Society of the Inner Light and a contemporary of Dion Fortune, mentions that

> *The symbol of Isis is the Ankh and it symbolizes the forces of life contained within the form of matter. Behind the individualized life form that is man there is the Great Sea of Life. Isis is the star that rises from the Twilight Sea, the star that is itself the symbol of the divine spark in man. The Egyptians called it Sothis; we call it Sirius.*[2]

Sirius is the brightest star in the night sky and was undoubtedly used, along with the North Star, by ancient mariners to guide them in their sea travels. It is quite near the constellation of Orion. Sothis, as Sirius was known to the Egyptians, was the star of Isis, while Orion represented Osiris, husband of Isis. Sirius/Sothis was quite important in Egyptian culture and religion.

Sirius is also near the constellation of Argo Navis, the great ship of Greek myth in which Jason and the Argonauts sailed in search of the Golden Fleece.

Though often referred to as the Dog Star—a reference to Orion's dog although it may originally have been a reference to the jackal-headed god of the dead, Anubis, sometimes depicted hieroglyphically as a dog—Sirius/Sothis, was associated with Isis-Hathor, who was depicted in the form of a cow with horns. Sirius was also deeply connected with the fertility of the land of Egypt as the star's first appearance in July's early morning sky was the indicator of the Nile's annual inundation, the flood that deposited rich soil from the uplands of Ethiopia on the Nile banks and ensured the viability of Egypt's dry lands.

Therefore, it was Isis-Hathor, as the Star of the Sea, who was linked with successful navigation, and thus, guidance in general, as well as with the land's fertility and prosperity, which is the basis of life itself.

Dion Fortune linked her also with the moon, saying,

> *But in the heavens our Lady Isis is the Moon, and the moon powers are Hers. She is also the priestess of the Silver Star that rises from the Twilight sea. Hers are the magnetic moon-tides, ruling the hearts of men. In the Inner She is all-potent. She is queen of the kingdoms of sleep. All the invisible workings are Hers and She rules all things ere they come to birth.*[3]

Mary, The Mother of God

> *Hail Queen of Heaven, the Ocean Star!*
> *Guide of the wanderer here below.*
> *Borne on life's surge, we claim thy care.*
> *Save us from peril, and from woe.*
> *Mother of Christ, Star of the Sea.*
> *Pray for the wanderer, pray for me!*
> (Catholic hymn)

Since Isis was, at the advent of Christianity 2000 years ago, the most popular goddess of the ancient Middle Eastern and Western European world, it is not surprising that her successor, Mary, Mother of the Piscean Age avatar Jesus, should fall heir to many of her titles and attributes.

In both a physical and a metaphoric sense, Mary has inherited Isis's title and role as the *Stella Maris*, or Star of the Sea. During the age of seafaring Mary was called on for safe voyages and was seen as a guiding star—guiding her children safely, as well, through life's tempestuous seas. Mary is often depicted with stars around her; sometimes she is wearing a crown of stars. Many Catholic churches are named after her in her role as Star of the Sea, and the verse at the beginning of this section is part of a lovely song to her in this aspect.

The History and Lore of Mary

What we know of Mary the mother of Jesus comes from the Bible and from Christian oral tradition, some of which was actually transcribed in various documents and gospels early in the Christian era.

Mary is also mentioned in the Holy Quran; what is said sounds very much like it derives from the same sources as the early Christian scriptures and oral traditions.

Mary's name and her story as given in Christian lore tells us quite a bite about her. She is Mary/Mari, daughter of Anna/Hannah—whose name means, in Hebrew, *grace*. In Hurrian, a Middle Eastern language spoken in parts of ancient and nearby Syria, Anna means *mother*. Mary's father was Joachim, whose name means, *God prepares* (also *lifted/ raised up by God/Yahweh*). Mary's birth was foretold by an angel. Her son's birth was also foretold by an angel, the Archangel Gabriel. Overshadowed and impregnated by the power of the Holy Spirit, Mary gave birth to Jesus, the sacred child of the Christian religion. She has been honored and venerated for two millennia. But who, really, is Mary?

Mary - Miriam

The name has been rendered as Mary, Mari, Miriam, Maryam, Mariham, Mariamne, and Mariam. Hebrew words are composed of consonants only; no vowels are provided, so the exact pronunciation used in ancient times is ultimately uncertain.

The most common interpretation of her name is *bitter sea*, which comes from reading the name as the Hebrew *marim*, (i.e. *maryam*) "bitter," which contains the word *yam*, meaning "sea." The word bitter was sometimes used to mean salty. So the *Bitter Sea* was also the Salty Sea—the salt waters of our planet—the Ocean. And with this we begin to see her link to the great ocean that birthed all forms of life on our planet. Since tears are salty, the word bitter is often used to refer to them and to sorrow in general. This brings in a more human element, that of emotion, and we get a glimpse of Mary/Mari/Miriam as the feminine power of emotion, who sheds tears of both joy and sorrow.

The name is sometimes interpreted as being related to the Hebrew word *mara*, which means well-nourished or fullness, both of which imply beauty. In addition to the usual definition, the word *fullness* hints at the great Void of creation, which is not really empty but *full* of all potentialities.

In Latin the word *mare* means "sea" and is from the Proto Indo-European root word meaning sea, *mori*, from whence marine, mermaid, and other such words derive.

The first biblical mention of this name comes from the Old Testament where we find a Miriam who was the sister of Moses. Those familiar with the Old Testament will recall that it was Miriam who tended the infant Moses—whose name is sometimes said to mean *drawn from the waters*—as his cradle basket drifted in the river, hidden by the river's reeds, and it was Miriam who watched over him and, mostly likely, drew him forth from the waters at night to bring him home. And when the day came that he was discovered by Pharoah's daughter and taken to be her son, it was Miriam who made sure that his own mother became his wet nurse. All of these are protective and nurturing functions.

The Old Testament names Miriam as the First Prophetess. In the story of the Exodus, it is Miriam who leads the Hebrew women across the Red Sea—another act that is rich in symbolism—as they are fleeing from Pharoah and his men. Once they are safely across and the Pharoah and his armies destroyed, Miriam and Moses lead the women in a sacred celebratory song and dance that has become known as the *Song of the Sea*.

Interestingly, the term *Red Sea* has proven to be a mistranslation of the Hebrew *Yam Suph;* which actually means *Reed Sea*, rather than Red Sea (i.e. sea of reeds), and was probably a reference to the Nile Delta, where the Nile empties into the Mediterranean Sea. The word *suph* actually denotes an edge, as in border or boundary, but was also used for what lined that edge (the boundary between land and water), which in this case were the water-loving plants called reeds, from which papyrus was made. So in a sense, the Sea of Reeds across which Miriam led the Hebrew women was the "edge of the world," the threshold between the known and the unknown.

Aiding beings and/or energies to cross a threshold from one form of life to another is very much a goddess function; it is also a priestess function. As mother, the Goddess births spirits into physical life; as the Dark Goddess of Death, she births them from physical life into the spirit realm. The death passage can also be viewed as a midwiving function.

Part of Miriam's lore concerns a well. When the Children of Israel wandered in the desert for 40 years, they were sustained by the clean, fresh water from Miriam's Well—a well that God caused, because of Miriam's virtue, to follow them wherever they went. Or so the story goes. The Bible mentions that when Miriam died there was no water for the community. Here we see Miriam most definitely linked with both water—the life-sustaining waters of the deep earth—and a vessel of water in the form of a well. Many in the Jewish community today set a special chalice, Miriam's Cup, on their Passover table to represent this well and the role Miriam played during the Exodus.

Miriam's connections with water—in the form of the river, the Reed Sea, and the well—show her connections with the Divine Feminine in the form of water's life-giving and life supporting functions. Similarly, Miriam helps midwife her people into a new life, beyond the Sea of Reeds. These actions—bridging the realms of known and unknown, past and future, spirit and matter— are in the nature of a priestess of the Goddess. Might Miriam have been a priestess of the Goddess at the time when the Hebrew people still honored the Divine Feminine? It seems very likely.

Mary the Mother of Jesus

Moving forward to the New Testament we again find a woman named Mary bridging the worlds, and bringing a powerful being/energy into manifestation—Mary the mother of Jesus.

Mary's mother is Hannah/Anna, a name which, as we have noted above, is said to mean "grace" or "gracious" in Hebrew, as well as "mother" in the Hurrian language of nearby Syria. Yet the name is remarkably similar to the Anu/Ana/Danu/Dana group of names we have already analyzed. The word Anu (i.e the syllable *An*) is, in fact, one of those remarkable sounds/words that shows up in several languages in many of the world's cultures. In Irish it refers to the giving, flowing grace of plenteousness, often seen as a river. In Sanskrit it means something like atom, or molecule (i.e. very tiny particle). In Yoruban it is said to mean 'mercy,' while in ancient Sumerian the word meant the 'heavenly one,' or simply, 'the heavens.' The word is quite likely related to the name of the pre-Roman deity Janus/Ianus, who was the double-headed god of doorways and thresholds, and for whom the threshold month of January is named. The word may also be related to the names of the Roman deities Dianus/Diana, god and goddess of the wildwood.

Therefore, Anna's name links her to both the tiniest building-block particles of the material world, the beginning of matter, and to grace—flowing, giving, and from the sky (quite similar to the Irish Goddess Dana, come to think of it!). Her name can, in fact, be seen as meaning heaven, the sky world, source of all being and manifestation. How fitting that Anna/Hannah's daughter, Mary/Miriam, who is in actuality her earthly counterpart, brings divinity across the threshold of the worlds and into material form.

Felix Coeli Porta

Ave Maris Stella,

Dei mater alma,

Atque semper virgo

Felix coeli porta.

Hail, Star of the Sea,

Of God, the young maiden-mother

Who was ever-virgin,

Happy gate of heaven.

In Catholicism, one of Mary's titles is *Felix Coeli Porta*, which means the "happy gate of heaven." Given Mary's function as both the threshold between the material and immaterial realms and the one who carries beings through that threshold in both directions, that's exactly what she is.

Mary, mother of Jesus, is not mentioned very often in the gospels of the New Testament. She is referred to in the accounts of the birth, infancy, and childhood of her son; she's part of the story of his first public miracle of changing water into wine; she's briefly mentioned in accounts of his ministry, and was noted to be present at his crucifixion.

Additional information about her comes from oral tradition and non-canonical holy books, which tell us a few things about her parentage, her life before motherhood, and her life after the death of her son.

From an early non-canonical scripture known the *Protoevangelium of James* (also known as the *Infancy Gospel of James*) we learn that Anna conceived Mary after a long period of barrenness, during which she and her husband Joachim prayed and beseeched God for a child. In the last of these beseechings, Anna promised that if God gave her a child, she would dedicate the child to service in the temple. At this point, an angel appeared to Anna to tell her that her prayers had been answered, and at the same time, an angel appeared to Joachim (whose name, please remember, means, "God has prepared") to tell him that his wife had conceived. Nine months later Mary was born, and when she was three years old she was taken to serve in the temple. At age twelve she was betrothed to Joseph.

Shortly after this Mary was called back to the temple to help weave a veil for the temple's holiest sanctuary[4], since this could be done only by virgins from the tribe of David and Mary was from the tribe of David. The veil, based on extant descriptions of the temple's layout, was one which divided the Inner Sanctum of the temple into two rooms—the Holy Place, which held an incense altar, the menorah, and the golden table of "presence-bread" (bread offered to the Divine Presence), and the Holy of Holies, the Temple's most sacred space which was said to house the very presence of God. The Holy of Holies of the Second Temple was empty aside from the Foundation Stone (and, by some accounts, two huge cherubim statues), upon which blood of the sacrificial animals was sprinkled by the priests during the Yom Kippur ceremonies. Below the Holy of Holies was a cave, today known as *Bir el-Arweh* (Arabic), meaning the *Well of Souls*, in which the sound of water could be heard. These sounds, it was said, were the sounds of the rushing rivers of Paradise as well as the whispering voices of the souls of the dead.

The Foundation Stone represented the sealed gate to the Underworld—which was the *Tehom*, the "waters below," the deep watery abyss of the Underworld. This Foundation Stone, known as *Shettiya*, was very significant. It was thought that the waters of Noah's flood came not only from the sky in the form of rain, but also sprang up from the underground waters of the deep. This stone represented not only the portal to the place from which they had sprung and to which they receded, but also, served as a seal—a "stopper" that closed off the portal to the chaotic watery Underworld. It is possible that it may have also represented the actual place of creation in Hebrew lore—the place where, as recorded in the early verses of Genesis, God "divided the waters which were under the firmament from the waters which were above the firmament" and began creation—a statement which is evocative of the Egyptian story of the emergence of the first land from the primeval creative waters of Nun.

Returning to the Protoevangelium's story of Mary, we learn that lots were cast regarding which of the maidens would spin the various colored threads, and it fell to Mary to spin the scarlet and purple threads.

Interestingly, red is the color of life/blood, and associated with the first chakra, while purple is the color of royalty and of connection to divinity and is associated with the seventh chakra, which is traditionally linked to one's connection to the Divine. These colors would seem to be, then, symbolic precursors of her role as mother of the divine king.

Similarly, the task of spinning the threads for the temple veil connects her with goddesses such as the Fates and the Norns—those who spin the universe into being and also spin and weave the threads of time and fate that create and sustain its pattern. The veil itself—which divided the Holy Place from the adjoining sacred chamber of the Holy of Holies that contained the Foundation Stone gate to the Tehom—may be seen as the veil between the worlds of spirit and matter. Once again, Mary is linked with that particular boundary; she is the *Felix Coeli Porta*.

It was as Mary was spinning these threads that the Angel Gabriel came to her, telling her that she, although yet virgin and unmarried, was, by God's power, to become the mother of God's son, whom she was to name Emmanuel, which means "God with us."

It might be said that, in this story, Mary herself is the veil whose threads were being spun, since she, like the veil, was being prepared to become the threshold by which the divine passed into physical form.

It is from these meager gleanings of oral tradition and canonical and non-canonical scripture that Mary's image in the Christian tradition began. They seem scarcely enough to account for the enormous Marian cult that was to unfold as the centuries marched on. Her image continued to form, since, as time passed, she became the heiress of many of the traditions of other important mortal mothers of divine sons.

Another of Mary's titles was *Ark of the Covenant*. The original Hebrew Ark of the Covenant was a wooden box covered in gold inside and out, with two golden cherubim atop it, facing one another. It was made during the time of the Exodus and said to hold the Presence of God, who occasionally appeared as a cloud between the two cherubim, a place called the Mercy Seat. The Ark held the Rod of Aaron (who was the brother of Moses), which he'd used to perform miracles to convince Pharoah to release the Hebrew captives; the two stone tablets on which the ten commandments had been engraved (supposedly by the finger of God himself); and a jar of manna, the divine food provided by God to the Hebrews when they were lost in the desert on their way to the promised land. These sacred objects—which represented to the people God's divine power, his law, and his nourishing care for them when they were in need—symbolized the "covenant" between God and the people. Since Christianity considered Jesus to be God, Mary, by bearing Jesus in her womb, was considered by Christians to be the "new" Ark, the vessel that had carried the "new covenant" between God and his people.

An Ark is a vessel, and Mary's title as the "new" Ark of the Covenant was not the only reference to her as a vessel of the divine. The Litany of Loreto—also known simply as the Litany of the Blessed Virgin Mary and supposedly dating back to the 12th century—refers to Mary as "spiritual vessel," "vessel of honor," and "singular vessel of devotion," references which point to her role as the vessel containing divine energy in the form of her divine son. This may be linked to the phrase "full of grace," which is used to describe her in the most famous Marian prayer, the "Hail Mary."

By the time of the church Council of Ephesus in 431 A.D. Mary was so important that her position as *Theotokos*—the Bearer (i.e Mother) of God—was formally recognized, although it had been mentioned in church writings for at least two centuries prior to the council.

This was very significant as it—in effect if not wording—proclaimed her to be, defacto, a goddess. For who else but a goddess could be the mother of one who, even as his humanity was repeatedly affirmed, was also said to be *wholly and completely* God?

The location of this church council, Ephesus, had previously been home to the cult of the Goddess Diana, known and artistically depicted as the "many-breasted one" to emphasize her fertility and maternal aspects. One legend from the church's oral tradition held that the Apostle John, to whom Jesus entrusted the care of his mother at the time of the crucifixion, took Mary to live in Ephesus, where she eventually died and was thence bodily assumed into heaven. Indeed, tourists are even today shown the remains of the house in which she lived. The commemoration of her Assumption into heaven was set for August 15th, a date which had previously been a feast day of the Goddess Diana of Ephesus (as was August 13th as well). Here again, we find Mary linked with an important goddess figure.

It should be noted that in the near eastern legends of "god-men" born of virgins, such as Mithras and Jesus, the mother is always mortal because she represents matter, while the father is a god, and represents spirit. Often, the mortal mother is later raised to the status of a goddess—exalted in some way, made part of the heavenly realm of deities—being made equal or near equal with the gods because she has borne this child. In the case of Mary, she was most definitely exalted—named as *Theotokos*, given titles such as Queen of Heaven, Queen of Angels and Saints, Star of the Sea, and others, and was said to have been "assumed" into heaven after her death.

The child who results from the sacred union of human mother and divine father represents the fusion of these two natures, and thus the perfect unification of matter and spirit, earth and heaven. The child has both natures, and is considered a divine human—an avatar, the incarnation of a deity who stands as a prototype of what all humanity can and should be; our highest point of possible evolution, if you will.

How much of Mary's story is actual historical truth will never really be determined. But from a mythic perspective, it is very significant. It represents a new mother goddess figure—who has just given birth to the Light of the New Age—taking over from the previous mother goddess figure, she who had birthed the previous Age.[5] And yet they are one and the same mother, but wearing different garb, one appropriate to the age that is just dawning.

Over the centuries the cult of Mary continued to grow, becoming deeply rooted in the hearts of the people. Despite the fact that she was not called goddess, she most definitely assumed the role of a mother goddess to her devotees. She was not only the Mother of God and Queen of Heaven, she was named queen of the angels, saints, and apostles as well. A great many churches, holy wells, and other sacred sites were dedicated to her.

It did not take long for her son, Jesus, to become identified with the pagan solar and agricultural deities, taking on their imagery of light, brightness, growth, and healing, as well as the feast days of their birth or rebirth, death and resurrection. This, in essence, made Mary into She Who Gives Birth to the Light—the Mother of the Light—and thus Life.[6]

Black Madonnas

Since light is born from the dark, it's important to note that Mary also had a dark aspect. Not only was she the queen of heaven and all the angels, she was also mother, like Isis before her, to all the souls still stranded on this earthly plane, as well as those who'd passed on into the Land of Death. She was queen, mother, and intercessor for them all.

Early in the Christian era statues of dark skinned "Black Madonnas" began to surface in Europe—statues of the Virgin and her child which looked very much like those that typically depicted Mary and Jesus but having dark or black skin. Later in time, many reasons were given as to why they were black—dark colored wood, soot from candle smoke, damage from church fires, or even just plain dirt. But the people who found and venerated these statues didn't seem to care why the skin was black, though the blackness was important to them. They knew this was Mary, their mother, and they loved her—light-skinned and dark.

Although there is no general consensus, modern scholars find clues to the mystery of these Black Madonnas in the pre-Christian traditions of earth and Underworld goddesses, especially those of Isis-Hathor (whose worship was widespread) in her spirit world/funerary aspects. For Mary, like Isis and many goddesses before her, was not only the Bright Mother who conceived, gestated and birthed life, she was also the Dark Sorrowing Mother who received life back into herself when it had ended. In Catholic terms this aspect is beautifully portrayed by Michelangelo's stunning sculpture, *Pieta*—the sorrowing Virgin Mother cradling the body of her dead son on her lap.

Yet since it was the Void that gave birth to the universe, it would be misleading to imply that the Dark Mother is always and only about death. It seems to me that the Black Madonna, who is always depicted holding her child, is, in a very literal sense, clearly representative of the Mother in both her bright and dark, creative and destructive aspects. Sometimes the goddess finds it necessary to take life as well as give it. Both aspects are part of One Thing—the cycle of life's manifestation.

To me, these images of the Black Madonna represent not just the earthly dimension of the Goddess, but the cosmic one as well. She is dark, like the depths of space, like the Void, and on her lap sits her divine child of light. She is the darkness that gives birth to the light—the stars, the sun, the Christ-light—and thus life.

Most likely, to the average, ordinary Catholic of the first millennium or so, all this was either unknown or unimportant. Mary was important to them as Jesus's mother—God's mother—and as their very own heavenly mother… especially when she began appearing to some of them…

Notes:

1) Fortune, Dion; *Sea Priestess*, Samuel Weiser, NY, NY, 1957, p 225

2) Ashcroft Nowicki, Dolores; *The Forgotten Mage*, The Aquarian Press Ltd, Thorson's Publishing Group, 1986, p 122

3) Fortune, Dion; *The Sea Priestess,* Weiser Publishing; Maine; p 234

4) In the Hebrew temple prior to Josiah's ouster of Asherah, her priestesses wove reeds to make curtains and shrines for her. Author Sabina Teubal, in *Sarah the Priestess* (Swallow Press, 1984), thinks that this may harken back to ancient Sumeria, where priestesses wove reed shrines for Inanna. One wonders if the virgins weaving the veil for the Holy of Holies, the dwelling place of the Divine Presence, was a remnant of this ancient practice.

5) This is also shown in legends of Joseph of Arimathea bringing the Virgin Mary to Glastonbury, Britain, a site previously sacred to the Goddess and which later was the site of the Lady Chapel

6) An interesting thread that ties together Isis-Hathor, Sirius, the Milky Way, and the divine Virgin together is this. At midnight on the night of the sun's rebirth at the winter solstice, the constellation of Virgo is rising on eastern horizon. The Star of Isis, Sirius, reaches its highest point overhead on midnight ten days later, at 14 Cancer. This is 14 degrees away from the Anti-Galactic Center-which is close enough to be called an opposition to the sun/dark rift/2012 conjunction point. Thus the Virgin in the East, Isis, gives birth to her son, the newly reborn sun who emerges in the eastern sky at dawn on solstice morning. Shortly thereafter the Star of the Sea lights up the middle of the night – which may represent the new wave of light and life just beginning on the earth.

Chapter Ten - The Lady Comes to her Children

The Lady Comes to Her Children

The Mother expresses herself to her children in different ways at different times, dependent upon their cultures and belief systems. In the western world of the last two millennia, it has been as Mary, the Virgin Mother of Jesus, that she has primarily shown herself.

The sheer number of confirmed Marian apparitions within the last two hundred years is staggering. With each of them comes a message, a warning, and a prescription for healing the spiritual ills of the world.

Although couched in the Catholic terminology one would expect coming from the mouths of the devoutly Catholic seers, her messages transcend religion and speak directly to the need for spiritual rebalancing in *all* her human children.

That was the message she gave to Catherine Laboure in Paris, France, in 1830; to the two French children, Melanie and Maximin, in La Sallette, France in 1846; to Bernadette Soubiroux in Lourdes, France, in 1858; and in the 20th century to the three Portuguese children—Jacinta and Francisco Marto and their cousin, Lucia Santos—in Fatima in 1917, and to several other seers over the last 180 years as well.

She is the Goddess, our Mother; make no mistake about it.

The First Apparition

According to legend, the first Marian apparition was to the apostle James in the year 40 A.D. After the Ascension of Jesus, it was said that the apostles began traveling and evangelizing. James's travels eventually led him to the Celto-Iberian province of Galicia in the northwest portion of Spain. Discouraged by his lack of success, he began to pray. Legend has it that Mary, although still among the living, came to him in vision to console him. She brought him a pillar[1] of jasper wood (hence, one of her titles in Spain is Our Lady of the Pillar) and a small wooden statue of herself, and asked him to build a church in her honor. The following year James arranged for a small chapel to be built there.

After his martyrdom in Jerusalem a few years later, his disciples brought his body back to Galicia, burying it in a field in the area. The legend says that eight centuries later his grave was rediscovered by a bishop who noticed an unusual formation of stars in the sky over the field; later a cathedral dedicated to St. James was built upon the spot. In honor of the star formation, the spot was called *Compostela*, which means "field of stars," or starry field.

The site gained prominence over the centuries and became a major Christian pilgrimage site. It is still popular today and many pilgrims still come to make the walking journey to Compostela, the starry field. This rather arduous pilgrimage route begins in the southern Pyrenees of France, crosses over mountains into Spain, and extends onward across varying terrains to Compostela, and beyond to the sea at Finisterre (which means "end of the earth"). There are those who relate this route to the Milky Way which stretches across the wide sky, just as the path to Compostela stretches across the mountainous countryside of France and Spain.

There are other legends associated with Compostela, including different attributions for the name.

But what, really, *is* the starry field, one might ask? Although the obvious answer would seem to be the route as a reflection of the Milky Way's path across the sky, there is no definite answer. There are many old stone monuments in the area, and ruins of a very old Celtic tower have been found on the site. There is evidence both the site and the pilgrimage route were sacred to local pagans before the legend of St James and his vision of the Virgin became attached to it.

Guadalupe

Mary's first appearance in the Americas makes it quite clear that she is the Mother of all. In the early years of Spanish rule in Mexico, during a time in which the Indians were being (often forcibly) converted to Catholicism, she appeared on December 9, 1531, to an Aztec Indian man, remembered now by his adopted Christian name, Juan Diego. It was early and Juan was on his way to Mass when he passed Tepeyac, a hill previously the site of a sacred shrine to the Corn Goddess, Tonanzin—whose name means "Our Mother." He was surprised to hear birds singing—apparently rare in the winter—but even more surprised when he saw a lovely young native woman standing near the top of the hill. She greeted him with maternal affection, calling him her "little son." A golden mist surrounded her, and she was wearing a dress covered with traceries of flowers and leaves, and a blue cloak with eight-pointed stars on it. (In the past the eight-pointed star has been a symbol of Inanna and the planet Venus) She identified herself as the Virgin Mary, the Mother of God[2], and said she wanted a temple built for her at that place.

In the days that followed, she appeared a few more times to repeat the request. It took several visits to the bishop by Juan and a stunning miracle on the part of the Lady to convince the bishop of the truth of the apparition, but the cathedral eventually built on the spot still stands today in Mexico City. And the miracle—her image on Juan's cloak, complete with the miraculous winter roses and the moon beneath her feet—hangs above the cathedral's altar for all to see.

The Lady also appeared to Juan Diego's dying uncle, Juan Bernardino, curing him of his disease and telling him the name by which she wished to be known: "The Perfect Virgin, Holy Mary of Guadalupe." But Guadalupe is a Spanish word; the Lady would have spoken to both men in their native tongue. Many believe the word was actually *Coatlaxopeuh*, which in the Nahuatl language meant "She who crushes the head of the (stone) serpent." In addition to the fact that there is a biblical reference to the woman (interpreted as Mary) who will "crush the head of the serpent," the word *Coatlaxopeuh* sounded very much like the Spanish word *Guadalupe,* which was the name of an important Black Madonna shrine in Spain.[3] At least that must have been how the bishop heard it because that was the name given to the apparition and the site. The Spanish word "Guadalupe" actually comes from an Arabic word that is said to mean—quite appropriately in this case—"river of love." [4]

The Guadalupe apparition was an extremely significant event for many reasons, not the least of which was that it marked a time when a new ethnicity, Mexican, was about to come into existence with the intermarriage of the Spanish and the Indian peoples in that part of Central America. The Lady of Guadalupe is, in a very real sense, the mother of these new people, and of all the mixed blood people of the Americas, and may, indeed, be America's own "Black Madonna."

Pontmain

The story of Mary's appearance in Pontmain, France, during the Franco-Prussian war of the 19th century is particularly precise in its Goddess imagery. Here's the story, along with my interpretations of the details, italicized and in parentheses.

On January 17th, 1891, a country child who was helping his father with the livestock one winter night paused to look out of the barn at the night sky. He noticed that there were no stars to be seen in one part of the sky, and called to his brother to look and corroborate this for him. *(This represents the Primal Goddess as the Void.)*

As he watched, that part of the sky suddenly seemed to open up, and an image of a beautiful woman appeared. *(The Goddess manifesting from the Void)*. She was clothed in a dark blue gown, speckled with golden five-pointed stars. *(Among the first manifestations of creation is light in the form of the stars; the five points may represent the four elements and spirit.)* On her head was a black veil that covered her hair and ears, and went down to her mid-back. Atop the veil she wore a golden crown with a large red stripe running across it. *(The crown illustrates her status as Divine Queen)*

The apparition went through five phases, during which the imagery changed. (Again, the number five is the number of the four primal elements or 'energy movements' of life, plus the 'element' of Spirit.)

At one point four candles appeared surrounding the lady (the four directions that create a space by serving as its boundaries); later these candles were lit by a star that emerged from her hands (she brings the first Light into being and the elements are activated). At another point a group of stars appeared beneath her feet, as if she were standing just above them. (There are stars within the earth, as the earth itself contains a starry fiery core) After that a small red cross appeared near her heart, later growing larger (Love comes into manifestation---perhaps this is her son, who is a further manifestation of light/fire.), and still later she was seen holding the cross. (She is the Mother of Form—which is built from the four primal elements, often depicted directionally in the shape of a cross referred to as the Cross of Matter. In addition, she is the mother of the incarnate deity.)

By this point in the apparition, neighbors and passers-by had gathered to see what was happening. As the children spoke of what they were seeing, the adults realized the children were seeing a vision of the Virgin. Someone present began to sing the song, "Ave Maris Stella" *(Hail Star of the Sea)*, after which the red crucifix disappeared.

Later, a tiny white cross appeared at each of her shoulders (she contains both polarities within herself. This may also represent the two middle sephiroth on the two pillars—the active and passive energies of force and form, respectively—of the Tree of Life as superimposed on the human body; these are usually shown near the shoulders). And finally, a white mist or veil began rising from below, covering her, till finally she was completely obscured. (She is spirit covered by the veil of matter—that is, she is spirit manifesting as matter in this world. When she comes to us the veil is lifted for a time, and when she takes her leave she again covers herself with the veil).

The above description might be more easily understood in the form of a chart.

A boy notices a part of the sky that has no stars.	*The Primal Goddess as the Void.*
A beautiful woman appears in the sky.	*Goddess manifesting from the Void.*
Her gown is speckled with five-pointed stars.	*Among the first manifestations of creation is light in the form of stars. The five points may represent the four elements and Spirit.*
She wears a crown.	*Crown illustrates her status as the Divine Queen.*
Apparition goes through five phases.	*Five is the number of the primal elements and Spirit.*
Four candles appear around the Lady.	*The four directions create a space by serving as its boundaries.*
These candles are lit by a star emerging from her hands.	*She brings the first light into being and it activates the elements.*
A group of stars appear beneath her feet, as if she were standing just above them.	*There is, in a sense, a star within the earth in the form of the earth's starry, fiery core.*
A small but growing red cross appears near her heart.	*Love comes into manifestation. Perhaps this is her beloved son, himself a manifestation of fire and light.*

Later, she is seen holding this red cross.	*She is the Mother of Form, which is built of the four primal elements, often depicted in the shape of a cross and referred to as the Cross of Matter.*
A tiny white cross appears on each of her shoulders	*She contains both polarities—the active and passive energies of force and form—within herself.*
A white mist or veil rises from below to cover her.	*She is spirit covered by the veil of matter; spirit manifesting as matter in this world.*

This particular apparition is absolutely stunning in its depiction of Mary as the Primal Goddess who gives birth to the light and then to all creation, and finally, reveals how her true reality is covered by the veil of matter.

Lourdes

The Lady of Lourdes appeared to Bernadette Soubiroux in a large, rocky, cavelike grotto—part of rocky outcrop known as Massabielle beside the River Gave de Pau—in 1858 on February 11th, a day that would have been, by the old calendrical reckoning still used in areas of Europe, the feast of the pagan goddess Brigid, the Catholic St. Brigid, as well as the Catholic feast of Candlemas. The word *grotto* is used because the cave was not very deep, though it opened into a larger cave that led into a mountain (called "Mountain of Caves") that contained many other caves. As we have previously noted, caves and rivers are both associated with the Goddess.

Garbed in a white gown with a blue sash and with golden roses on her feet, the Lady appeared to Bernadette a total of eighteen times, praying the rosary with her each time and instructing her to drink from the spring, and wash in its water. Seeing no spring, Bernadette began to dig in the dry ground, and came to a damp spot from which water began to trickle forth. Within hours the trickle increased, and today that spring provides hundreds of gallons of healing water per day. At the end of the cycle of apparitions, after repeated requests for her name, the Lady said, "I am the Immaculate Conception."

The Virgin Mary's appearance in Lourdes was at a place that had previously been sacred to the Roman Underworld Goddess Proserpina[5], and quite likely to a native Underworld goddess before that. Proserpina is the Roman equivalent of the Greek Persephone—the maiden goddess and daughter of the Great Mother, who was taken by the Lord of the Underworld to be his bride and queen; she is the Dark Goddess of the Underworld.

But one cannot help but notice the similarity of the Lady of Lourdes to other apparitions recorded in folklore of the "White Ladies"—young, beautiful, female spirits dressed in white, who often appeared near the caves and caverns of the Pyrenees, especially those near a water source such as a river or spring. Often the spring was known to be a healing spring. The White Ladies usually sought interaction with passers-by, and it is interesting that the Lady of Lourdes also sought interaction—by her request to the asthmatic, under-nourished Bernadette to drink and wash in the waters of the spring. This request resulted in the discovery of a spring, perhaps long hidden in the rocky earth of Massabielle, which is now world famous as a healing spring.

The Immaculate Conception

The Catholic Church has long held that Jesus had been conceived by divine intervention, without the aid of a physical father. Although born of a human woman, he was declared to be without the "soul-stain" brought about by the Original Sin of Adam and Eve, which was said to be, thereafter, passed on to their descendants—every human being ever born.

But how could this be unless his mother was equally free of such sin?

The great minds of Christianity pondered this for years and came to the conclusion that Mary herself must also be free of sin. But how could a mere human be without the stain of the original sin?

Several theories were proposed: that her conception was as virginal as that of her son; that God granted her the special privilege of sinlessness at the moment of her conception; that her physical conception had occurred in the normal way but that her spiritual conception—the infusing of soul into body—was the part that was sinless. As one might imagine, this opened the door to even more thought and theorizing as to the soul condition of her parents, and the part played by normal sexual desire—called concupiscence—which was often equated with sin.

So at one point in its evolution, the doctrine of the Immaculate Conception sought to extend the nature of Jesus's conception—sex-free and desire-free—to that of his mother as well. This version did not make it into the final and formal doctrine, but it was quite seriously considered and debated for many years.

During the 1830 apparitions to Catherine Laboure, the Lady requested that a medal be struck with a prayer on it saying. "Oh Mary, conceived without sin, pray for us who have recourse to thee." This may have served to reignite interest in the subject, since the doctrine was finally and formally proclaimed by the Church in 1854, and thus was only four years old when, in 1858, the Lady of Lourdes said to fourteen year old Bernadette Soubirous with great intensity and emotion, "I am the Immaculate Conception."

While the Church might have finally decided that the concept they'd been considering for years—that Mary's own conception was virginal and asexual—was not correct, it is interesting to ponder what this doctrine, and Mary's statement, mean on a deeper, more esoteric level.

To begin with, the idea of a person being born of a human woman yet fathered by a spiritual power was not a new one. Many other gods, avatars, and prominent spiritual teachers in the ancient world were considered to have been thus conceived. It is not at all surprising to find the Church considered Jesus's conception to have occurred in this manner; indeed, it would have been surprising had they thought otherwise. But it was quite significant that they decided the same was true of his human mother. This, combined with the 4th century proclamation of Mary as *Theotokos*—Bearer (i.e. Mother) of God—quite neatly recognized her inherent divinity without actually committing the sin of blasphemy by calling her a Goddess.

The word "immaculate" means very clean, very pure, and without stain. Metaphysically this can be seen to mean the condition of pure spirit—before matter came into being. "Conception" is the first spark in the process of coming into being, into manifestation.

Therefore, the phrase *I am the Immaculate Conception* means one who came into material manifestation by purely spiritual means; no physical realm influences playing a part. This is quite profound, as what it *really* states is that such a being is inherently a *being of pure spirit* taking manifestation in human form and is thus both human and divine. This places Mary in the same category as her divine son and other divinely conceived—and therefore themselves divine—avatars of other religious traditions.

But this point of view is based on the traditionally Catholic understanding that there is a huge inherent difference and separation between things physical and things spiritual, between human and divine. If one does not accept that position, if one holds that the physical realm is but Spirit in Manifestation, that we are *all* pre-existent spirits manifesting in human form, then things begin to look different.

Seen in this light, the Immaculate Conception may mean that Mary is the very essence of pure Spirit in the exact moment at which it sparks into material manifestation, or begins its movement into physical reality. This would mean she is the Void itself, as well as the Void as it births manifestation, bringing energy into being, light into darkness, and ultimately, energy/force into form. Thus, in her simple statement to Bernadette, the Lady proclaims herself the Primal Source and Creatress.

Conception is a process—a verb as well as a noun.

There is another way to view this that takes into account old pagan traditions of the Goddess and her daughter, who is inevitably a later version of her Mother though she often evolves individual characteristics of her own. In this scenario, Hannah (better known in Christianity as St. Anne), the mother of Mary and grandmother of Christ, is the Void from which All comes forth. Her daughter, Mary, is the first form the Void takes—the vast Sea of Being/Sea of Space/the Prima Materia, which births the rest of the universe. This accords well with the actual meaning of the name Mary, which is *Bitter Sea*, and may link St. Anne with the primal Celtic Goddess Ana/Anu/Dana/Danu in her form of Don/Domnu, the Watery Abyss and Sea of Space. Thus the *Immaculate Conception* represents both Hannah and Mary—as the Void at the very moment it brings forth that very first idea of form.

Beauraing

The teaching of the Immaculate Conception was apparently reaffirmed in the Marian apparition that occurred in the small Belgian town of Beauraing in the winter of 1932-33. Between November 29, 1932 and January 3, 1933 the Lady appeared thirty-three times to five children (three girls and two boys), ages nine through fifteen. The Lady appeared by a hawthorn tree in a convent garden near a school attended by one of the girls. She appeared to all the children, though not all heard all her messages, and she seemed to have some special messages for each child. On December 21st (Solstice Eve/Mother Night) she revealed her identity to the children, saying "I am the Immaculate Virgin."

At the end of the vision of December 29th, she opened her arms to the children, revealing her heart of gold to them. Surrounded by eight glittering rays, it looked like a small sun shining upon her white-robed chest.

This imagery captures well the bright blazing warmth of divine love, pouring outward to all of creation. The Lady's essential message to the children was to pray and to be good.

Significance of the Dates of the Marian Apparitions

It should be noted that many of the Marian apparitions occurred on or near days previously sacred in the old pagan calendars. The Lady of Guadalupe appeared to Juan Diego on December 9th, the day following the December 8th Catholic feast day of the Immaculate Conception (originally established in 1476), a date quite near the start of the week long Roman Saturnalia festival that both preceded and encompassed the winter solstice. So also were the apparitions of Beauraing close to the winter solstice. Beginning on Nov 29th and continuing through January 3rd, these apparitions occupied the entire 35 day period before and after the solstice, a time during which various winter festivals had occurred in the past, including the Germanic feasts of the Goddess Berchta and Mother Night, as well as the twelve day Egyptian festival of the birth of Horus.

All of these festivals mark the birth of the light, which was often anthropomorphized as the "divine child of light." And of course in the Christian calendar this time period encompasses Advent, the Christmas season, and most of the Twelve Days of Christmas. The Twelve Days of Christmas end at the feast of the Epiphany, January 6th, when the newborn light is revealed to the world, as represented by the visiting magi, or wise men—now thought to be astrologers—who came from afar to see the holy child.

The apparitions at Beauraing, starting at Advent and finishing at Epiphany, encompass the season of the Virgin Birth—the birth of the light from the dark—the season of the Immaculate Virgin Mother and her Child of Light.

The Lady of Lourdes appeared first on Feb 11th, which was Imbolc/Brigid by the old calendar. She announced her name on March 25th, just past the Spring Equinox, which starts the season of increasing light, warmth and growth. March 25th is also the Catholic feast of the Annunciation, which commemorates Mary's miraculous conception of Jesus after the Archangel Gabriel appeared and told her this was God's wish. The Lady of Fatima first appeared on May 13th, very near the date of Old Beltaine. The Lady of Pontmain put in an appearance on January 17th, the old Roman feast of the Goddess Felicitas (happiness, good luck) and just after the feast of the Goddess Concordia, goddess of harmony and agreement (interesting in that the Lady of Pontmain came to tell the people of a coming time of harmony and happiness—that the war threatening them would not affect them and was about to end). The Lady of La Sallette first appeared on September 19th, just a few days before the Fall Equinox, while Catherine Laboure's Lady of the Miraculous Medal appeared on July 18th-19th, the approximate time of the rising of Sirius, the annual Nile inundation, and the ancient Egyptian festival of the marriage of Isis and Osiris (which later, as mentioned, became the feast day of Mary Magdalene).

Fatima

The most important and famous Marian apparition of the 20th century was to three shepherd children—Lucia Santos, age 10, and her cousins Francisco Marto, age 9, and Jacinta Marto, age 7—in Portugal in the year before the end of the First World War. The war, with its aircraft and new forms of weaponry, was the first of the modern wars, and was a new, exhausting, and terrifying experience for all concerned. It brought bloodshed, loss, and death on an unprecedented scale.

The apparitions actually began in 1916 with the appearance of a beautiful and brilliantly glowing young man who identified himself to the children as the Angel of Peace and bade the children to pray with him. He came to them three times during 1916, speaking to them of prayer, repentance, and of the Immaculate Hearts of both Jesus and Mary.

It was May 13, 1917 when the Lady first appeared to the children, arriving in a little globe of light that settled over a small holm oak tree in a place called the *Cova da Iria*, or Cove of Irene where the children were tending sheep. The word Irene means *peace*, which is interesting in light of the messages about to be given and the name of the angel who had appeared the previous year. Greek mythology records a goddess with the name Irene.

The Lady was beautiful, dressed all in white; she radiated a light "more brilliant than the sun."

The Lady appeared a total of six times between May 13 and October 13, 1917. Each time her message was, like that of the angel, about prayer and reparation for sins. She warned the children that there was much evil in the world and God was greatly hurt and offended by it. She warned that God's instrument of chastisement would be Russia, which would "spread its errors throughout the world," bringing wars, persecutions, death, and even the annihilation of nations if left unchecked. To prevent these things the

Lady requested, in addition to repentance, prayer, and daily recitation of the rosary, that Russia be consecrated to her Immaculate Heart, and that special devotions to her be undertaken.

Word of the first apparition spread like wildfire, and by the second apparition crowds were pouring into the area. Some people asked for a miracle to prove the reality of the apparitions, a request that Lucia dutifully reported to the Lady. The Lady agreed to this, and set the date for October 13, 1917. And on that date there *was* a miracle, witnessed by a crowd of at least 70, 000 people, some of them not even at Fatima itself but in other villages in the area. The crowd consisted of believers and scoffers alike.

According to the reports of many eyewitnesses, it had been raining that day and things were quite muddy and soggy as the apparition began. But after a bit Lucia pointed to the sky and shouted, "She is going! Look at the sun!" A somewhat pale, silvery sun had come out from behind the grey clouds, and as people watched it began to "dance," to revolve and spin around in the sky, sending out rays of rainbow colored light. People watched in wonder, staring at the sun without the usual eye discomfort as it whirled around and around, casting off constantly shifting beams of rainbow colored light that lent their coloration to everything below. After a few minutes of colorful spinning, the sun, now fiery red, appeared to detach itself from its normal position in the sky and began to fall, or so it seemed, zigzagging rapidly toward the earth. As the fiery spinning disc came closer and closer, it appeared larger and larger, and the people's wonder turned to panic and fear for their lives as it looked as if the sun would crash into the earth. People began screaming and running about, thinking it was the end of the world; terror prevailed. People cried out in both panic and prayer. Then, as quickly as it had begun, the sun stopped in its downward course and began ascending again, coming to rest in its rightful position.

A stunned silence fell over the crowd, during which people began to notice that the ground around them was completely dry from the earlier downpour, and their soggy, muddy clothing was now clean and dry. And then, realization of what had just been witnessed and experienced swept through the crowd, and the people erupted in cries of joy and prayers of love and gratitude to the Virgin for the miracle.

The entire event had unfolded over a ten minute period of time.

Since this solar event was witnessed by approximately 70,000 people at the apparition site, a crowd composed of both believers and nonbelievers alike—newspaper reporters, priests and other religious, and ordinary citizens—and was seen by even more people over a 40 mile radius of the apparition site, mass hysteria must be ruled out.

Newspaper headlines the following week said, "Revolt in Russia; Miracle in Fatima," because within one week of the miracle at Fatima the Russian communists had launched their "October Revolution," which led to the overthrow of the Russian government and, eventually, to the formation of the officially atheistic Soviet Union. As we all know, the

Soviet Union did indeed go on to spread its "errors" as far throughout the world as it could.

Although the Lady's messages are laden with traditional Christian/Catholic terminology, with use of words such as sin, repentance, and phrases such as "sin hurts God,' and "war is God's punishment for sin," the messages may be restated in terms less specific to particular religions. When looked at in a spiritual rather than simply religious way, the messages are a wake-up call for moral and spiritual change, for humans to take responsibility for their thoughts, words, and deeds.

At their core, the messages at Fatima were very much about peace and goodness, and contained much imagery pertaining to fire, heart, and love. The fires of love are mentioned. References to how much Jesus and his mother love humanity were frequent. And Jacinta once remarked "If only I could place in the heart of everyone the fire which I have in my heart which makes me love the Heart of Mary so much!"

The Immaculate Hearts of Jesus and Mary are mentioned several times, and in powerful ways. Speaking of the fate of humanity, Mary said to the children, "Only I can help you. My Immaculate Heart will be your refuge and the way that will lead you to God." She also said, "In the end my Immaculate Heart will triumph.... and a period of peace will be granted to the world."

The painful and destructive powers of fire are mentioned as well; the children saw a vision of the torment of souls in hell—the hell of the punishment of being eternally separated from the presence and love of the Divine Source. The fire of the sun also played an important part, in ways both beautiful and terrifying. Yet the visions were really about the love God has for his mother, the love she and her son have for humanity, and their desire that humanity not destroy itself with its own evil. When looked at in a universally spiritual rather than strictly religious way, this is reminding us that our thoughts and actions have consequences: we reap what we sow.

By her message in these visions, Mary made it known that *she* was a power to be reckoned with, rather than acting as simply a veneer or mouthpiece for her son. Reading between the lines we can see that there has been an emphasis shift in the usual Catholic hierarchy. She says that her son and his father are offended and hurt by humanity's sins, but they are offended and hurt on *her* behalf. She told the children, "Sacrifice yourselves for sinners, and say often to Jesus, especially whenever you make a sacrifice: O Jesus, it is for love of Thee, for the conversion of sinners, and *in reparation for the sins committed against the Immaculate Heart of Mary.*" (emphasis mine)

She also told the children that God wished to establish in the world devotion to her Immaculate Heart. This was being done, she said, in order to save souls from the punishments of hell and to bring peace to the world.

If we consider Mary, as the Goddess, to be the primal "mother of form," her message is telling us that grave offenses are being committed against the sacredness of form, of matter itself, and that this threatens material existence itself. We need only look at the modern weapons of war to know this is true, although its truth may also be found in the pollution of our lands, waters, and atmosphere, our abuse of animals, as well as our attempts at genetic manipulation. Indeed, we do not respect even our own human forms, and our lack of self-respect can manifest itself in self-destructive behaviors such as chemical addictions, excessive risk-taking behaviors, lack of appropriate self-care, and the like.

The material realm is not just a mistake on the part of God, the message seems to be reminding us; it is a precious part of God's creation and must be loved, respected, cherished, and cared for. Metaphysically, of course, the world of form, the material realm, is a manifestation of the divine (body is the temple of spirit), and is just as divine and holy as the realm of pure spirit. Therefore, grave offenses against the material world are sins against the very vessel in which the Divine Spirit manifests itself.

How interesting it is that the Lady's message states that God wants humanity to refocus on her, the Mother of the World, and her loving Immaculate Heart, so that peace and harmony may be restored.

Because of the emphasis on the rosary, the Lady of Fatima is known as "Our Lady of the Rosary." She stressed the importance of both the rosary and herself by requesting its daily recitation and saying, "Only I can help you."

To bring all this around to the theme of this book, here we have, less than a century ago, a statement by Mary, Virgin Mother Goddess of the Piscean Age, telling us that we are reaping what we've sown, but that she is still our Mother and wants to help us and see us succeed in creating good, honorable, and peaceful lives for ourselves and our planet. She returns at this time of the end of one Age and the birth pangs of another, to tell us that *we* are making the New Age; that *we* are setting its tone by our thoughts and actions; that *we* bear the responsibility and consequences for what we are creating, and that it is a process which *we* can still affect by our positive energies in the form of prayer, love, and our choice of action.

The Universal Mother

The rate of Mary's appearances seem to be increasing within the last forty to fifty years. She appeared to four young girls in Garabandal, Spain in 1965; to thousands in Zaytoun, Egypt, in 1968, where she was seen atop a Coptic Church in a series of apparitions that went on for two years. Sometimes at night the apparitions were accompanied by the presence of several white or golden luminous doves, which flew and hovered around the apparition. In 1984 she appeared in Medjugorje, Bosnia-Hercegovina. As recently as mid-December 2009 she appeared in Warraq, a poor district of Cairo, Egypt, accompanied, once again, by luminous doves or pigeons. Over the course of several nights she was seen by thousands—Christians and Muslims alike—as a brightly glowing female image, clad in blue and white—atop the church's domes. Many present took pictures with cell phone cameras and posted videos to youtube.com, and the events were widely covered by both Egyptian and international media.

It is important to remember that Catholics do not own Mary. As a manifestation of the Divine Mother—Mother of God, Mother of Form, Primal Goddess—she is mother to us all. She came to Catholics wearing an identity that they could recognize and to which they could easily relate. Her message was one of repentance and virtue. These are applicable to all of us, no matter our religious orientation. She is asking us to be virtuous, kind, loving, and respectful.

When she appeared to the three children at Fatima she promised special rewards for the regular recitation of the rosary. She didn't say that only Catholics could say the rosary, or that only Catholics would receive the rewards. This was made clear to me by a deeply moving but very personal experience several years ago that showed me that Mary is, indeed, the Goddess—mother of all.

So what is the rosary and how can non-Catholics say it? It is a structured prayer, calling out to Mary, affirming certain beliefs about her, and requesting her help in our lives and at the time of our death. That's it. But it is the pattern, its energetic aspects, and the intention behind its recitation that makes it important, that makes it more than just a simple statement. It is the repeated calling out and making of the request, over and over and over, that makes it effective. By this repetition, it burns itself into our psyche, putting us into a meditative, receptive but focused alpha state, which allows us easier access to inner worlds, inner world beings, and the energies which flow there. When these are wedded to our intentions, the recitation of the rosary becomes a powerful magical tool.

I believe that Mary is coming as a mother to her children, as the mother birthing the New Age, to prepare us for the upcoming Changing of the Ages and all the turmoil and change that will bring to our lives, and also to remind us that, to a great extent, we co-create our reality.

The modern world is out of balance. Hatred, greed, and warfare seem to be the constants of our modern world—always happening one place or another on the planet. Deforestation is occurring at a rapid rate, as are problems such as air pollution and desertification. The Antarctic ice is melting, the ozone layer has holes in it, water pollution is nearly pandemic in scope, many species are mutating in unhealthy ways, and global warming is a fact. Yes, the planet *does* go through cycles of its own, but human interference and human-caused pollution have now interfered with the natural cycles, causing us to endanger our planet's ability to support advanced, complex life forms, including our own. The planet itself will survive, the bacteria will survive, and probably insect life will survive. But will we?

Poisonous chemicals used in households as well as manufacturing, residues of drugs and pesticides flushed into sewers, radioactive wastes from nuclear power plants—the pollution we humans have created has poisoned our world and poisoned our bodies as well. The toxic chemicals that flow through many of our rivers and streams flow through our blood streams, cellular liquids, amniotic fluids, and breastmilk as well. What the long term repercussions of this will be remain to be seen. The ocean—mother of life on the planet—has a huge patch of floating garbage and debris, largely plastics, in the area of the North Pacific Gyre, between California and Hawaii. This patch is twice the size of Texas, and presents grave dangers to birds and marine life, which often mistake the plastic debris for food. What happens to the chain of life, including human life, when we damage and despoil our great mother, the ocean?

I feel that these urgent issues of Age change are the forces behind the resurgence of interest in the Goddess in the mid to late 20th century. One cycle is ending, another being born. Birth requires a mother. Is it surprising, then, that the most well known Great Mother figure of the last two millennia is making her presence felt? Is it surprising that she is asking her children to get things in order so that a safe birth of a healthy entity can take place? Because all these things she is asking—prayer, love, respectfulness, goodness, virtue—are all *frequencies of energy* that will help "shape" the form that the new incoming energies and impulses will take in years to come.

Being of Help

A situation such as this seems to call on those of good heart to render assistance. Things are falling apart; old things are dissolving; new things are coming into being. The worthwhile things must be carried into the future; that which is outworn must be released. Not only does the planet do this during these Age changes, but it also must be done by each of us in our own lives. What can we do to get things in order, and help shape the new age by weaving the energies of balance and harmony into the new energies that are coming in? Some suggestions will be offered in the chapters that follow.

The Holy Spirit and Wisdom

There is another form in which the Goddess, the Divine Feminine, has survived into our era, and that is as the Holy Spirit.

As mentioned in *Chapter Seven*, the New Testament tells us that before he ascended to heaven Jesus told his disciples that he would not leave them alone and comfortless but would send them the Comforter, the Consoler—the Holy Spirit. The Christian feast of Pentecost, also referred to as the Descent of the Holy Spirit upon the Apostles, commemorates the occasion when this promise was fulfilled. At that first Pentecost, the sound of the rushing wind was heard and small tongues of fire were observed over the heads of the apostles. The Bible indicates that they were "filled with the Spirit,"—inspired—and began preaching to the crowds of Jerusalem, where each person listening heard the words in their own language.

Though portrayed in most of Christianity as the third person of an all male trinity, the Holy Spirit is feminine: she is the same being that the first Jewish temple called the

Ruach HaKodesh, Spirit of God, the Shekhinah—the divine presence that resided within the temple's most sacred inner sanctuary, the Holy of Holies.

It is this same divine feminine being—the Spirit of God, the Shekhinah, Wisdom (and as, we noted in *Chapter Seven,* the Canaanite goddess Asherah)—known to the Greeks as Sophia—who is the Holy Spirit of Christian tradition, the Comforter and Consoler that Jesus reminded his apostles would be with them always. Jesus was referring to Wisdom, the Shekhinah, when he counseled his disciples to be "as wise as serpents but as harmless as doves" (Matthew 10:16); both creatures are associated with Asherah.

The Church considered Jesus to be the embodiment of God's divine wisdom. The Gospel of Thomas quotes Jesus as saying that his "true" mother is the Holy Spirit.[6]

As the years rolled on, the Catholic Church gave many of Wisdom's attributes to the Virgin Mary, bestowing upon her the title "Seat of Wisdom," much as the Egyptian Goddess Isis had been known as "the Throne," and Hathor as the "House of (womb that bore) Horus."

In the Eastern Orthodox churches Mary is even more directly equated with Wisdom, with many referring to her as Holy Wisdom and displaying beautiful icons and images of the Virgin Mary depicted with the symbology of the Old Testament figure of Wisdom.

Notes:

1) It should be noted that pillars, along with trees, staves, poles and other similarly tall, thin, upright objects, have long been associated with sacred sites as symbols of the "axis" which connects heaven and earth. It may well be that Compostela was once a site sacred to earlier cultures.

2) In actuality, what she really said was that she was "the forever whole and perfect Saint Mary, honorable mother of the True God, honorable mother of the giver of life, honorable mother of the creator of men and women, honorable mother of the one who is far and close, honorable mother of the one who makes the heavens and the earth," attributes which identify her as the Aztec goddess Coatlique, also known as Tonantzin Coatlique, mother of the Gods. For more on this see *The Aztec Virgin,* John Mini, 2000. pp118-121.

3) www.holymary.info/didshesayguadalupe.html

4) *wad-i al-hub*; Arabic Place Names, www.billcasselman.com/place_names_of_the_world/arabic_place_names_one.htm

5) The iconography of the Lady of Lourdes portrays her as a young woman, despite the fact that Bernadette's original description indicated that the apparition appeared to be a girl of about 12 or 13 years of age, referring to her as "uo petito damizelo," which means "tiny maiden." Bernadette's description seems much more in keeping with the age of Goddess Persephone/Proserpina at her abduction by Hades, and indeed, with the supposed age of Mary when she gave birth to Jesus.

6) Gospel of Thomas, Logia 101.

Chapter Eleven - The Miriam Tradition

The Miriam Tradition and the Sea Temple

From ancient times there has been a line of priestesses and holy women who have served or in some important way represented the Sea Temple. I sometimes refer to these Sea Priestesses as the Miriam Line, and the Sea Temple priestess tradition in which they serve as the Miriam Tradition[1], from the Hebrew word *Miriam*, meaning *Mary*, which in Latin, *mare*, means sea. This priestesshood served the divine feminine—the Goddess—and stretches back at least as far as the Temple of the Moon (also known as the Sea Temple) in Atlantis.

This temple was spoken of in the writings of early 20th century British magician Dion Fortune,[2] and was referred to, though not by name, by the American psychic Edgar Cayce, as well.

The tradition is demonstrated historically in goddess traditions associated with both the moon and with water—including rivers and the sea—and is associated with items symbolic of water such as cup, cauldron, chalice, bowls, and other vessels.[3] Ships, arks, and boats of all kinds may be numbered among these as well, considering that they are most definitely connected with both "containment" and with water. The planet/deity Venus is also closely associated with the tradition.

Since the tradition is also associated with "coming into form," it is linked with fertility, conception, gestation (and, quite obviously, the womb), and nourishment of the young. Because of the nourishment aspect, it may also be associated with milk—both as the first food of the young and as a nourishing substance for the rest of the community. In addition, the Miriam line and Sea Temple are associated with DNA, genetic lines, and the many waves of life of all species on earth, including humanity.

In addition to its associations with the waters of creation and sustenance, the Sea Temple is also associated with the creative and formative powers of the both the Underworld and the Upperworld—the waters below and the waters above.

The goddesses we have detailed in preceding chapters have these associations with the moon and with water—in the form of river and sea—and thus they belong to the Sea Temple and are part of the Miriam Tradition. Many of these goddesses were also associated with the planet Venus, who was, as we have seen, associated with Inanna/Ishtar.

In the Sumerian stories, Inanna was the daughter of the moon deities, Nanna, and his wife, Ningal, (also called Nikkal),[4] who were the patron deities of the Sumerian city of Ur. It was from Ur that, according to the Old Testament, Abram and his wife Sarai (later to be known as Abraham and Sarah) were said to have begun their divinely-commanded sojourn, one that took them first to the city of Harran, whose patron deities were also Nanna and Ningal, and eventually to the land of Canaan, and south to the village of Mamre, where Sarah lived for many years toward the end of her life. The goddess Nikkal was also worshipped in Canaan. Author Sabina Teubal, in her book, *Sarah the Priestess*, has made a very good case for Sarah being a moon-priestess of the Mesopotamiam tradition who attempted to preserve and carry on her tradition in her new land amidst a rising tide of patriarchy.[5] There was a holy well at Mamre, so perhaps we may consider Sarah as an early priestess of the Miriam Tradition.

It would seem likely that Miriam Traditions of old were to be found near bodies of water—the seas, rivers, wells, and lakes. This persisted even into the Christian era. Speaking of the cult of the Black Madonna, French author Jean Markale says, "The Marian cult cannot be viewed apart from the ancient worship of the waters."[6] This is true, whether that water be wells, springs, ponds, rivers, oceans, or the rains.

Christianity absorbed much of the Miriam Tradition in the form of the cult of the Virgin Mary, and remnants of the tradition are to be found in depictions of Mary where the crescent moon and/or the sea feature prominently. This description is used in the Bible, in the *Book of Revelation* where the apostle has a vision of a woman who is "clothed in the sun and with the moon under her feet." This is an important image and we will speak more of it in subsequent chapters.

In some of the very early cultures of the Middle East, the moon was sometimes seen as masculine and associated with a god, but the planet Venus was most often seen as feminine, and associated with the goddess. The Venusian power was feminine, the embodiment of fertility and fruitfulness, while the moon god represented the male fertilizing force. The moon, whether seen as male or female, always has to do with some aspect of fertility, cycles, and the emergence of new life forms. Often, the moon/Venus imagery is combined, and a crescent moon is pictured with a star, which is, in actuality, the planet Venus, hanging just beside it.

The Sumerian Inanna was associated with Venus, and also with storms, rain, and fertility. The Akkadian/Babylonian Ishtar was associated with the planet Venus as well, but one of her epithets was "Cow of the Moon God Sin," in which capacity she ruled over plants, watering and caring for them, and making them grow.

Many of the goddesses of the Miriam Tradition have the usual but confusing (to our modern minds at least) tendency to exhibit traits which seem to be contradictory. As

Raphael Patai says about the Middle Eastern goddess who seems to be the prototype of all the others, "her personality exhibited everywhere the four basic traits of chastity and promiscuity, motherliness and bloodthirstiness."[7]

This would seem to demonstrate that the ancients may have realized that these opposites were, on a deep level, complementary rather than simply conflicting. A goddess of *Form*—of "life-in-substance," is, of necessity, also a goddess of death since all things born must eventually die.

As must be evident by now by our examination of several of the most significant goddesses of the ancient world, they all spring from one source—the original goddess, the divine feminine power who was and is the mother of form itself. She begins as the Void from which all else emerges—the primordial darkness—but as the manifestation of this spiritual energy into form occurs, she ultimately becomes the mother of the stars, the mother goddess of our planet itself—both land and sea—and thus mother of all physical life.

The Miriam Tradition serves this Great Goddess—the feminine aspect of divinity—by serving the power that conceives, gestates, nourishes, and ultimately destroys and recycles the material forms of life. This "service-to-goddess" is made manifest by service to Life—the other beings with whom we share the planet and the planet itself. This service, this priest/esshood, is also about learning to mediate energies from the invisible to the visible world—bridging the worlds, as does the birth-giving, death-dealing goddess.

This feminine, mothering/destroying divine principle, the Great Goddess, manifests differently in different areas of the planet—some of her contradictory characteristics more pronounced or less pronounced—because she manifests through the landscape. Landscapes vary in form, providing different filters for the energy to pass through.

In much the same way, the land—and what humans need to do to survive on it—creates the culture. Mother Nature presents different faces in different areas, and the deities and culture of those areas reflect that fact; although when human development accelerates and civilizations are created, nature may often become less of a factor in the culture and religion than it was early on. The religions begin to mimic the human structures of kingship and empire, rather than being solely based on the manifestations of natural forces. As time goes on, the deities, who began as sentient personifications of natural energies, celestial energies, and landscape forces, assume all the trappings and foibles of humanity and human culture, including the human form. They become quite individual, still related to a "type" of natural power, but with distinct and individual characteristics—similar to how humans, while being individuals, are all still part of "humanity."

It would seem that one of the sacred symbols of the Miriam Tradition still exists in the form of an amulet known today among Jews as the Hand of Miriam, and among

Muslims as the Hand of Fatima. The Hand is a talisman of protection—the protecting hand of the goddess—originally used to ward off the evil eye, but later worn for general protection. In Judaism it is said to be the hand of Miriam, sister of Moses, while in Islam it is thought to represent the hand of Fatima, beloved daughter of the Prophet Mohammed.

But before the amulet represented either of these good ladies it was sacred to the Phoenician/Carthaginian lunar goddess Tanit, whom, as we have seen, is related to the Canaanite/Phoenician Anat, the Egyptian Neith, the Akkadian Ishtar, but ultimately, to the Sumerian Inanna—all of them "Queens of Heaven," and/or "Ladies of the Sea." Tanit was worshipped in both Phoenicia and its African colony of Carthage, as we have previously noted. In Egyptian, Tanit means "Land of Neith."

Lineage of the Tradition

The Miriam/Sea Temple Tradition goes back to the ancient Sea Temple priestesses of Atlantis and other archaic and unrecorded civilizations that have come and gone over untold ages. While there has been no definitely identified physical evidence for the Atlantean lands and civilization, there's been plenty of lore, legend, and metaphysical evidence—among which may be counted the detailed readings of American psychic Edgar Cayce. The earliest mention of Atlantis comes to us from the writings of Plato, who said it was a tale he learned from a man called Solon, who told him the story dated back several thousand years.

In her writings about the Sea Temple, Dion Fortune stated that one of its main functions was that of seership. The priestesses were trained to be seers—that is, they were trained to open psychically and reach into the invisible realm to receive and read the patterns emanating from that realm, and interpret these patterns and subtle energies. Thus, these priestesses also served as prophetesses.

According to Edgar Cayce, the priestesses of the Atlantean temples were also trained to communicate with that realm, the realm of Divine Spirit. A few lines in one of his readings jump out as pertaining to this. In this case it seems that the priestess tuned into the spirit realm with the use of a special white stone:

> ....*in Atlantis, a priestess, a keeper of the white stone, or that through which many of the peoples, before the first destruction in Atlantis, kept their accord with the universal consciousness through speaking to and through those activities.*[8]

Sea Temples were often associated with nearby Sun Temples. Dion Fortune tells us that while the Sea Priestesses were seers, the Sun Priests were magicians, and that the Sea Priestess function was the higher one spiritually, accessing, as it did the deep spiritual realms and energies, while the Sun Priest function was to preside over the outer aspects of life and religion.

THE MIRIAMS OF THE BIBLE

Miriam, Sister of Moses

Let's look a bit further at the characteristics of the major Miriam/Mary figures from the Bible and oral tradition.

In the chapters where we have spoken of Miriam, sister of Moses, the roles she played as prophetess and leader of the women during the Exodus showed her to be a leader in her own right. The Hebrew women obviously respected her and saw her as such. Her activities, including taking issue with her brother Moses when she disagreed with him, suggest a strong-minded priestess role.

Miriam may well have been a priestess of this Miriam tradition as it existed among the not-yet-completely-monotheistic religious tradition of the Hebrew people living in Egypt during the time of the Exodus. We can see that she was a woman of power. As we have already noted, she has connections with water—the Nile, the Sea of Reeds, and her traveling well that sustained the children of Israel as they wandered for forty years in the desert. The fact that she was known as a prophetess links her to the tradition of seership that is an integral part of the Moon/Sea Temple and the Miriam Tradition.

Mary, Mother of Jesus

Mary, mother of Jesus, accepted the role as the *felix coeli porta*—the "happy gate of heaven" who allowed herself to be overshadowed by pure divine spirit, mediated by an angel—to bring through a divine child. We have already spoken of her in the preceding chapter, but in terms of the Sea Temple/Miriam Tradition, please recall what has been said about her as the Star of the Sea, as well as depictions of her wearing a halo of stars and with the crescent moon beneath her feet.

Mary Magdalene

Mary Magdalene is mentioned twelve times in the New Testament in conjunction with the ministry, crucifixion, burial, and resurrection of Jesus from which we learn that she was a devoted follower of Jesus and helped provide for him and his apostles from her own resources.

In recent years there has been a renewed interest in Mary Magdalene and a new understanding of her role in the life of Jesus. The non-canonical scriptures referred to as the Nag Hammadi have more to say.

From the *Gospel of Mary* (i.e. Mary Magdalene) we learn she was a much favored disciple of Jesus, his respected and much loved companion. Due to her innate spiritual intelligence and deep understanding, he shared many teachings with her that he did not share with the rest of the apostles. After he had departed the earth plane the apostles asked her to share some of these teachings with them. When she did so, they immediately became jealous, particularly Peter, and wondered why Jesus chose to share these things with her, a mere woman, rather than with them?

In the *Gospel of Philip* it is said that Jesus loved Mary Magdalene more than the other apostles and used to kiss her often; this, too, made the other apostles jealous and resentful. The Gospel of Philip seemingly equates her with Divine Wisdom, saying she is "the mother of the angels," a title previously accorded by the early Hebrews to the Goddess Asherah.

Though mentioned only a few times in the New Testament, legend has much to say about her. Recent interpretations of both biblical and non-canonical scripture show her to be a strong figure, chief disciple of Christ, first witness to his resurrection, "Apostle to the Apostles, "and a missionary of his good news to the people of Gaul (modern day France). A fresh interpretation of legends and traditions of southern France and of the apocryphal gnostic Gospels of Philip [9], Thomas, and Mary suggest she was the chief and most favored disciple of Jesus, and that she may have been his spouse and mother of his child.[10]

This interpretation would cast her in the traditional role of daughter (other self) of the goddess, the goddess in this case being Mary, mother of Jesus. In many ancient mythologies there is a quaternary of deities—a father god, a mother goddess, and their son and daughter, who inevitably mate (incest not being an issue with deities) and produce offspring. The hidden tradition of Mary Magdalene's marriage to Jesus places her firmly within this ancient mythological setting.

The implications of a marriage between Jesus and Mary Magdalene are enormous. Could it be that the Jesus, portrayed as sexless and celibate, actually possessed the characteristics of a normal human male, capable of sexuality, desirous of love and marriage?

In Christianity, Jesus is said to be not just the *Son* of God but also divine *himself*—a god. Therefore, mythically speaking Jesus was, as we've noted previously, a "godman" (son of a god but with an ostensibly human mother)—with a human wife, Mary Magdalene.

These new readings of the Mary Magdalene stories say she may have borne a daughter and that this daughter, Sara (whose name means "princess"), was the ancestress of many of the royal houses of Europe. This child, then, would be representative of the new (new because the Piscean Age was just dawning) evolutionary development in which the divine blood—that is, the power of the spirit world—not only manifests fully and physically in the world in the form of that particular person, but its power is spread down through the succeeding generations, gradually working its way down through the bloodlines of humanity over time, thereby transforming humanity by infusing it with the power of divinity.

This new understanding of the Magdalene suggests that, in a sense, she herself is the "Holy Grail" of legend, because she, as the mother of Jesus's child, was the "vessel" containing his "holy blood"—his child—within her very body, very similar to what is said of the Virgin Mary, whose body, quickened by the power of God's Spirit, was the vessel that held the divine infant, Jesus. But more than that: the logical extension of this new understanding posits that Magdalene is important in and of herself, as the feminine aspect of divinity's manifestation for the new age. Jesus and Mary Magdalene are thus seen as co-avatars or "archetypal bearers" of the Piscean Age.[11]

Such a vision of the Holy Grail is intimately linked with the Sea Temple because the Sea Temple is about bloodlines, reproduction, motherhood, new life, and cycles and rhythms. The Jesus story dates from the beginning of the Piscean Age. Mary Magdalene, as the mother of the human-plus-divine child of Jesus, might be viewed—along with her mother-in-law, Mary—as Goddess (of the "exalted woman" type) of the Piscean Age.

Pisces is a water sign, the sign of the hidden and often murky depths of the ocean. There is much secrecy about it—secrets which may be revealed later when they are finally "pulled up from the depths." The nature of Pisces is dual; its symbol is two fish swimming in opposite directions. Pisces wants to go both ways at once, which indicates an inner conflict and duality that it often tries to conceal. Given this, it is not surprising that the Divine Feminine figure of this age would have been split into two very different figures—the virginal Mother Mary, and Mary Magdalene, considered until quite recently to be a prostitute. It's also unsurprising that the divine son of the Piscean Age, Jesus, would be portrayed as above and beyond normal human sexual desire, when in reality he may well have been a husband and father. [12]

Some legends about Mary Magdalene tell us that she and some companions traveled across the sea in a small rudderless boat, making landfall in what is now Provence, southern France—a place where the Isis cults were still flourishing. The somewhat crescent shape of such small boats are reminiscent of the crescent moon, and this iconography links her and her fellow travelers to the Sea Temple and the Miriam Tradition.

Some say her companions were her sister Martha, her brother Lazarus (whom Jesus had raised from the dead), a youthful maidservant named Sara, and a priest called Maximin. Others say her companions were Mary Salome (Salome is related to the word *Shalom*, meaning *peace*), mother of the apostles James the Great and John the Beloved, Mary Jacobe (called Mary Clopas in the gospels), who may have been the mother of the apostle James the Less, and Sara, sometimes said to be either Mary Magdalene's daughter or maidservant.

Sometimes Joseph of Arimathea is cited as one of her traveling companions; it is said that Joseph and Mary Magdalene traveled to Britain and spent time there before going to the south of France.

These Three Marys—Mary Magdalene, Mary Salome, and Mary Jacobe—were said to have been present at the crucifixion and were the three women (according to the Gospels of Mark and Luke) who went to the tomb to anoint the body of Jesus, only to find the tomb empty. [12 & 13] These three Marys, and Sara as well, are still honored today in southern France, where the legends about them are strong. There is a town on the Mediterranean Sea in the Carmargue region called *Saintes Maries de la Mer*—the Saint Marys of the Sea. The church there is called the *Church of the Marys*, and has statues of Mary Salome and Mary Jacobe, as well as an underground crypt with a shrine to St. Sara, who has become quite special to the Gitans, or Gypsies. St. Sara is depicted as black, much like the Black Madonnas. On May 24th every year Gypsies gather in the Carmargue for a festival in her honor; they dress the statue in beautiful and elaborate clothing, and take it in procession into the sea and back to the church again.

The traditions of this area tell us that the Magdalene was said to have preached the gospel and converted many. She was also known as a healer and some say as a prophetess. The legends tell us that towards the end of her life, she retired to a cave outside the city where she spent the remaining years alone, ministered to by the angels. Caves, as you will recall, are representative of the Underworld realm of the Dark Goddess, and are places where people have traditionally gone for meditation, retreat, and quiet reflection in their search for wisdom. Thus caves are related to Wisdom, who is depicted in the Bible as female—the first-created and greatly beloved creation/emanation of God who helped him create the universe. And Wisdom is, of course, the meaning of the Greek word *Sophia*, the goddess-like being who was greatly honored in her own right as the Wisdom of the Divine.

Whether or not Mary Magdalene was the spouse of Jesus and mother of his children, she remains, in her own right, a powerful figure—beloved chief disciple of Jesus, first witness to the Resurrection, and Apostle to the Apostles. Of greater significance, however, is the implication that as the beloved and favored disciple of Jesus, she was actually his spiritual partner in the work he came to do for the world.

Some legends seem to suggest that she may have been a priestess of the Divine Feminine—Asherah, Astarte, or perhaps Isis since at least one source indicates that she may have been trained in a Jewish temple located in Egypt.[14]

The Seven Demons

Something quite interesting is possibly suggested by a single phrase in the *Gospel of Luke's* first mention of Mary Magdalene:

> *"....Mary Magdalene, out of whom seven demons had been cast."* – Luke 8:2

For centuries bible readers have wondered about the meaning of this phrase. Is it to be taken literally? What, or who, were these demons? Were they actual beings—evil spirits with consciousness? Or were they similar to what later became known as the "seven deadly sins"—wrath, greed, lust, laziness, pride, envy, and gluttony? Note that this text does not refer to Jesus casting them out of her, just that they had been cast out. This is mentioned again in Mark 16:9, which does say that Jesus had cast them out of her. However, this section of Mark has been deemed to be a later addition to that gospel.

The word demon is from the Greek word *daemon* and means simply a spirit, neither human nor divine, that operates in the realm between heaven and earth; daemons can be beneficent or malevolent.

Seven was an important number in the ancient world. There were many significant sevens—including the seven known planets (the sun and moon were counted as planets). The ancients had a conception of the heavens as being multi-layered; the layers were referred to as heavens—a concept mentioned in the Bible but that probably goes back to Sumeria—and had to do with the seven planets. The regions of the planets in the sky were seen as being different spheres, with different influences, vices, virtues, and rulers. The highest heaven, the eighth, was the abode of the Most High, and reachable only by traveling through the seven previous heavens. Each of the seven heavens had a guardian, or administrator, whose job it was to challenge the soul in order to assure it had earned its place in that next heaven by overcoming the vices and acquiring the virtues associated with that heaven. This entitled the soul to travel upward to the next level. This process is described in the *Gospel of Mary*, as a teaching given by Jesus to Mary during a vision. In the Gnostic traditions of early Christianity, these vices were sometimes personified and referred to as archons.

I believe Luke's words about Mary Magdalene and possibly Mark's as well refer to this seven heaven cosmology, and that Mary's words (in the *Gospel of Mary*) describe the process of ascending to the highest heaven and the guardian/archon/challengers to be met along the way.

This teaching was conveyed to Mary as being about what the soul undergoes after death but it might well apply to a spiritual practice of the old temples, an initiation in which the initiate, who has experienced a spiritual form of death during the process of initiation, ascends the Tree of Life—whose sephiroth represent the planetary heavens—on the way to the place above them all, the eighth and highest heaven, which was the throne room of God. Mark telling us that Jesus cast out Mary's seven demons is perhaps a way of saying that Jesus guided her through this particular initiation.

Something very like this was practiced by the priesthood of the first temple, Solomon's temple, a practice that survived in Judaism in the form of a tradition that later became known as *Merkavah* mysticism. *Merkavah* means chariot and the priests envisioned a chariot as the vehicle of their ascension.

Mary's knowledge of this ascension process, as well as her ability to understand the more deeply esoteric concepts taught by Jesus, might imply that she was an initiate in the Judaic mystical traditions of the day, traditions in which she may well have been trained within the Egyptian Jewish temple in Leontopolis, Egypt, that existed between

163 BC and 73 A.D. and was recognized by the Jerusalem temple as valid. Leontopolis maintained, as best it could, the traditions of Solomon's temple, including the ones removed by Hezekiah's and Josiah's extreme reforms of the 6th century BC during which the goddess had been banished. Because of this, one may assume that there were priestesses as well as priests who served this temple.[15]

It should also be noted that some of the old gnostic traditions considered Mary Magdalene to be an incarnation of the Shekhinah/Sophia—Divine Wisdom, that is, the Holy Spirit.[16] This links her with the Black Madonnas mentioned in the previous chapter. Wisdom is associated with darkness because she existed from the very beginning—even before light—and helped in the creation. Perhaps the Black Madonnas are black because rather than representing simply Mary Magdalene or the Virgin Mary, they represent Sophia—the Wisdom that fashioned the world—with the child on her lap, depicted as holding a globe and usually considered to be Jesus, representing the creation.

Notes
1) I wish to make it absolutely clear that "Miriam Tradition" is my name and definition of these priestesses, rather than an archaic one found in ancient records or books.
2) According to Dion Fortune priests also served in the Sea Temple.
3) "As we all know, humans are milk-giving creatures. An interesting, quite natural, but often overlooked cup symbol of the goddess is the female breast. The nursing breast contains the milk that sustains the life of the infant, similar to how cauldrons of plenty were known to provide sustenance and nurture. In other words, life emerges from a feminine source, and is sustained by a feminine power. While we are familiar with images of Isis nursing the infant Horus, lesser known are the images of Mary nursing the infant Jesus. But they exist. References to the "Madonna Lactans" go back to the middle of the 6th century, and artwork still exists that show Mary nursing Jesus, sometimes in a pose reminiscent of the Isis images. The earliest of these images is from the middle of the 3rd century; they began to die out in the 16th century when church began to discourage the use of nudity in religious artwork. Some of these images may be found here: www.fisheaters.com/marialactans.html
4) Though she is sometimes said to be the daughter of Anu, the high god (i.e. the heavens).

5) Teubal, Savina J; *Sarah the Priestess: The First Matriarch of Genesis*; Swallow Press, Ohio University Press; Athens Ohio; 1984. There were also large magnificent oak trees at Mamre, which was the site of an ancient oracular Canaanite shrine.

6) Markale, Jean, Cathedral of the Black Madonna: The Druids and the Mysteries of Chartres, Inner Traditions, Rochester, VT, 1988, p 175.

7) Patai, Raphael, *The Hebrew Goddess*, Avon Books, NY, 1967; p 136

8) Cayce, Edgar Evans, *Edgar Cayce on Atlantis*. A.R.E. Inc, Virginia Beach, VA, 1968; Reading #5037-1, April 19, 1944

9) Gospel of Philip, Gospel of Thomas, Gospel of Mary; The Nag Hammadi Library; James M. Robinson, editor; Harper & Row Publishers, San Francisco, 1981.

10) This subject has been covered convincingly and in great depth by Margaret Starbird in her books about the Magdalene. www.margaretstarbird.net

Starbird, Margaret, *Goddess in the Gospels*, Bear & Company Publishing, Santa Fe, NM, 1998, p 141

12) It might also help to explain why so many wars were fought in the name of Jesus, the Prince of Peace.

13) Mary the mother of Jesus was also present at the cross and the tomb, according to the gospels.

14) www.marymagdaleneshrine.org Click 'Testament of Mary Magdalene', then click 'Egyptian Initiation.'

15) In *Mysteries of the Bride Chamber*, author Victoria LePage says, "It is significant that Solomon is proverbial for his prodigious knowledge, for the hidden name of the Goddess Asherah was Wisdom, later to be known as Sophia in the Jewish Wisdom writings and still later as the Shekhinah of Judaic lore. Asherah would have had her priestesses and her secret schools of female wisdom, and we can confidently assume that, following the Egyptian model, female sacerdotal orders played no small part in the cultural life of ancient Israel. This is an assumption strengthened by the findings of archeology and biblical research. Carol Meyers, an American archaeologist and Professor of Religion at Duke University, notes that Israelite life in the early monarchic and pre-monarchic period was relatively free of gender bias and that an unusually large number of prominent and powerful women prophets were to be found in it. Moses' sister Miriam is cited as an influential prophet in the book of Exodus, and in the book of Judges the prophetess Deborah is also a judge, an office that carried with it the highest intertribal authority. Early Talmudic rabbis have written the women's orders out of the Hebrew scriptures, but in 2 Kings 22:3-14, Huldah the prophetess has escaped the scribal editing of a later age. We learn that she lived in the Jerusalem college around the time of the prophet Samuel, a woman evidently of great spiritual prestige who offered oracular information and counseling to the temple officials. Female priestcraft can therefore be assumed to have been well established in ancient Israel at that time. (LePage, *Mysteries of the Bride Chamber*; Inner Traditions, Rochester, VT, 2007, p xx)

16) More information about the gnostic traditions and the gnostic gospels can be found at www.gnosis.org

Chapter Twelve - Medicine Dreams and the Age of Aquarius

Dreams, Dreams, and More Dreams

In the spring of 1986 I had a curious dream. I cannot recall all of it but at the very end I was told about a soon-to-born child who was to be very important in the future; in fact, this child wasn't so much an individual person but was, rather, a representation of the energy of the New Age about to dawn. At the end of the dream I was shown the child. This child, who was utterly beautiful, looked to be about three years of age, had short golden curly hair, intensely blue eyes, and was wearing pink blanket-type sleepers. The gender of the child was impossible to determine. When I was shown the child I was shocked because the child was laying on the ground—asleep but with open eyes—right at the edge of a small stream. At first I thought the child was dead—had drowned in the stream—but I was given to know, in that strange way that dreams have, that the child was not dead but rather, not yet ready to awaken. When I awoke I knew that many others must be dreaming about this child, and many of us were being called to midwife the child's birth.

I dreamed about this child several other times over the years, and came to call it the "Golden Haired Child," and the "Child of Promise." I began to realize that the depiction of the child in the dream was telling me things about the Age to come. Although I kept wanting to refer to the child as a boy, I knew this wasn't correct. The pink sleepers made me think of a little girl, and yet I knew this wasn't correct either. Since the child's gender was truly impossible to determine, I sensed that the energy of the Age to come had to do with a balance of male and female energies. The child's eyes were open yet it wasn't awake; this led me conclude that it wasn't yet time for it to be awake. The fact that the child was so young told me that the energies of the Age were still flowing into formation and not yet ready to present to the world. It wasn't till much later that I realized how similar the child at the edge of the stream was to the Star card of the Tarot, where a woman (mostly likely the Star Goddess) is pictured at the edge of the stream or pool, pouring water into it. Rulership of this card is given to the sign of Aquarius, and it represents healing, hope, and renewal for the future.

* * *

Like so many others, I have been pondering the meaning and implications of the Age of Aquarius for many years. I've spent a good bit of time reviewing the history of the last 2000 years, discerning the threads of Piscean and Virgoan themes in that time period, noting the ups and downs of human progress, and doing a lot of reflecting on what the Age of Aquarius might mean—not just for humanity but for all the life-streams on the planet.

For years I have kept a dream journal and recently, as I was pondering the Age of Aquarius, I remembered another dream I'd had many years ago.

Something Big is Coming

Midmorning on August 18th, 1994 I awoke from a dream that felt to be of great significance.

In the dream, I was in a house with several dearly beloved, spiritually-minded friends. We were ablaze with excitement and anticipation because Something Big Was Coming. We could feel it. I looked out the front window and saw signs of it in the twilight sky, with its grey clouds and the sun shining through them. I could feel the expectant earth singing in joyful anticipation. We could feel this energy in our bodies and in our minds. We were humming with it.

What was coming was magnificent and amazing, and my friends and I were all preparing for it. The preparation included sleeping, because time passed in this dream—days and nights—and the sleep state was essential to properly receiving what was coming. In the waking state we could feel the energy of what was to come—which included a huge sense of joy. In our waking state the sensations were very strong; but during our sleep state we were receiving the full sense and strength of it. Sleep seemed essential to receiving this Something Big, as did the passage of time. As we continued to receive more and more of "it," our anticipation and excitement grew in leaps and bounds, and we began to be desirous of bringing our loved ones along with us into this wondrous state of being. We went searching for them, imparting to them what we were feeling, and many of them decided to join with us in our conscious preparations.

The energy continued to build. The message was "Soon! Soon!" The Something Big was coming closer and closer to full fruition, and our excitement continued to increase, along with our conscious reception of the energies. I had a distinct body and even cellular sense of these energies, which grew stronger and told me their fullness would arrive soon. Then I felt the Something Big arrive fully, and the sensations of joy and wholeness I experienced were so great they pushed me up, out of the dream, and back into a waking state, where I continued to experience them for several more hours. "This is the future," I thought....

But I didn't want to leave this dream, and kept fighting to stay in it, so I spent quite a bit of time in that in-between-waking-and-sleeping state. Before opening my eyes I mentally asked my dream guides what it had meant. I was told that a new phase of our evolution is kicking in now, and the dream was me experiencing the final countdown to its arrival. Strangely, because I didn't really consider myself Christian at the time, what it felt like was the approach of the Second Coming of Christ. Another explanation possibility given to me was of the return of Quetzalcoatl, the Feathered Serpent of the indigenous Central American traditions.

My dream guides told me this phase of evolution had to do with *Brain Transformation*— how we use our brain, how we think about our brain, and the brain's relationship to the rest of our body and self, the rest of nature, and other aspects of our life.

What we are coming into is a time when the focus will be on becoming whole. I was told—quite emphatically—that we would begin to realize that our brain, by which was meant our consciousness and our awareness rather than simply the physical organ, did not reside merely in the head but within the entire body. Whole-Body-Brain; Cellular Brain, Cellular Memory Access, Energy Field. The energy field that connects all parts of our physical being would be the new "brain." Something in us is evolving and it involves all parts of us—our physical selves, including our electromagnetic vibrations, and our soul and consciousness as well. My conclusion was that we are being 'rewired' for the new age. Or perhaps our pre-existent wiring is being reactivated. Our consciousness will be expanded by this, and we have the potential to develop a new form of collective consciousness—knowing ourselves to be part of a larger whole—while still retaining our own individual consciousness.

This powerful dream took years to properly interpret. It clearly informed me that big changes were coming into the world, to humanity. These changes were expected, had been foretold; it was part of a natural order of evolutionary change. The energetic shift was represented to me in the form of the return of some powerful avatar type energy. As I've mentioned, at the time I felt it to be the Christ/Quetzalcoatl energy. It was bright and shining; it illuminated us, expanded us, and turned on our inner senses in a huge way. It expanded our consciousness to the point that our consciousness and awareness, normally thought of as located in the brain, would be located throughout our body and energy field, and that we would, as a species, awaken to this fact. So what I was seeing and sensing in the dream was the arrival of the Quetzalcoatl energy, the second coming of Christ, the arrival of the Aquarian Age and what it would bring. And while I could understand how the feathered serpent symbology of Quetzalcoatl fit what I had felt in the dream, I had never taken the idea of the Second Coming of Christ very seriously, and was surprised that this analogy had been given to me. Being both a child of the 60's and a budding astrologer, I was aware that "this is the dawning of the Age of Aquarius," but hadn't given too much thought to what that Age might be like.

A few days after this dream took place, I learned that a white buffalo calf had been born in Janesville, Wisconsin, the first such birth in many years. Many Native Americans took this as the beginning of the fulfillment of the prophecies associated with one of the most sacred figures of the Plains Indians, White Buffalo Calf Woman. This birth, happening so soon after my dream, seemed somehow to underline the significance of the dream.

The Age of Aquarius

For centuries the Sign of Aquarius was considered to be ruled by the planet Saturn. In 1781 the planet Uranus was discovered and is now considered the co-ruler of Aquarius. Until Uranus was discovered, Saturn was considered the furthest edge of our solar system. The discovery of Uranus pushed the boundary out further and, in a way, its discovery might be considered one of the harbingers of the modern era. The years just preceding the discovery saw the American Revolution, while the years just following saw the French Revolution—both big harbingers of change in how people saw themselves, their rights as humans, and what their system of government should be. In short, these revolutions were about freedom, a type of freedom previously unknown to the average human being. Freedom and the breaking of previous restrictive boundaries are among Aquarius's principal themes.

These years might well be considered a bridge between one era and the next, past to future—staid and limiting Saturn guarding the past at one end of the bridge while wild, futuristic, and humanistic Aquarius beckons from the other.

As I have previously noted, the Age of Aquarius does not come into being in one fell swoop or one moment in time. It inches its way in over several years through various astrological aspects and the energetic windows of power and opportunity they open for us. Things shift gradually but indisputably.

Some sense of the age to come can be gleaned by a very rough glance at the astro-dynamics in place as the Age of Aquarius truly dawns.[1] The sign of Aquarius will be, of course, on the eastern horizon as the sun rises on the day of the Spring Equinox. An astrological chart drawn for dawn that day would show that Taurus is at the midheaven, Leo is on the descendant, and Scorpio is at the root, or nadir, of the chart.

Scorpio is the root energy, that which wells up from the depths and brings things forth from the hidden places to be dealt with. Scorpio is a sign of powerful transformation, transmutation, and regeneration...the snake shedding its old, outworn skin, so that it may live again in its new one. This is the serpent power energy, the *kundalini*, the life force itself as it rises through the body/situation. Scorpio is about raw life energy power pouring forth, uncovering and helping to release all the muck that must be transmuted. It is about transmuting that muck, and clarifying and purifying the channel through which the life force must flow, that regeneration might occur. Another image for the sign of Scorpio is the phoenix, that legendary bird that bursts into flame, consuming itself, and is then reborn from its own ashes.

Aquarius on the Ascendant (i.e. Aquarius Rising) says that the New Age will present itself to the world with Aquarian characteristics. The Ascendant can act as a filter through which the rest of the chart is expressed. But sometimes it can be a mask that shields the real self and issues.

Aquarius Rising will show the things that are facing us—the wonderful possibilities as well as the jobs that need to be done—although perhaps, at least at first, it will show these in a very idealistic way. But Aquarius is about information, and will give us that information if we're paying attention, pulling back the misty and emotional Piscean veil that has hidden the facts for so long. Aquarius on the Ascendant will bring things to light. Aquarius also has to do with humanity, human values, and also, electro-magnetic frequencies. And since it is ruled by Uranus and co-ruled by Saturn, sudden upheavals and disruptions (including earth changes) might well be part of that unveiling and informing.

Leo on the descendant, the descendant being the 7th house of relationships and partnerships, shows us how these things are to be worked out—in mature, heartfelt, and rightful relationship with each other, caring for the tribe, strategizing for the common good, loving one another, and protecting the young. Leo can exhibit a tendency to be self-absorbed so the possibility for that is definitely present, but the highest manifestation of Leo is true Kingship—that is, self-sovereignty and caring for others.

Taurus at the Midheaven shows us how these Aquarian Age themes and struggles will show up in the bright illuminative glare of the midday sun—as issues of security and insecurity, prosperity and scarcity, public values and private values, fertility and sterility, beauty and ugliness are spotlighted. Since it is at the Midheaven, Taurus will display and highlight these in a public way. There could be a tendency for society to point only to the good things and try to pretend all is well, but the polar opposite Scorpio Nadir will not permit that ignorance or illusion to last long, and will continue to bring forth that which must be dealt with if all are to survive.

At its best, Taurus at the midheaven will provide an ongoing display of how beautiful and life-friendly things could be if we would just get busy with the job of transmuting the hidden muck, as well as giving us a push to get going on manifesting those Aquarian ideals by working hard to bring real beauty to the world. But Taurus at the midheaven could possibly turn things into an even bigger tug of war between the haves and the have-nots of the world. I like to hope that Aquarian Age humanitarian ideals will win the day—or rather, the Age.

Air, Water, Fire, and How It All Gets Earthed

Although an Air sign, Aquarius has a connection to the element of Water, as well. It is located in the southern part of the sky where many of the water-related constellations lie, and it is the sign of the Water Bearer, the celestial being who nourishes the earth and humanity by pouring down the heavenly waters—some say of information and knowledge, some say the rains of spring—from its starry vessel.

The tarot card associated with Aquarius is the Star. Its imagery depicts the Goddess [2] by a body of water. Her right foot is upon the water while her left knee is upon the land. She holds a pitcher in each hand. With her left hand she pours the waters of life onto the land, while with her right hand she pours these regenerating waters into the body of water before her. The card symbolizes healing and renewal and the Goddess pictured is considered to be the great feminine divine power known by Kabbalists as Binah, or Understanding. Binah, the Great Mother, pours her waters of life and renewal from the Above World, the spiritual realms, to the Below World, the material realm.

In astrology the Sun is representative of the essential self, the core of one's being and nature. Just as the sun is at the center of our solar system's circle of planets, our essential self is at the core of all the other aspects of who we are. The vernal equinox sun rising in the constellation of Aquarius will bring the work of understanding and embodying the essential human self to the fore. It will bring us the information we need, but it is up to us to use it to our spiritual advantage. At its best, it will allow us to balance emotion with intellect and information, harmonizing head and heart.

As the sign of the age, the nature and values of Aquarius will be the dominant themes of the next couple thousand years. Yet they will be in a dance with the themes of Leo, the sign which is opposite from Aquarius across the zodiacal wheel, just as the themes of the Piscean Age have been in a dance with those of its opposite sign, Virgo, for the last couple thousand years.

The constellation of Aquarius depicts a human form and Aquarius is about the human, both individually and collectively. It's about humans—the value of humans, human rights, and human values. It's about ideas, information, and the mental realm. It's about the evolution and expansion of human consciousness. Although I didn't quite understand it fully at the time, that's what my dream was trying to tell me back in 1994. During that dream I was with others while I was feeling the intense energies, and my desire to share it with others who were not present, specifically family members, was very strong—an imperative, in fact. The dream was telling me that the coming changes were about this very important evolution and expansion of human consciousness. What I've come to realize in the years since then is that this expansion has the potential to eventually result in a state of unity, as the individual consciousness expands and touches into that of others, and then into the greater unitive field of which we are all part, which is consciousness itself—the Divine Mind.

As we grow and evolve with these Aquarian energies, our expanding consciousness wishes to share our thoughts and ideas with others. And indeed, communication is an important aspect of the Aquarian Age. Speech, whether oral or written, gives form and voice to our thoughts. As we articulate our ideas, our voice sends forth the vibratory frequency of our thoughts and ideas; as others receive this—and we receive theirs—the energies start to form patterns and build structures. "In the beginning was the Word." But the Word is not merely a sound, it is a vibratory frequency containing the energetic pattern and structure of our thoughts and ideas. The Age of Aquarius, with its mass communication technology, communicates these vibrations farther and faster than ever before possible, allowing a more rapid spread of thoughts, ideas, and changes. The sign of Leo, on the other hand, is about the sovereign, mature, heartful, centered self; and in its highest manifestation, about using one's power "heartfully" and generously in service of others.

Will we each learn to become kings/queens in our own castles during the coming age? Is this about learning and practicing the sovereignty of our own selves, as well as about respecting the sovereignty of others? The possibility of recognizing the actual value of each individual self—you are another myself—is very strong here. But we only learn these things by being inside them. So we must learn this by being inside of issues of self-sovereignty and situations which teach us the value of other human lives, situations that trigger compassion and camaraderie.

Self-Sovereignty. Leo. Aquarius. The Age of Aquarius is the Age of Humanity. It's about us. The spring sun rises in Aquarius, and we are becoming the sun/son/children....*We*, in our most evolved, heart-centered selves, are, in fact, the Second Coming of the Christ—sun-god/son of god, the wise and loving avatar of the Piscean Age reborn in collective form. The Second Coming will be in each of us as we become "Christed"[3] beings; this can only happen with the return of the Divine Feminine—the Goddess, the Holy Spirit, the Holy Sophia, Holy Wisdom, the Presence of God—into our lives. It is her power that allows us to rebuild ourselves, our reality, and our world if we let her into our lives.

Twelfth century medieval mystic and theologian Joachim de Fiore, whose main area of study was the emergence of divinity in history, predicted that the next "Age" of the world would be the Age of the Holy Spirit.[4]

Leo, whose ruling planet is the sun, is the sign of royalty, and it is the Queen, as the Lioness Goddess, who gives birth to this new age, the new humanity, with its potential for divine and balanced androgyny. She gives birth to humans and gifts us with the potential to be all that we can be—fully human, the sacred human with the elemental powers balanced, the psychic powers balanced and almost instinctive, in full expression of our core solar essence, our Christ selves.

The goddess is giving birth to the new age—and the new sun. *We* are that new sun; it's about us.

What does it mean to be becoming the sun? It means human consciousness will expand, because it's time for us to grow up and become who we really are—to fulfill our potential as Suns, as suns/sons/children of God, as Godlike beings: to "shine," to radiate the expanded consciousness of our solar selves to one another for the benefit of all.

True kingship/queenship, true sovereignty, is not simply about "power over." It's about power within and service to others. A sovereign's job is to serve his/her people by seeing to their welfare and making decisions for the common good. In order to do this effectively, a king must first be king over himself, and a queen be queen over herself. This means coming to maturity, as well as gaining self-knowledge and inner security. Once again, the Age of Aquarius is about humans coming into their full potential, their true sovereignty, by coming to maturity as a species.

The nature of the Lion Goddess is that of female lions in general. They are good hunters and smart strategizers. They realize the value of cooperation and do so often for the common good of their pride—their tribe. They cooperate in hunting, in breeding, and in cub-raising, often nursing cubs not their own (and occasionally baby animals of other species); they are excellent mothers. Their whole agenda is about cooperation for mutual survival. Yet they still remain very powerful as individuals.

This gives us clues as to how to develop our self-sovereignty—by cooperation and nurturing!

Just about everyone is familiar with the Egyptian Sphinx. This amazing stone being was one of the seven wonders of the ancient world. The Sphinx, with its lion body and human head, seems to embody the combination of lion and human energies that characterizes the Leo/Aquarius axis.

In astrology, the cusp between the last degree of Leo and the first degrees of Virgo is known as the Sphinx Point.

Within the constellation of Leo, at a point near the ecliptic, is the bright fixed star Regulus. The name of this star, which is located at a point in the constellation said to be the heart of the lion, means *kingly* or *royal*. The sign of Leo governs the heart and is ruled by the sun, which is the heart of our solar system.

The Age of Aquarius/Leo is asking us to let the actions of our head be governed by our heart, the two of them working together to bring balance. It is asking us to develop maturity and balance, to value our individualism but to learn to work cooperatively for the common good. It is asking us to look at others and see/feel "another myself."

Lions and the Goddess

The combination of lion and goddess is not new. As we have previously noted, in past ages several goddesses have been linked with lions, or have had leonine qualities—among them we may count Inanna, Elat, Astarte, Asherah, and Sekmet.

Brigid

In addition to these, the Celtic Goddess Brigid comes to mind when I think of a goddess who exhibits the qualities of the Age of Aquarius/Leo. In many ways, Brigid—whose legends as goddess and saint are inextricably interwoven—displays very leonine qualities.

As St Brigid, she was an abbess, a leader and woman of power at a time when women did not have much religious or secular power. There's even a legend that she was consecrated a bishop. She is associated with healing, care-taking, and cooperation. Her legends and imagery link her with fire; and yet there's a connection with water as well, and many healing wells in Ireland are named after her. And as we have mentioned previously, Brigid was linked with cows and milk, things that show her ancient roots as a goddess of sustenance and nurture.

As goddess, Brigid was the giver of inspiration and was the matron deity of poetry, smithcraft, and healing—all of which represent the power of fire combined with the power of air—mind/head, skill/hands, and heart/skill and compassion. Her feast day was the first of February, which falls midway through the Air sign of Aquarius, and the inspiration that she was known to impart was a very electric, divine-frenzied, "bolt out of the blue" Uranian type of energy.

An interesting story concerning Brigid is found in the writings of 19th century writer Fiona Macleod. It comes from a little volume called *Winged Destiny: Studies in the Spiritual History of the Gael*.[5] In this story the author encounters an elderly woman named Mary MacArthur who tells him of a dream encounter she'd had with St. Brigid many years before. Brigid was very precious and dear to the Gaels; they regarded her as the foster mother of Christ, and this encounter touched Mary McArthur deeply.

This was the dream that Mary McArthur recounted to Fiona Macleod. A woman of great beauty came up to Mary as she was at the seashore gathering driftwood to kindle her fire. The woman threw the wood into the sea, saying she was throwing away Mary's sorrows with the wood. She identified herself as Brigid, and Mary exclaimed aloud in wonder and praise, and went down on her knee. Brigid looked at her and said:

> "I am older than Brighid of the Mantle, Mary,
> and it is you that should know that.
> I put songs and music on the wind before ever the bells of the chapels
> were rung in the West or heard in the East.

> I am *Brighid-nam-Bratta* (Brighid of the Mantle),
> but I am also *Brighid-Muirghin-na-tuinne*
>   (Brighid of the conception of the waves),
> and *Brighid-sluagh* (Brighid of the immortal host),
> *Brighid-nan-sitheach seang* (Brighid of the slim faery folk),
> *Brighid-Binne-Bheullbuchd-nan-trusganan-uaine*
>   (Brighid of sweet songs and melodious mouth),
> And I am older than *Aona* (Friday)
> and am as old as *Luan*. (Monday)
> And in *Tir-na-h'oige* (Land of the Ever Young)
> my name is *Suibhal-bheann* (Mountain Traveller);
> in *Tir-fo-thuinn* (Country of the Waves)
> it is *Cù-gorm* (Grey Hound);
> and in *Tir-nah'oise* (Country of Ancient Years)
> it is *Sireadh-thall* (Seek-beyond).
> And I have been a breath in your heart.
> And the day has its feet to it that will see me coming
> into the hearts of men and women like a flame upon dry grass,
> like a flame of wind in a great wood.
> For the time of change is at hand, *Mairi nic Ruaridh Donn*—
>   (Mary, daughter of Rory Brown)
> though not for you, old withered leaf on the dry branch,
> though for you, too, when you come to *us*
> and see all things in the pools of life yonder."

This interesting passage, wherein Brigid refers to a time of change close at hand, would seem to speak of the Aquarian Age which will soon arrive, as well as the major time of changes we are now experiencing and which are leading us into the new age.

Older than Friday—creation's final day, when all living creatures had come into being—and as old as Monday—the second day of creation, when God began creation by separating the waters, creating sky and sea, Brigid is telling us she is older than earthly life and was there at the very beginning—just as was the Biblical figure of Wisdom.

She is Lady of the faeries, the sea, and the songs in the wind. Brigid says that she has previously been like "a breath in your heart," but that the time is coming when she will enter into people's hearts like a flame upon dry grass and a flame of wind in a great wood.

Thus she identifies herself as a major player in the future; a powerful being who will help bring about, in the age to come, the very changes she foretells.

Asherah

There is one Middle Eastern Goddess who seems to bring together many of the themes mentioned above. This goddess is Asherah, about whom we learned in *Chapter Seven*. Within the image and lore of this great Semitic Mother Goddess we find connections with lions, fertility, sexuality, motherhood; with doves and the Divine Spirit; with the sea, with healing, with serpents[6] and (possibly) the body's kundalini energy, and also with the Tree of Life itself—in the form of the asherah pillar that symbolized her. Thus, Asherah seems to exhibit many of the associations and qualities of the eternal Mother who births the Ages.

As can be seen by the above examples and those in *Chapter Seven*, the Goddess is about all the elements—earth, air, fire, water, and spirit—because she is the Mother of Form.

The Woman Clothed With the Sun

One night during the writing of this chapter I awoke from a dream wherein I saw an image of the Goddess, her cloak shining brilliantly as if lit from behind by the rising sun. I heard the words *"A woman clothed with the Sun and the Moon under her feet,"* ringing in my ears. I realized these words were from the Book of Revelation in the Bible and I knew immediately—in that way that happens with dreams—that they referred to the Goddess giving birth to the Aquarian Age. She was "clothed with the sun" partly because the astrological sign of Leo is opposite that of Aquarius (just as Virgo was opposite Pisces during the Piscean Age), and rules the sun. As we have mentioned, astrology often works in these polarities, and just as Virgo gave us a Virgin Mother goddess, Leo will most likely give us a Leonine one.

When I awoke again in the morning I looked up this passage in the Bible. I found that the complete text was:

> *"And there appeared a great wonder in heaven; a woman clothed with the sun, and the moon under her feet, and upon her head a crown of twelve stars: And she being with child cried, travailing in birth, and pained to be delivered."* [6]

She is clothed with the sun, crowned with the stars, and has the moon under her feet. What more clear image could one ask of the Great Mother Goddess—crowned by twelve stars representing the twelve signs of her zodiac—giving birth to the new age? And the fact of the matter is that because she is "clothed in the sun," she births every new astrological age. These lines from Revelation were written almost two thousand years ago, and therefore referred to the Piscean Age then dawning. But such an image is timeless—and as significant and valid for our times as it was two thousand years ago as an image of the goddess birthing a new age, though the interpretations will vary with each age.

In Church iconography, the woman "clothed with the sun and the moon beneath her feet" is sometimes depicted with a serpent near the moon, and the woman's foot upon the serpent. The Church's interpretation of the serpent is that it is Satan, and the Virgin foot is crushing his head, destroying him.

Here, then, are my interpretations of the image as it appeared in my dream. This is what I "knew" in the dream, and what came forth strongly right after waking.

The woman is "clothed with the sun," which means not only does she birth the sunrise into a new sign, but also that as the goddess of this new age she will exhibit solar qualities—brilliance, illumination, warmth, fierceness, love, and the possibilities of abundance those things can bring. Here is the goddess seen in a leonine aspect—since the sun rules the sign of Leo. No more the meek virgin, she will be the Lion Queen, full of fierceness, but also of leonine motherliness and protectiveness as well. Her brilliance and illumination give proper nourishment to her human children—affording them just what is needed for the growth, evolution and expansion of their consciousness and their relationships with one another and the rest of earth's life forms.

The crescent moon is under her feet. The image of the crescent moon has long been linked with ships, boats, and arks. So here we have the moon-boat, the ark, the sacred vessel which carries us from age to age. The moon-boat is under her feet, so the Goddess stands and is carried on the boat, but in truth, she *is*, herself, the boat. She carries us all, including the sun, from day to day, from age to age, through the waters of time and space. In addition, there is a relationship here with the womb, the vessel that holds and nourishes the next generation as it grows into being.

The moon rules the sea—its magnetic tides and rhythms—and since all life on the planet was birthed from the sea, this means that she is related in a very physical way to the lifestream of this planet, and the new life she brings will be more than simply an evolution of consciousness; it will have physical aspects as well. And as there are positive and negative (from the human perspective at least) in all things on this plane of existence, one has to wonder if this bespeaks the effects of pollution and global warming on the planet's oceans and life-streams during the coming age.

The moon is representative also of time, its phases being used by ancient people to measure the passage of time. Time is a function of matter, of form; so the goddess standing on the moon represents divine energy in form—spirit in substance—that is, the divine power within the earth and all physical matter. The serpent beneath her feet emphasizes this meaning as it may represent the divine feminine kundalini energy, called the serpent power, waiting to rise up and grant us expanded consciousness but held back by her foot till we are ready for that expanded consciousness.

The imagery of the moon beneath her feet brings us full circle from very early understandings and imagery of the Goddess as Mother of Form and linked with Stars, Sea and Moon, to Mary—the Virgin Mother of Christ, who is traditionally pictured with the moon beneath her feet.

Another possible (or additional) explanation for the moon beneath her feet is based in astrology. In astrology, the moon refers to instinct (i.e. in particular the survival and generative instincts) and the unconscious mind, the "moon under her feet," may also refer to these instinctual and unconscious parts of the self. Because the woman with clothed with the sun, the moon under her feet may refer to these instinctual and unconscious parts of ourselves coming into the awareness of our solar selves—our heart and mind in a more illumined and informed state of being. From the darkness of ignorance and blindly reactive instinct is born the light of mind and heart.

A good summation of all of the above may also be given in Kabbalistic terms: The "woman clothed with the sun and the moon beneath her feet and upon her head a crown of twelve stars" is the Goddess of Life, the Tree of Life—with her feet (roots) upon lunar and foundational Yesod, her body shining with the solar garment of Tiphareth's beautiful harmonization/integration of creation's opposing but complementary forces, and her head/consciousness crowned with the stars of the Divine Supernal Triangle of Kether-Crown, Binah-Understanding-Discernment, and Chokmah-Wisdom.[7]

With this new age, a new wave of life is being born; it is cresting on the shore. This woman clothed with the sun is rising from the sea, whether it be the sea of instinct and the unconscious, the sea of space, or the physical sea itself that births life-forms on the planet.

We are living in some pretty dark and challenging times; quite often it seems we are blind to the humanity of others and the worth of the rest of creation. The Aquarian Age to come offers the promise of humanity evolving from the *domination* of its dark, blind, instinctual side to a state of expanded consciousness and awareness of our full potential—physical, mental, emotional, energetic, and spiritual—as humans; instinct and intelligence working together. It offers the promise of humans finally recognizing their siblinghood with each other, as well as their kinship with all other life forms on the planet. We all came from the sea, we were all born from the same mother....

The woman clothed with the sun is laboring, crying out in pain, awaiting the imminent birth of her child. The child she is birthing is the new Age of Aquarius. Yet this goddess is *our* mother as well, and her pain and cries are also for us as we struggle to be born into the new age of expanded consciousness. She is concerned for us, and full of grief at the shortcomings which make this such a difficult process for us. As was stated in the previous chapters, she has expressed this sorrow and concern repeatedly in her apparitions over the last few hundred years. She is the mother of the Ages, but also, the Mother of Mercy and Compassion.

It should be noted that the Catholic church has traditionally held the "woman clothed with the sun" to be the Blessed Virgin Mary.

The next verses from Revelation tells how, after the man child is delivered, he is "caught up to heaven," to the throne of God, while the mother takes up residence on earth in a protected place, specially prepared for her—reminiscent of the great Shekhinah—who lovingly sacrifices her place in the heavenly realms to dwell with her earthly children while they evolve to a recognition of, and are able to embody, their own innate divine wisdom.

She is a new *form* of the Goddess, bearing many of the aspects of the ones mentioned, but in a new way. She is the Star Mother, showering her radiant celestial energies upon the earth once again to enliven, refresh, and regenerate life for the new age.

The Goddess of the Aquarian Age

In the text above, we have begun a description of the Mother Goddess who births this age; she cannot be fully known to us from our perspective in this one particular lifetime. She will reveal herself more fully as the Age unfolds, just as her "child"—those Aquarian characteristics and energies—will manifest in us as we move into a state of being wherein our inner male and female energies are coming into balance.

Aquarius is about humanity, but it also has to do with space, mind, intellect, consciousness, and with the balance of male and female energies—an honoring of both polarities and a realization of the necessity of both. Aquarius the Water Bearer pours out the waters. As previously mentioned, these are variously said to be the waters of knowledge, poured out to quench the thirst for knowledge in the soul of humanity; the waters of spiritual life, poured out to nourish the soul; or simply the waters of life, such as the rain waters from heaven that physically sustain life. Aquarius's ruling planet is Uranus, which is about sudden and often unexpected and shocking upheavals and changes that can break through restrictions and limits. These changes can bring utter chaos, great liberation, and/or very important and necessary awakenings. Its co-ruler is Saturn. Saturn is about limits, structure, law, stability. In previous eras Saturn was also about agriculture, the land and its bounty—all necessary things for building up a suitable foundation for humanity to live and thrive.

Above all, Aquarius has a very sudden and radical type of energy and a very high vibrational frequency. This frequency is what I was feeling in my Big Dream; that "high" feeling, full of joy—all circuits open and receiving. The openness and receptiveness can lead to understanding the relationship between all beings, and valuing all beings.

This is what Aquarius promises, what it has to offer. It is what humanity desperately needs at this juncture in time. What we choose to do with this promise is up to us.

Notes:

1) There are differences of opinion as to when the Age of Aquarius actually begins; dates range from 2012 to

sometime in the 24th century.

2) Some call this goddess Astraea, which means Star Goddess, which in turn may harken back to Inanna, earliest of the goddesses associated with Venus, the Morning Star. Astraea was the Roman goddess of justice and the scales of the constellation Libra are hers. The Greeks identified her as the virgin of the constellation of Virgo.

3) Christed may be defined as the "higher" consciousness, with head and heart faculties awakened and able to work together; an awareness of one's "oneness" with the divine source.

4) Joachim's scholarship of the Book of Revelation and his inspired prophetic vision led him to see the emergence of divinity in three stages, or eras. The first era, that of Old Testament times, was the Age of the Father, a time ruled by the fearful power and might of God the Father, governed by the "law of severity." The second era was the Age of the Son (Jesus Christ), was governed by the "law of love"—the teachings of Jesus as taught by the Church. The third age he saw as the Age of the Holy Spirit. It would begin with the "Second Coming," which he felt referred to the Holy Spirit rather than the person of Jesus, and would lead humanity to a time of universal joy and love, and great spiritual freedom with no need for the hierarchical governance of the Church's structures. Needless to say, this did not go down well with the Church hierarchy.

5) Macleod, Fiona (William Sharp), Winged Destiny: Studies in the Spiritual History of the Gael; William Heineman, London, 1913; p 213

6) Revelation; *The Holy Bible*; King James Version

7) On the Tree of Life, Yesod, the Foundation, is the world of images – templates for the "form" that will come into being in Malkuth, the plane of physical manifestation. Tiphareth is the Sphere of the beauty and integration that occur when opposing forces are harmonized, while the Supernal Triangle of Kether-Chokmah-Binah represent Source's first manifestation of consciousness—awareness, awareness/consciousness of the divine pattern and its inherent harmony and wisdom.

Chapter Thirteen - The Future and the Art of Navigation

From the Past to the Future

From the Babylonian Epic of Gilgamesh comes the story of Ut-napishtim.

The god Enlil had become very annoyed with humanity. They had become so noisy and bothersome he could endure it no more and decided to eliminate them and all that lived on the land. He was determined to cause a great flood to drown them. He met in council with the rest of the gods and convinced them to agree to his plan. But as the time grew closer, another of the gods, Ea, grew uneasy with this plan and decided to save some creatures so that the earth could be repopulated. He selected a good and upright man named Ut-napishtim and ordered him to build a large, waterproof boat in which to ride out the flood. The boat, later referred to as an ark, was built and a breeding pair of each animal species was loaded onboard, along with Ut-napishtim, his family, a pilot, and the craftsmen who'd helped him build the boat.

The rains began and they lasted for many days and nights. Everything was flooded; even the mountaintops were covered by the flood waters. Finally the rains stopped, the water level began to drop, and after a while the ark came to rest atop a high mountain. Several days later Ut-napishtim sent out a dove, knowing that if it found dry land it would not return. But it returned, and so did the bird he sent next. But the third one did not return; the waters had receded to the point where the bird was able to find food and a place to land. So Ut-napishtim knew it was safe to leave the ark and commence the beginning of the new era.

If this story sounds familiar it's because it's pretty much the same story as the one found in the Bible in which the main character's name is Noah. Which one of these stories is the original and which is a copy is still being debated by some. The truth of the matter is that it's an ancient story, the earliest version being from Sumeria, that was prevalent all over the Middle East and thus found its way into the sacred writings of most of the local cultures.

In a way, living in these times is like getting ready to board Ut-napishtim/Noah's ark. We may not be facing 40 days and nights of rain, but we are facing the end of one era, one way of being, and the beginning of another. What is it that we should bring along with us on this trip? Which life-forms are to be loaded, two by two, onto the ark that shelters us as it moves us into the future? Which of the forms and patterns of our era need to be brought forward, and which will be left behind? Which things will be useful and workable in the age which is to come? The skies are overcast; when will the rain start and when will it stop? When will it be safe to get out of the ark and start the rebuilding process?

Pondering these questions even briefly results in the realization that the answer is not fully in our hands. Yet in a way, some of it *is* in our hands by virtue of the choices we make.

Packing the Ark

The analogy of an ark is apt. An ark is a vessel, often a boat. Like all boats, it carries one across waters—in this case the waters of time—to a destination, hopefully with skilled navigators plotting the course and steering the vessel.

However, the voyage is itself as important as the destination, and may help determine the vessel's ultimate destination.

Similarly, the ark may be seen as a womb—a safe and enclosed space which protects us as we gestate in preparation for birth into a new life.

For some years now we have been in the early stages of this particular voyage into our future. One age is ending, another is beginning. Such times of transition always involve some things being saved and carried forward in the future, while others are left behind or destroyed. The new age will be constructed in part from the (hopefully) useful remnants of the old. In addition, it will be constructed from what will eventually come into being from the new energies and patterns that are currently emerging from the cosmos and flowing into the sea of our consciousness. In other words, we are co-creators of the new age; a lot depends on what we do with what we currently have, and also, with what we are being given.

This is true on both physical and metaphysical levels. On the physical level, one has only to think about the huge air, land, and water pollution problems we face, and their impact on our planet's ability to sustain itself, in order to realize that modern humanity's ways of thinking have led us into ways of being that must change if we are to survive.

So as a species, we have the two-fold problem of mental pollution and physical pollution—our ways of thinking have led us to ways of being that the planet—and our bodies—cannot ultimately sustain.

How do we navigate this crisis? How does humanity, as a species, sail safely into the New Age?

The answer to this is multi-fold, and all aspects of it will not be dealt with here as they may be found in the many excellent books that have been written on cleaning up pollution and maker saner lifestyle choices. But just for starters, it would be wise for us to try to live our lives in ways that contribute as little as possible to the pollution load of the planet. "Reduce, Reuse, Recycle" are always at the top of the list.

What we will talk about here is the spiritual aspect. There is work to be done. We *can* help, in our small ways. And if *many* of us help in our small ways, it's not so small anymore. Remember, in her apparitions of the past two centuries, the Mother has repeatedly been calling for prayer and change of heart. These things are energies, and what she is calling for is an energetic shift. If we devote ourselves to prayer, visionary work, to ritual action, and to the creation of beauty (i.e. harmonious 'forms'); and if we allow ourselves to be guided by the Goddess and her inner world workers and priest/esshoods, we can help shift the vibratory frequencies and thus make a difference. Remembering, of course, that all of this starts on a day-to-day basis with ourselves, our own lives, body, and environment.

Navigation

From ancient times till quite recently navigation was linked to the stars for the obvious reason that, when out on the vast deep sea, mariners had no other reliable way to ascertain their directional orientation than by the stars. Modern equipment has changed this but the long tradition remains.

But navigation is also linked with the stars in a poetic and metaphoric way. The sky itself has been likened to a sea. Sailing vessels navigate the world's oceans just as the stars and planets (ours included) navigate the skies.

Belief in the power of the stars to influence destiny and affect humanity has been widespread in human history, and the idea of stars navigating their way through the night sky was not just an astrological metaphor but one that described times and tides in the affairs of humanity. Human society navigated its way through oceans of time, tossed on the tides of historical events, was cast adrift, cast ashore, or even drowned by great changes and calamities. Sometimes the stars brought good fortune; sometimes bad.

Stars were seen as sources of power that could shape the affairs of humans, and stellar movements and positions were carefully watched by those trained in the art. Troublesome stellar aspects gave rise to "disaster," the literal meaning of which is "bad star" or "sundering of stars." Stars were also thought to affect conditions on earth, such as the weather.

Similarly, the stars were thought to affect human mental states and consciousness as well. This belief in the power of stars to influence the planet, the weather, and human affairs became codified as the art and science of astrology, the beginnings of which date back at least as far as the Sumerian and Babylonian empires of 4000-5000 years ago. In fact, it may well have begun before the Sumerian civilization, in Ireland, where more than 5000 years ago stone monuments were built that tracked solstices, equinoxes, and the movements of several stars.

These beliefs did not come out of nowhere. They did not come out of simple superstition. They came out of centuries of stellar and earthly observation, record keeping, and of "connecting the dots." They had a basis in fact.

The reason the stars were thought to be so powerful and influential was because they were thought to be beings, huge heavenly beings—gods, or at least godlike. Much larger than humans, they were also more powerful, and had an influence on the planet and human life. Some sense of this survives in modern day astrology, where the influence of our solar system's planets are measured, plotted, charted, and defined. There are also specialized branches of astrology where the influences of various other things, such as asteroids and fixed stars, are taken into account when charts are drawn for specific events.

The belief in stars/planets as godly or angelic powers was widespread in many parts of the ancient world, and such beings were sometimes referred to as the "host of heaven," or the "heavenly assembly." Heavenly bodies in general were referred to as stars, without our modern distinction between stars and planets. But the planets—the wandering stars—were usually considered a pantheon, or family of gods, complete with a father god, a mother goddess, and their offspring, all having various functions and areas of rulership.

So, if the stars and planets are seen as beings, astrology is learning to navigate life by knowing the influences these beings bring to bear on our lives—on both an individual and collective level.

But the primary stellar pattern that concerns us here is the star-current of the Precession of the Equinoxes that is leading us from the Age of Pisces into the Age of Aquarius. And the primary question right now is how we may gracefully navigate this current and the stormy sea-crossing that leads from Pisces into Aquarius. What, if anything, can we do to help make the crossing successful and keep ourselves and our fellow travelers as comfortable as possible?

The key to this lies in realizing that, since one of the main facets for humanity of the shifting of the ages is the evolution of human consciousness, the waters we navigate are those of our own development—our own growth into an expanded consciousness—as well as the physical challenges brought by earth and life changes. How do we grow from these challenges and changes? How do we develop character? How do we use spiritual energy (as well as physical) to navigate this passage and help others to do the same?

It should go without saying that the basic requirements for this type of work are personal integrity, deep introspection, brutal self-honesty, and a willingness to face and clean up our own messes, both inner and outer.

A Mother's Guidance

It seems to me that the only way to do any of this is with recourse to our Great Mother, who is the source of all life, all form. Once again I am reminded of that old Catholic hymn:

> *Hail, Queen of heav'n, the Ocean Star,*
> *Guide of the wand'rer here below;*
> *Thrown on life's surge, we claim thy care:*
> *Save us from peril and from woe.*
> *Mother of Christ, O Star of the Sea,*
> *Pray for the wanderer, pray for me.*

What is required of us at this time is selfless and willing participation in changing the energy, shifting the vibrational levels so that we may move forward in the best way possible. And the time honored standards of prayer, good works, ritual, inner visionary work, work on ourselves, and working with spiritual energies are still the most effective tools we have at our disposal.

Our task is to balance and reseed things for the future. We are in the beginning of a big shift toward a new planetary consciousness. Although our modern world is technologically very advanced, it's important to remember that all the current amazing development and advances we so take for granted have happened in just a few centuries—a rather short period of time compared to the many thousands of years of world history. Though much change has occurred even within our own lifetimes, we are in the barest beginnings of the big changes which are to come. With climate change, pollution, global warming and the like, it would seem that we are in the destructive phase of the changes, as destruction of the old and outworn always precedes rebirth. In fact, quite often the phases overlap—and we see destruction but also the first glimmerings of the new as well. We will not live—in these particular bodies at least—to see how it all evens out a few centuries from now.

But we can still work at influencing the course of events, making course corrections by our redemptive magical work with some of these happenings. We can, by our prayers, rituals, inner work and outer work, offer caring, compassion, and healing to those suffering and in need. To *do* it, we must *be* it—we must become the change we want to see, to quote the famous Mahatma Gandhi.

We can also work with the innerworld, with the land, and with whichever spirit beings choose to work with us—mediating whatever spiritual influences we are asked to mediate from inner world to the outer world.

We are now in a time when the very physical matrix of the bloodstreams and cells of earth's creatures are being terribly polluted by toxic chemicals and genetic engineering.

Something new is indeed emerging, but is it doomed to be unnatural and disfigured, or can we turn things around and bring them back into harmony with nature again?

Chapter Fourteen - Elements and Temples

The Work of the Elemental Temples

Let's move now into the practical spiritual work that we can do with the help of spiritual beings during this time of transition in which we live. This is work that falls under the province of what I refer to as the Sea Temple, or, since the themes are interrelated, the Temple of Moon, Sea, and Stars. But let me start by explaining about the Temples themselves.

The Elements and the Temples

The spiritual traditions and pathways I follow make use of, as do many other traditions worldwide, the ritual structure of the four directions and center. The four directions are correlated with the four classical elements as follows:

> East — Air
>
> South — Fire
>
> West — Water
>
> North — Earth
>
> Center — Spirit; Beginning and End of all

The four elements are the building blocks of creation—and in particular, of life's physical manifestation. The four elements are innerworld energies; our outer world is the manifestation of the expression of these great innerworld energies that are, in actuality, movements and frequencies of energy—as spirit manifests itself as matter.

Renaissance Era physician and alchemist Paracelsus taught that the four elements have two states of being: one is the physical manifestation with which we are all familiar; the other is the primal "subtle" energy of the element, which he referred to as its *elemental essence*.[1]

Inherent in this four direction/center structure is the concept that the power in the center is the power of Spirit, and the energies of the elements/directions are particular frequencies and manifestations of the power of Spirit. At each of the directions the power of spirit flows forth in a particular frequency and with particular characteristics.

These are the basic energies—the basic units, which, in combination, create form and substance.

This four direction/center structure can be worked with in many ways. Throughout the ages, various magical and spiritual traditions have viewed the innerworld wellspring of these elemental powers as landscapes, kingdoms, watchtowers, lodges, castles, or temples—complete with courtyards, outer courts, inner courts, inner sanctums, as well as sacred fires, stones, rivers, lakes, pools, or trees to mark the center. In actuality, it doesn't really matter which imagery you use since it is the basic four directions/elements and center imagery, as well as the powers and beings springing from each of them, with which you are working. All of these are useful, depending on one's purpose in a magical working. The imagery is merely the imaginative structure by which you link into the energies.

For the purposes of this book the model I have chosen to use is one I call the Elemental Temples.

All things begin and end at the Center. Each temple contains the power of the Center as it expresses from the Void of Potentialities through that particular element, or movement of energy.

Thus in the East this power expresses as Air. This is the first movement—a great whirlwind of movement/sound-vibration/change spiraling out of the void. On the inner lever the power of air expresses as the mind, consciousness, and awareness.

In the South it expresses as Fire—representative of the star fires of heaven (including our sun), the star-fire core of the inner earth, and the volcanic creative fires of inner earth which, in interaction with the sea and the mineral kingdom, create lands and life on earth's surface. On an inner level the power of fire expresses as the "fire of mind" which is the power that inspires and allows creation, growth, and expansion in the realm of consciousness and ideas.

In the West it expresses as Water—the great flowing sea of being, the great Ocean Mother of planet Earth from whose womb all life-forms on this planet came forth. The ocean leads—by way of the horizon—outward and into its Upperworld counterpart, the Great Sea of the starry depths of space. Things come into formation and are gestated here as energy begins to organize itself into somewhat fluid and flowing patterns in the West Temple. On the inner level the power of water expresses as the movements, rhythms, flows, and tides of emotional, physical, and mental energies.

In the North it expresses as Earth—as structure and pattern, wherein the patterns of energy are fixed into more stable, dense structures, and eventually into material forms. On the inner level this expresses as our belief structures and systems, things that form the foundation of our world-view constructs.

From these movements of energy all life forms in the universe and on this planet have come into being. These energies are not just the physical elements; they are the energies behind the physical elements, and from which the physical elements emerge and manifest.

Last, but not at all least, we have the Center, which is the place from which all spirals forth, and to which all returns. The movements of energy that are the elements come forth from this place of Center, and eventually will return to it at the end of the cycle.

Depending on the realm of life which is being accessed by use of the temples, there can be many "centers," but all are harmonics of the Cosmic Center. The Cosmic Center is the great Mother Void from which all is birthed. From the perspective of our particular solar system, the center is our sun. On earth, the center is the star in the heart of the earth—the planet's fiery molten core. And within our physical bodies, the center is the area encompassing the heart and solar plexus chakras—representing heart-mind and will-mind, respectively.

Correspondences of the Elemental Temples and Their Directions

In brief form, here are the correspondences associated with the Elements and the Elemental Temples. While there is much more that could be said about each temple, our work in this book is that of the Sea Temple, and what is offered below is to give context to the Sea Temple work.

East - Element of Air, The Temple of the Winds

In the East is the Temple of Air, sometimes called the Temple of the Winds. Magically, East is associated with the element of Air and with the mental realm, and with beginnings. Air has to do with mental things—thought and areas of thought, ideas, beliefs, information in general, and also the communication of these. It has to do with many kinds of communication, but especially with words. "In the beginning was the Word," as the Bible says; quite likely this refers to the first vibration that emerged, as sound, from the void. Emergence implies movement, and the East/Air has to do with movement, and movement brings change.

While information and communication have always been important to humans, we currently live in an age of an explosion of information technologies that allows the proliferation of information of all kinds—informative, speculative, empowering, manipulative, true, untrue. We are in a "war of words," a phenomenon which has both its good and bad sides.

The Air Temple is also about inspiration (i.e. the inbreathing, or drawing in, of spiritual influence) and education (i.e. to draw out that which is within), both of which give rise, on the outbreath, to culture, arts, sciences, religions, and belief systems of all kinds.

With regard to religion, it has to do with the religions of "The Book." These are idea-based religions; they are based on personal revelations—considered unique and important and coming from divine inspiration—that were first spoken or recited, then later written down, formulated into doctrine and dogma, and promulgated. Historically, these revelations come to one individual (the "Great Man" syndrome), whose followers then crystalize the inspiration into the "form" of sacred scriptures, practices, and churches/religious institutions.

The pronouncement of these doctrines and dogmas was followed with endless and ongoing interpretations of the sacred words, but eventually one interpretation was agreed upon by the majority of the followers (with the opposition sometimes ruthlessly suppressed), the doctrines codified, set in stone, and not changed significantly in the years that follow.

The Air/Wind Temple has to do with both giving and receiving inspiration, instruction, education, and expressing these not just through words, but also through the harmonic arts of music, dance, color, shape, and sacred proportion. The old sacred technologies teach us much about these things, but there are new ways emerging as well. We must receive them, and learn how to share them, as the work of this temple now is the carrying forward of information both old and new into the New Age.

South - Element of Fire, The Sun Temple

The Sun Temple is located in the Direction of South and is associated, magically, with the element of Fire. The Sun Temple, also known as the Fire Temple, has to do with spirit, and particularly with the individual spark of spirit that glows within each living being and is generally referred to as the soul. Thus this temple has to do with the life force itself (and our individual spark of it) and its expression in the manifest world, and is about light and warmth, creativity and growth, blossoming, passion, illumination, and brilliance.

Since light *illuminates*, when inspiration occurs and is *communicated* (i.e. "In the beginning was the *Word*"), it can then be *illuminated* (made visible) by interpretation. A flurry of growth and creativity then follows until the all coalesces into a "form" (a process that also involves the elements of Earth and Water). Because fire illuminates, it is linked to vision and perception.

With regard to religion, the Sun Temple has to do with religions built around this illuminated vision and perception, and also, around the Divine Fire—those who worship or honor the fire because they see it as the embodiment of the Divine Spirit. Many cultures have honored this divine spark. The fire altars of Zoroastrianism come to mind, as do the sacred fires tended by the Vestal Virgins of Rome, Brigid's priestesses in Kildare, Ireland, and the Cherokee veneration of the sacred fire, referred to as "Old White." In all these cases the fire was seen as the Sacred Center, the omphalos, in whichever land it was revered. Thinking about the importance of the sacred fire and the widespread mythology of sacred mountains as omphaloi, I've often wondered how many of these sacred mountains may have been volcanos—combining both sacred mountain and fire-as-center motifs.

Other manifestations of this Sun Temple/Divine Fire are various sun gods and goddesses/light gods and goddesses of various religions both ancient and modern, of which Christ may be the most well known example. The Goddess Brigid is another example, as we have seen in previous chapters.

These deities (or saints, as the case may be) are ones who illuminate our life's path with their revelations or by the example of their lives, and inspire us to reach for the divine—God/dess—as well as the spark of divine within our own being.

The Sun Temple is also the realm of the fires of the material world—the starfire of nuclear fusion, the fiery core within the heart of the planet, the power of fire as it operates within our body and spirit. In particular, for us in this work, it has to do with the kundalini fire, or serpent power—a major part of the body's subtle energy system that resides, while asleep, at the base of the spine, but when awakened, rises up the spinal cord, enlivening each of the chakras in turn, heightening our awareness, raising our consciousness, and opening us to the spiritual realms. It is my feeling that this part of us is up for major rewiring and retuning in the age to come.

West - Element of Water, The Sea Temple

The Sea Temple is found in the West and is the place of tides, cycles, flows and rhythms. Thus, it has to do with anything that has a cycle or rhythm, including the Astrological Ages which cycle through time. It has to do with the moon, whose cycle of wax and wane is clearly visible in our night sky over the course of a month. These associations also link it with women's menstrual cycles, and hence with motherhood, as well as the cycle of life—birth, growth, flowering, decay, death–and thus, also, with the ancestors. Since all life comes from the sea, the Sea Temple is associated with the birth of new forms. And because the sun sets in the West, the Sea Temple is also associated with endings—the end of a day, a month, a year, an astrological age, a cycle and/or form of any kind. In addition, it is associated with the time just past that ending—similar to the period of twilight that follows sunset, as the sky gradually deepens into darkness.

Birth and death are both a changing of form. The Goddess is the Mother of Form, so it is not surprising that we find her in the Sea Temple in her role as Mother Goddess; in particular, as the Virgin Mother Goddess, from whom all things spring and to whom they return after death. In her role as goddess of death she is sometimes called the Crone Goddess.

The polarity-in-action between East and West should be noted here. Generally speaking, East is the place of origination, of beginnings. Yet West is the place of the Mother and Mother Ocean, who is the inception/conception/birther of all things manifest. The difference is partly an issue of spirit and matter. East is the place of origin in a spiritual sense—spirit first begins manifestation here, though in subtle form, while West is the place where it manifests physically—through the Mother who, all in good time, brings form into being. East is the place where Spirit gets things started; South is where things are enlivened and West is where the creation of the form occurs. North is where the form finally becomes manifest as physical being—and in another turn of the wheel, where the form begins its dissolution from physical being back into energy.

The West is also is linked with the ebb and flow of the emotional realm. The Sea Temple governs the tides of life, which includes, in addition to the strictly biological, our tides of both thought and emotion, and indeed, anything that has a tidal ebb and flow, from blood to thought. While it may not seem that emotion and thought have their tides, they do indeed have an ebb and flow, even if not with the regularity of the sea tides. Tides are governed by the ever-cycling moon, so the moon also falls under the province of the Sea Temple.

With regard to religion, the Sea Temple has to do with religions built around ancestor cults, birthing rituals, the Virgin Mother, and deities of the sea and stars.

There are many themes found within the province of the Sea Temple, and because it is our main focus in this book, we explore these in greater depth in the next chapter.

North - The Element of Earth, The Earth Temple

The North is the place of midnight and darkness. The Earth Temple is found here, and it is the temple having to do with both destruction and regeneration. While this might sound contradictory, the Earth/North Temple is about the material realm, and the cycle of creation and destruction is the nature of the material plane. The Earth Temple is the place of substance, of structure, patterns, and forms. This is the place where the Dark Goddess of death and regeneration holds sway. It is a place where structures and patterns are both formed when needed, then destroyed when they have outlived their usefulness. This includes *all* structures and patterns that manifest in our world—on both the physical plane and the more formative astral plane—and encompasses everything from stars to planets to our own physical cells.

The Earth Temple is the place of the final contraction of spirit into dense matter, which subjects it to the laws of the plane of matter—cycles of birth, growth, decay, and death.

Because they flow into one another and interact, the functions of the Sea Temple and the Earth Temple sometimes overlap and can often work together.

If the Sea Temple is about endings, the Earth Temple is about what happens after the ending. All deaths are merely changes of form, and form is at the heart of this temple's activity and work. Because this temple has to do with structures and form manifesting it is, along with the Sea Temple, very active at the moment because of the earth changes. Things are being destroyed, things are being created. This is always true, but more true now in this time when the ages are changing and the earth changes seem to be more frequent and dramatic.

With regard to religion, the Earth Temple has to do with the life cycle of religious forms, from their growth into solid forms and patterns to the final stages of those forms and patterns. In the Earth Temple these religious impulses have evolved into structures, with fixed doctrines and ways of practice. If the form is flexible enough to continue to evolve and grow, it will last for a while because it continues to be useful. But if it's not, its rigidity will cause it to weaken, decay, and finally to break apart and collapse. This is the way of all Form, the cycle of all manifest things, and is why the Goddess is *both* the Mother of Life and the Mother of Death—the womb and the tomb.

In short, the work of the Elemental Temples may be expressed thus:

The Temple of the East - mediation of the Word
The Temple of the South - mediation of the Spirit
The Temple of the West - mediation of the Cycles and Rhythms
The Temple of the North - mediation of the Powers of Destruction and Regeneration

Although this book focuses on the West Temple, the Sea Temple, all the temples work together to a certain extent, so some basic information on all of them will prove useful in your work.

In the next section we will take up the concept of West, and what it has meant in the Middle Eastern spiritual traditions that have fed into our modern religious and magical precepts.

WEST AND THE BIRTH OF THE WORLD
Sunset and the West: Endings and Beginnings

The Wheel of the Year glyph illustrates the relationships between light and dark, life and death. An interesting thing about it is that, depending on one's perspective and needs, the cycle can start on three of the four major points of the wheel. It all depends on how one designates or defines a beginning.

Although there are exceptions, the timing of a year's beginning typically has fallen into three categories, each related to the light/dark cycle of the equinoxes and solstices:

- ❖ The Spring Equinox or dawn of the year—the time when the light increases over darkness.
- ❖ The Fall Equinox or sunset of the year—the time when the darkness increases over light.
- ❖ The Winter Solstice or midnight of the year—the time when the dark hours have reached their maximum number, the sun is reborn, and the light hours begin to increase.

The direction of West is associated with sunset and with the element of Water. The western quarter of the circle of the year includes the astrological signs of Virgo, Libra, and Scorpio; it is the time of the year when light moves into darkness.

Because it is the time of sunset, the West is about endings. Yet every ending is the necessary prelude to a new beginning. So in actuality, the West is about endings followed by beginnings—the end of one cycle and beginning of another. West is the place of "going into the darkness" but it is the darkness of not only rest and repose, but also one wherein the new light and its cycle of new life is gestated.

There are many beginnings and endings in the cycle of life: from life into death and death into life, from night into day and day into night, from one season into the next, from one year into the next, to decades, centuries, millennia, and astrological ages. Both beginnings and endings are usually marked in some way. Endings are often marked by rituals of assimilation, assessment, judgement, completion, and letting go of what is finished. Beginnings are frequently marked by celebrations of a new start—the laying out of new goals, plans of new destinations to be reached, and the planting of new seeds for the future.

Endings and beginnings are most definitely related to the Sea Temple as it is always the Virgin Mother who gives birth to the New Age and its particular stream or manifestation of life.

The constellation Virgo is the astrological sign of this Virgin who has the great and seemingly paradoxical power to give birth. And yet it is not really a paradox. *Virgin* originally meant one who was complete within herself (i.e. containing the energies of both polarities within) rather than a woman who had not yet had sexual relations. The Virgin has no need of an "other" to complete her.

Virgo is the constellation associated with the month of September, although astrologically the sign of Virgo is the time between August 23 and September 23. It also contains the September 8th birthday of the Blessed Virgin Mother Mary, carefully placed by the Catholic Church nine months from the feast of her Immaculate Conception on December 8th.

Also falling within the sign of Virgo, though sometimes within the early part of Libra, are the sacred and significant Jewish feast days that mark the end of one year and the beginning of the next—Rosh Hashana and Yom Kippur. These undoubtedly had their origins in a pre-Judaic time, most likely as harvest festivals, but are important in Judaism today and tell us much about the ancient Middle Eastern metaphysical beliefs that fed into Christianity, and thence into much of western civilization.

The Jewish calendar reflects the ancient feasts and festivals of the specific area of the Middle East where Hebrew culture arose—the areas of ancient Phoenicia and Canaan. Because of similar geography and conditions, similar festivals were widespread in the entire Middle East area, from what had been the ancient lands of Sumer (present day Iraq) to Persia (Iran), Syria, Arabia, and Egypt. The Greek Eleusinian mysteries were also celebrated near this time of year.

In fact, a look at the Hebrew fall festivals gives great insight into the cosmology of the world's *Fertile Crescent*, which is one whose influence spread far and even today affects many of the worlds religions.

The High Holy Days of Judaism

While various cultures have celebrated the start of the new year at various times, it is interesting to find that Middle Eastern people celebrated it near the Fall Equinox, which represents the "sunset"—(the West) of the circle of the year. Sunset proceeds into the darkness of night, and in the morning, sunrise heralds the new beginning. The year must die before it can be reborn.[2]

The High Holy Days of Judaism are comprised of the festivals of Rosh Hashana, the Ten Days of Awe, the Day of Atonement, Yom Kippur and Sukkot. This approximately month long cycle [3] of festivals commemorates both the end of a world and the creation of the new world. In Judaism it is a time of inner reflection and self-assessment, a time of getting straight with God, of dealing with one's past imperfections and sins, and of closing the book on the old year and making way for the blessings and abundance of the coming year.

The self-examination time of Rosh Hashana marks the beginning of this process and is the start of the Ten Days of Awe, the time during which God's seven day creation of the world is both remembered and ceremonially reenacted within the self—thus aligning the self with what is going on in the greater sphere of being—the world—that is, the process of ending and beginning again. This leads up to the Day of Atonement, then the renewal of Yom Kippur, which is celebrated as the day God completed the creation of the world. This is the start of a new cycle and in Jewish tradition is celebrated as New Year's Day.

The word *Atonement* is particularly relevant here. While we are accustomed to understanding this word to mean compensatory action to right a wrong; implicit in this is the sense that such compensation will balance the scales, level things out, make them even and "at one" again. Atonement/"At-One-Ment" really means "becoming at one with." These festivals, coming at the time when the sign of the Virgin is giving way to the sign of the Scales of Balance, are about coming back to a oneness with the Divine Source.

The Autumn Equinox, which falls on September 23rd or 24th, is the day when Virgo the Virgin gives way to those Libran scales, marking the official start of the season of Autumn/Fall in the northern hemisphere.

Traditionally, the shofar, or ram's horn, was ceremonially blown every day for the month preceding Rosh Hashana (except for the day before), on Rosh Hashana itself, and to mark the end of Yom Kippur. In Judaism, it is considered very important that one hears the sound of the shofar during these times, as its piercing sound is considered to be the cry of the soul yearning to be close to God. The use of a ram's horn for this ceremonial instrument seems to be another item which harkens back to the Age of Aries the Ram, the time during which this religion was taking shape. Since these High Holy Days celebrate the end of one year and beginning of the next, perhaps the custom of the ram's horn may have originally heralded, for the people of Canaan, the end of the Age of Taurus and the beginning of the Age of Aries—approximately 2300 BC.[4]

Like the rest of the Levant area of the Middle East, the early Hebrews used a lunar calendar; the moon god Sin, after whom Mount Sinai was named, was an important deity in the Levant. Rosh Hashana begins with the sighting of the first crescent of the new moon near the Fall Equinox—usually about two days past the actual new moon—and by the time Yom Kippur occurs the moon is nearly full.

The day after the following full moon is the joyous feast of Sukkot, or Booths; it was also called the Feast of Tabernacles, and the Festival of the Ingathering. It commemorates a time very early in the history of the Hebrews, a time when they were still wandering in the desert on their way to Canaan from Egypt and living in temporary booth-like shelters. It is also a harvest festival (perhaps its original significance), and another interpretation holds that the festival harkens back to the time when farmers lived in such booths during the busy time of harvest. It was time of pilgrimage, when people gathered in Jerusalem, the country's "center" and most important city.

From the above it may be seen how the early Hebrews celebrated these festivals as a time of endings and beginnings—not just of the year, but of themselves as a people.

Omphalos—The Holiest Place in the World

The story of the Jewish fall festivals is the story of fresh starts—the end of one year and the beginning of another. But it's also the story of the beginning of the world.

The central location for all of these events is the Primal Place, the Void—the place from which all else springs—which was represented in the early temples by a central chamber referred to as the Holy of Holies; the *Kodesh Kodashim* in the Jewish temple. The Holy of Holies was considered to be the dwelling place of the *Shekhinah*, God's Presence. *Shekhinah* is a feminine word, showing that the presence, or spirit of god, was considered to be feminine.

This innermost sanctuary of the Jewish temple was, with a couple of significant exceptions, an empty room. In the First Temple it was empty save for the Ark of the Covenant and the two huge gold cherubim statues which guarded the Ark. By the time of the Second Temple the Ark of the Covenant had been lost, so the chamber may have been empty. However, author Raphael Patai, quoting Josephus and Philo, says that the sanctuary was not empty but contained huge gold Cherubim statues—new versions of the ones which had previously stood alongside the Ark as guardians in the First Temple—and hints that these Cherubim were "in marital embrace." This seems to indicate that early Judaism viewed the Divine as the sacred union of opposites, rather than simply as a lofty old gentleman with a white beard.

The Holy of Holies was entered only one day in the year. Because it was believed that Yom Kippur was the birthday of the world, at a certain hour on Yom Kippur—the Day of

Atonement and observance of the world's *first day*—the High Priest would enter the Holy of Holies wearing his elaborate ceremonial garb. He would utter the name of God—a name so sacred that it was spoken only on this one day—and would sprinkle the stone with the blood of the sacrifice.[5]

The Holy of Holies had been built upon the Foundation Stone—a large, flat rock on the top of Mount Moriah (sometimes called Mt Zion) traditionally held to be the place where Abraham was sent to sacrifice his son Isaac.

Mythologically speaking, the Foundation Stone was the Omphalos, or "center" of the world for the Jewish religion, that "first place" around which the world itself had been woven by the Creator.

But the Foundation Stone was significant for other reasons as well. It was thought to be the stone stopper that plugged the hole leading to the great deep abyss of the Tehom, the waters below—the waters that had risen up and joined with the rain during Noah's flood. As we have seen, the flood story is nearly universal in the mythologies of the Middle East and Mediterranean, so may well be representative of some actual historical event.

The temple site on Mount Moriah was also known as Aranauh's threshing floor because the previous owner, Aranuah, whose name seems to mean "lord" or "king," (and who is also referred to as Omar the Jebusite) had used it as such before selling the land to the Hebrew King David. It's interesting that the threshing floor became the site of a temple whose most sacred ceremony took place very close to Sukkot, a time just past the High Holy Days when a celebration of the year's harvests had traditionally been held.

During the time of the Second Temple at Jerusalem there was an interesting ceremony during Sukkot, which occurred on the full moon just after the High Holy Days of Rosh Hashana and Yom Kippur. The ceremony was called the "Joy of the House of Water-Drawing," and involved a joyous nightlong celebration that included the lighting of many torches and candles and much music and dancing. This was followed, in the predawn hours of morning, by the drawing of water from the Well of Siloam, situated just west of the Temple. After a quiet procession out to the well the water was solemnly drawn by the High Priest using a golden pitcher, after which the water was ceremonially carried back into the Temple and poured into a silver bowl on the west side of the altar. There was another bowl on the east side of the altar into which wine was poured. Both bowls were then poured out as libations. The wine went into a vat or cave below and southwest of the altar, while the water went down a series of shafts which led directly below the Foundation Stone, finding its way eventually into the waters of the "Deep" which lay far below. This was most likely an offering to feed the waters of the Deep, that they might be increased in the form of plentiful water from springs, lakes, and rivers.[6]

The Direction of West is emphasized a few times in this ceremony—the water was taken from the Well of Siloam to the west of the temple and poured into a silver bowl on the west side of the altar. Silver is traditionally associated with the moon, which is also associated with the west. The west was the direction from which the rains—as well as endings, beginnings, and thus new life—came.

Since this ceremony was held at the beginning of the rainy season, scholar Raphael Patai sees this as an ancient rain-making ritual—the waters of the Deep being fed and increased so they could rise up and nourish the earth along with the coming rains.

It may well have been that, but I also see in this libation echoes of a ceremony of appeasement to the waters of the Deep, lest they rise up too high and once again destroy the earth.

So here in the rites of early Judaism we see not only remnants of probably much older pagan rain-making rituals, but also an offering to the Primal Waters and an acknowledgement of water's vast power to both nourish and destroy.

As we can see, the West is about endings and beginnings, and the primal waters of life.

Notes:

1) Hall, Manly P.; *The Secret Teachings of All Ages*, CV, The Philosophical Research Society, Inc., Los Angeles, CA, 1988.

2) In a more mundane sense it represents the end of a particular growing season, the harvest and a thanksgiving for that harvest, and the beginning of a new season.

3) This accounting is from the day of Rosh Hashana to the end of the Sukkot period. Since the preparation for these High Holy Days often begins at the beginning of the previous month, some count this time period to be that much longer.

4) There is much evidence that some of these festivals did not originate with the Hebrews but were agricultural/pastoral festivals indigenous to the area of Canaan in which they lived. Over time, as Judaism grew, the festivals took on different much deeper spiritual meanings for the Semitic people who became known as the Hebrews.

5) Actually, the entire ceremony was long and involved and the high priest entered the Holy of Holies three times— once to bring in the incense and shovel, once again to sprinkle the bull's blood, and finally, to remove the incense and shovel.

6) Patai, Raphael: *Man and Temple in Ancient Jewish Myth and Ritual*, KTAV Publishing House, Inc., NY, 1947

Chapter Fifteen - The Temple of the Moon, Sea, and Stars

Because the stars are the seeds of life on earth, and because the moon governs the tides of the sea, the Sea Temple is also referred to as the Temple of the Moon, Sea and Stars.

Moon Magic and Lore

There have been hundreds of volumes written about moon facts, moon lore, moon goddesses, moon gods, and moon magic, containing all kinds of very interesting material, most of which I will not repeat here. Relevant to the subject of this book, suffice it to say that there are obvious and deep connections between the moon and the sea in the form of the sea tides, the inner psychic and magical tides, as well as the corresponding rhythmic influence between the moon and our internal fluidic tides. Indeed, our bodies are approximately 80% water, and the moon's magnetic pull exerts an influence on our own biological tides. The most obvious example of this is women's menstrual cycle, although some of our hormonal secretions—and thus our emotions and nervous systems reactions—may also be linked to lunar influences.

While the earth's turning and the sun's movements establish our year, the moon's cycle is related to much more intimate cycles—those of our days, weeks, and months. The pattern of sunlight on the moon's surface as it travels through the sky relative to earth gives us our new, waxing, full, waning and dark moon cycles—the rhythm of the month, whose very name, originally 'moonth,' is tied to the moon.

The moon is about cycles and rhythms: the rhythms of our bodies (physical, mental, emotional) and the tides of the sea. While the mechanical intricacies of the moon/tidal connection is beyond the scope of this book, it is well known that the sea brings us, almost twice daily, high tides and low tides. The tides of the New and Full Moons are called Spring Tides, and the tides of the Waxing and Waning part of the lunar cycle are referred to as Neap Tides.

Because of the sea's intricate tidal relationship with the moon, the most appropriate timing for Sea Temple workings is one based upon the lunar cycles. The type of working to be done can be keyed into the energy of a particular part of the lunar cycle. In very basic form, the Moon's cycles and their associated energies are given in the table below.

Phase	Quarter	Energy
New	First Quarter	Beginning
Waxing	Second Quarter	Increasing
Full	Third Quarter	At Peak
Waning	Fourth Quarter	Decreasing
Dark	End of Fourth Quarter	Ending

The moon's orbit is slightly irregular, and therefore, its cycle is between 27-29 days, depending on whether one is looking for it to return to a particular phase, or to a particular point in the sky. The complete cycle of its phase changes are what give us our month. The moon's approximately 28 day cycle relates it to the planet Saturn, whose path around the sun takes 28 years. Thus, Saturn's cycle and the moon's cycle are both divisible by the number seven—a number rife with esoteric significance and symbolism, and often referred to as the "virgin" number. Saturn's cycle of sevens has been used by esotericists to define the seven year stages of human life, while the moon's relationship with seven has given us our seven day week. Thus, both moon and Saturn, as well as the number seven, refer to the passage of time in a cyclical manner.[1]

The moon, in a magical sense, is about instinct and intuition, emotions and feelings. It is also about flow and patterns of flow—and here is a link to its governance of cycles and rhythms, including blood, both its circulation throughout the body and blood in the genetic sense of ancestral blood. Astrologically the moon is related to the feminine, particularly the mother, which provides another very direct link to the blood of the ancestors via the mitochondrial DNA.

In a sense, pregnant women are Sea Temples, since pregnancy is a condition wherein the mother's body forms the child, containing and gestating it within a sea of salty amniotic fluid. The mother's nutrient intake, general state of health, amount of sleep, and emotional states all have an effect on the growing fetus.

Historically, there have been both moon goddesses and moon gods. Quite often the moon gods were thought to impregnate women, or to have an effect on the impregnation of women; so they, too, are related to the themes of the cycles of fertility and reproduction, which also includes the theme of the rebirth of the ancestors into the tribe. All of these themes fall within the province and work of the Sea Temple.

The Moon Temple and I

My own work with this temple began in the mid 1980s. I had been involved in esoteric work for about twelve years at that point, and several years previously had read Dion Fortune's books, including the *Sea Priestess*. I had recently gathered together a small group of people for occasional magical work, and it was as I was pondering aloud one morning what we might do to celebrate the upcoming full moon that the initial contact was made. Standing in the kitchen, talking to my husband, I gave voice to this question, after which I distinctly heard a voice say, "Take them to the Moon Temple in Atlantis." My immediate responses were "What?" "How?" At that moment my inner vision opened up and I began seeing not only the Moon/Sea Temple itself but a route to get there. It was as if I was viewing a movie, the story unreeling itself before my eyes as I continued to ask questions—much to the confusion of my husband who was standing nearby and thought I was speaking to him. I was taken inside the Temple during this waking vision and shown several things; I noticed other things too, but was told I would learn about them at another time.

I've worked with the Temple on and off since then—the impulse to work there seeming to come and go periodically, like the tides of the sea.

Themes of the Sea Temple

As we have noted, the Sea Temple is about Life coming into Form. In the cosmos, this happened in the Sea of Space; on our beautiful planet, it happened originally in the oceans. Life manifesting in form has a life cycle—a rhythmic tide that carries it from conception, through birth, through growth, to maturity, and finally to death. Thus the Virgin Mother who births all Forms is a major part of the Sea Temple, as is the Dark Goddess, the Mother of Death who receives those Forms back into herself again, and regenerates their substance and energies for a new birth of some kind. Since life continues by reproduction, the Sea Temple is intimately involved with reproduction—conception, birthing and nurturing the young—and also with genetics, which is the transmission of DNA through family lines. This involves not just us, the present time and our current life, but our ancestors and descendants as well.

The Sea Temple is about cycles and rhythms since the cycles of hot and cold, light and dark are important to the development and growth of life forms.

From the basics above, the following basic themes of the Sea Temple may be drawn:

- ❖ The Virgin Mother
- ❖ Fertility
- ❖ The Rhythm of the Tides and the Cycles of Change
- ❖ Emotions

- ❖ The Mother of Destruction and Regeneration
- ❖ The Ancestors

We will elaborate on these in the chapters that follow.

Keys to the Sea Temple

There are several symbols that have come to me as being "keys" to the Sea Temple. These keys are symbols of things that have to do with the generation and formation of physical life. They may be used in journeys and ritual work.

- ❖ **A Crescent**—This can be the moon, the boat, the ark, or the chalice; the pelvic girdle is the chalice of the female body, in that it is the place that holds the seeds of new life and provides a place for them to grow.
- ❖ **An Ark**—A more elaborate boat than the crescent, the Ark is the boat that carries life into the next age. In the story of Noah, the animals were loaded "two by two," breeding pairs of each kind, into the Ark. This represents the male/female, active/passive, projective/receptive polarity necessary for life to procreate and continue.
- ❖ **An Anchor Within the Crescent with Rope Twisted Around It**—This is essentially the same image as the rod/staff of the Greek healer Aesclepius—a pole with a serpent winding its way up—but depicted in a crescent shaped boat. The Aesclepion Rod itself has been a symbol of healing since at least the time of ancient Greece. The crescent shape links it with the feminine symbols of the ark, chalice, and moon. But the image predates Aesclepius and traces back to Sumeria, where the healer god Ningishzida was pictured as a pole encircled by two snakes.
- ❖ **A Caduceus**—A pole or staff with two snakes circling it is called a Caduceus. Both crescent and anchor symbols are related to this very old symbol, which goes back to Ningishzida's serpent-entwined pole and is related to the Hindu concept of the Kundalini, or life-force "serpent" that sleeps at the base of the spine. When awakened, it circles its way up the spine in the form of the two currents of energy, positive and negative; the crossover places marking the chakras.
- ❖ **The Vortex or Whirlpool**—To me the vortex, or whirlpool, represents the first and immediately subsequent movements that arose within the Great Void—the basic energy movement pattern that brings things in and out of existence.
- ❖ **Blood and Amniotic Fluid**—Both blood and amniotic fluid, the waters that fill the human womb and nourish, support, and cushion the baby during gestation, are very similar in chemical makeup to the waters of the ocean.

- ❖ **Sea Water and Sea Caves**—Sea water is the amniotic fluid of the planet: it fills the womb of life. The somewhat crescent shape of the entry and body of sea caves combines the Sea Water Key with that of the Crescent Key, forming a vessel, a cup—a chalice filled with the planet's amniotic waters.

Service in the Sea Temple

As we begin to move into the new age, the Sea Temple calls us into service. There are forces at work that need to flow through us. There are new influences coming in that need to be embodied. There are obsolete factors in our world that need to be energetically dismantled. There are ancestral imbalances that need to be redeemed and/or released. There are environmental issues, especially concerning the world's oceans, that need to be addressed from both an inner and outer perspective. There is physically regenerative work that must be done for our physical world. And last, but not least, there is inner, energetic work we must do on our own body, mind, soul, and spirit, that we may move gracefully into the new era.

The new age will bring its Aquarian influences to bear on these issues, but it is up to us what we actually do with them.

Notes

1) Explanation of the meaning and significance of Saturn's cycles can be found through a study of astrology but in brief, every 28-29 years Saturn returns to the same place in the zodiac as it was when we were born. In astrology this is referred to as the "Saturn Return" and marks a significant transition from one stage or phase of life to another. It has to do with gaining wisdom and perspective as we age. The lessons hopefully learned and wisdom gained during those 28+ years aid us in moving forward into the next Saturn period. If not, we often keep making the same mistake over and over, and worsen our situation.

Chapter Sixteen - At Work in the Sea Temple

At Work in the Sea Temple

In all ages humans have worked to align themselves with the Spirit World and work with the beings and powers of that world in order to create positive change for themselves and their communities.

By virtue of our consciousness and power of intention, humans have the ability to act as bridges—natural mediators of energy—between the heavens and the earth, the above and the below, between the outer world and the inner world. This ability to bridge, to mediate, is inherent in humans, but must be consciously practiced and refined. When it is consciously cultivated in this way it becomes a priestly function.

In this book we have spoken of many goddesses in many cultures by way of illustration of how the Primal Goddess of Sea and Stars manifests through time, land, culture and deity forms. This was done to give you a background in understanding the Goddess in order to help you work her in the emergence of the new era. But it really doesn't matter which of these goddess forms you work with; choose one that you feel comfortable with, or work with the most primal form of goddess energy. Because the real point is to work with the emerging energies of the Age of Aquarius; to act, in a sense, as a birth attendant or midwife for the new Age. Bearing this in mind, please adapt the spiritual work and practices to however you decide to approach your work as birth attendant.

What follows below and in the next chapters are suggestions and aids for working magically in the Sea Temple. These make use of the traditional model of Four Elements and Center, mentioned in *Chapter Fourteen*. Since the particular emphasis of our work here is with the Sea-Moon Temple, which is about the sea, water, moon, tides, rhythms and cycles, it might prove beneficial to your work if you work with the lunar, solar and stellar rhythms, or at least the lunar phases. If you live near the sea you may want to follow the tides of the sea, as well. Your work can be in the form of prayers, practices, devotions, inner journeys, mediating energies, and ceremony.

But it is important to remember that these are just suggestions. Once you start the work in earnest, it is likely that spirit helpers—members of the inner Sea Temple priesthood—will show up to guide you further.

Since you most likely will be working with the lunar cycle you will want to keep track of it by visual observation during the month; a lunar calendar is also handy for noting the zodiacal sign through which the moon is passing.

Preparing for the Work – Assembling Your Ritual Objects

Necessary Items

There are only three things that are necessary for this work: an altar space; a candle, preferably dark blue; and a glass or earthen bowl filled with seawater or salted water.

The bowl of water represents all the seas of the world and, by extension, all the waters of the world. The clay of the bowl (or sand, if the bowl is glass) represents the substance of earth, from which all life is formed. The round shape of the bowl represents the primal roundness of the cycle of life—birth into life, growth and flowering, wither and decay, death, rest, and rebirth into life again.

The candle, whose color should reflect the color of either the sea or the night sky, represents the Void from which all things emerge. When lighted it represents the primal spark of life/energy emerging from the Void.

I prefer to use a simple midnight or cobalt blue candle but these are not always easy to find, so most of the time I use a white or blue votive candle in a dark blue candle holder. I decorate the base of the blue candle holder with a wreath of silver foil stars. Of course, the kind of candle you use is your personal choice but the color should be appropriate for Sea-Star Temple work.

Helpful But Not Strictly Necessary

If you feel like creating a more elaborate altar to enhance the beauty of your altar and help you tune into the appropriate energies to do the work, you might consider adding whatever appeals to you from the following list:

To Represent Fresh Water—A silver cup containing unsalted water to represent the waters of rivers, streams, lakes, and ponds.

To Represent the Sea—A picture of the sea; some seashells (I use abalone, oyster, and scallop shells), dried seaweeds, and pearls. Or perhaps just a sea-blue or blue-green bowl filled with salted water.

To Represent the Sky and Stars—A picture of a starry sky; a black or midnight blue altar cloth, a black or midnight blue bowl, a smallish 7-9 branched candle-holder (a menorah works well) with colored candles to represent the planets.

To Represent the Moon and the Goddess—A string or rosary of moon-colored pearls or beads, alternating, perhaps, with cobalt or midnight blue beads.

Other Items

Buy or make a shawl or stole with cloth of sea colors, or perhaps with seaweed patterns on it. Magically charge it to be your sea priest/ess stole, to be used when doing workings. The shawl should be long enough to fit around your neck and shoulders and drape down your back a bit; the ends should be long enough to wrap around your arms. The stole is a long narrow (4-6 inches wide) piece of cloth, the center of which is placed around your neck so that its long arms flow down your front. It may be decorated with magical symbols related to the sea temple.

Ceremonially (i.e. with intention and focus) robing yourself with a magical garment before doing your work helps you move from a mundane state of consciousness to a more spiritual and ritual state of consciousness.

Personalizing and Dedicating Your Ritual Objects

It is important that you put some personal effort into making these things, or at least personalize them in some way, because then you are partaking of the nature of the mother goddess who makes and shapes all Form. The short dedication ritual below may be used, with modification, for any of your ritual objects.

The Candle and Bowl

Unless you are a skilled potter, it is best to shop for the ritual bowl. Wash and smudge it carefully, and hold it in your hands for a few minutes before dedicating it using the ritual below. The same goes for the candles you use. After purchasing them, smudge them briefly and prayerfully, then hold them between your hands to imbue them with your energies before you dedicate them in the Sea Temple.

The Prayer Shawl

As above, buy or make a shawl or stole in a color associated with the sea. If you purchase it, add your own energy by sewing or crocheting some form of sea or star-themed decoration to it, your mind focused on the Sea Temple while you do so. Your contribution to the shawl or stole can be as simple as hemming the fabric, or sewing on a decorative edging, such as an appliqué of stars and moons, or sacred symbols that have personal meaning for you.

When it is finished, dedicate it using the simple ritual found near the end of this chapter, or one of your own choosing.

Getting Focused: Why Are We Doing This?

Before you begin each work session in the Sea Temple, it's a good idea to sit down and think why you are doing it. This may sound somewhat trite, but it really does help one get centered and focused.

When I sit down to do a session of work I begin by silently asking myself a question. The question is: "What am I doing and why am I doing it?" The response, spoken aloud in the manner of a recitation, is "I am here to attune to the Sea Temple and the Element of Water for the purpose of being a vessel or mediator for whatever priest/essing work I am asked to do." As I say this to myself I meditate on the words, reaching into the innerworlds and allowing my mind to sink into "priestess mode," a mode that allows me to put aside my personal self and "put on" my priestess self. Afterward I externalize this by "robing for the ritual"—placing my priestess shawl or stole around my neck and shoulders.

The altar can be set up either before or after this focusing session.

Working in the Temple

The process of working in the Sea Temple is actually very simple. The very first step is to practice the spiritual basics of grounding, centering, and using the imagination to enter the inner worlds.

The next step is to use the suggestions given below to make your first journey to the Sea Temple. Follow the guidelines in the journey and try to get a good sense of the appearance (however it appears to you) but most importantly, the *feel* of the Sea Temple. Repeat this journey a few more times over the next several days, allowing the Sea Priests and Priestesses of the Temple to show you around and teach you more about the temple.

In your Sea Temple work, there will be times when you will feel a distinct inner call to work in the temple. When this happens, make a plan—either on your own or from your inner guidance—for what you want to do in the Temple. And realize that once you are in the temple, the priesthood there might have a completely different list of things for you to do, so be prepared to set aside your own plan and do what you are asked to do.

After you've settled on a plan, set up your working space if you have not already done this. Then settle down to the work at hand.

Start by slow deep breathing to calm and settle yourself, and state your intention to work in the Sea Temple. By use of prayer and intention, open yourself to the guidance of your innerworld helpers; ask them to be with you and guide you.

Travel in vision to the Sea Temple and respectfully open yourself to the beings there. Either tell them why you have come and ask their assistance, or ask them what they would like you to do while there, then do it. At the end, thank everyone who has been of help, and slowly return to waking consciousness. Record your experiences in your magical journal before the details have time to fade away.

Sea Temple work can be very free flowing in terms of structure but there has to be a rhythm, as with the sea tides. One must alternate between inner work and outer work; between vision journeys (active and passive) and outer ritual, between prayer (talking) and meditation (listening).

Sometimes we can pick a task; sometimes we are given one to do. We carry out it in the above way—alternating between the poles of the rhythm, making use of the moon cycle. We can do this with the help of the particular goddess with whom we work, or by whichever goddess shows up to assist us. Generally speaking, during the time of the dark moon we work with the dark goddess, the Black Madonnas, and the Void Goddess. As the moon waxes we can work with the growing light in the form of the stars, and our own star, Sol. When the moon is full we work with the bright goddess, the mother goddesses, and the Virgin Mary. During the times between the phases we work with the goddess in whichever form she chooses to appear to us.

Visiting the Sea Temple

The first work that needs to be done is to create your inner Sea Temple structure through a process of visualization and journeywork.

To Begin

- ❖ Prepare your physical working space by determining the Four Directions, then sweeping the area clean both physically and psychically.
- ❖ Sit down, ground and center.
- ❖ Do the Focus work.
- ❖ Put on your priestess stole or shawl of moon and stars.
- ❖ Set up your altar, thinking about each item and its purpose as you place it on the altar.

Getting There

There are several methods by which the Sea Temple can be approached. The two approaches I use most often are given just below.

It is important to realize that the journeys provided in this book are to introduce you to the temple, show you what's there, and provide a framework for visiting and working there in the future. It's important to do these journeys as written the first few times, to get that structure into your head. But as you proceed in your work you will find that it's important to allow your journey to go "off-script" when necessary, so you can follow out what is actually happening at the moment. For example, a priest or priestess who's guiding you may want to show you or tell you something, or ask you to do something that is not in the script.

Another important thing to realize is that the scripts of these journeys—the imagery used—are only there to provide structure, scaffolding if you will, for our consciousness to contact and connect with the innerworld powers. Structure provides a pattern along which the energies organize themselves as they flow, and by which the inner patterns and powers may be accessed. Since organization of information is central to understanding and using it, the use of these structures will also aid in understanding our experiences in the innerworlds—the Sea Temple in this case. By making use of these structures we can access the priests and priestesses of the Sea Temple, and other inner beings as well. The structures help us communicate with them, and work under their guidance in our Sea Temple work.

Please note that the use of an ellipsis (…) in these journeys indicates the need for a slight pause, to allow time for your own inner experiences to unfold.

Journeys to the Sea Temple

Journey One

Settling before your altar, you light the candle at the center. Become aware of the Four Directions that surround you—East, South, West, and North—then return your attention to the candle. As you gaze at this center flame, breathing slowly in and out, you find that you are becoming more relaxed, calm and serene with each breath. When you are completely relaxed and settled, close your eyes, seeing the candle with your inner vision. As you look upon it, you feel yourself moving through the web of dimensions, and notice that the flame you are seeing with your inner vision is growing larger and brighter till finally it coalesces into a column of flame, a pillar of fire.

You see that you are in a large open space…and the pillar of flame is in the center. There are many beings present around the flame. seemingly in communion with it. This is the inner realm Convocation of Light—an expression of the enlightened collective consciousness of the planet's adepts of wisdom.

You are drawn to the pillar of flame and walk closer to it. This flame is the Hearthfire of the Cosmos, the flame of life and being, as it burns in the many worlds.

You gaze into the Hearthfire for a few moments, communing with it….. Then you turn and notice that there are four arched gateways which lead from the open space and the center flame, going off into the four directions of East, South, West and North. The Eastern gateway is white with gold spirals. The Southern gateway is of the many hues of fire, with flames that seem to flicker and spark as you watch. The Western gateway is blue-green, and decorated with many seashells. The Northern gateway is black stone, inset with rocks, crystals, and bones, and although it is black it seems to emanate a soft glow.

Through each of these gateways you can see a temple. You look at each of them in turn but feel drawn to the Western gateway, so you turn your steps in that direction. You step through the Western gateway and walk into the courtyard of the Sea Temple, which seems to be filled with pools, springs, and fountains of water. You walk up to the door of the temple and knock on it. The door is opened by a priestess who is clad in a silver-blue gown.

She invites you to step inside and shows you around the temple. The main floor is a large open chamber; off to the right a staircase ascends to the second level where you can see several doorways. To the left you can see a curtained doorway; she tells you that behind the curtain is a staircase that descends down into a chamber within the earth. Straight ahead of you there is another doorway. The priestess opens it and leads you into a long rectangular stone room, with many niches in it. Some of the niches contain items, such as candles, lanterns, icons, seashells, seaweed, and rocks, but many are empty.

There is another room beyond this one and now the priestess leads you through the doorway into that room. As soon as the door opens you hear a loud sound of rushing water. You see before you what looks to be a huge seashell filled with water; it is fountaining huge gushes of water that fill it, then rush over the edge and flow down the sides of the shell like ribbons of water. As these touch the ground they become small rivers, and flow off in each of the eight directions.

The room is filled with immense power. The priestess tells you that this is the Inner Court of the element of water, and that this shell-fountain, deep in the heart of the Sea Temple, is the power of the Void as it comes into manifestation as the element of water. You spend a few moments experiencing this power…..

Slowly you become aware of another presence in the room…. You turn and are surprised to find a beautiful woman standing beside you before the great shell-fountain. She wears a cloak of azure blue, and a crown of stars rests upon her head. Beneath her cloak her gown is a deep midnight blue sprinkled with silver stars. You gaze upon the Sea Mother from whom all life springs and to whom all life returns, and she smiles in welcome, filling you with great love and a sense of quiet stillness and peace…. You spend a few moments communing with her…..

It is time to leave. You reach into your heart and offer the Goddess the gift you find there…. She accepts, and in turn dips her hand into the waters of the shell-fountain. She sprinkles the shining drops over your head. You close your eyes and receive the gift of the Goddess, feeling the power of water seep into you. When you open your eyes the Goddess is gone, but you know that she is always with you.

Then the priestess leads you out of the room, through the room with the niches in the wall, and out to the main chamber again. She leads you to the door...walks with you through the courtyard..through the archway...and to the area where the Hearthfire burns. The two of you stand there for a few moments, communing with the Flame of Life.... Then she begins to speak. She invites you to come to the Sea Temple again and learn its mysteries, that you may be of service to others. She bids you farewell and you thank her for her help.

She walks back through the Western Gateway; you watch her as she goes. As you turn back towards the Hearthfire you see that it has become a wall of flame....The flame billows out...enfolding you...and urging you to step deeper into it...so you do. You stand in the center of the flame for a moment, and feel enlivened and refreshed by it. Then you step through the flames and out to the other side. As you do, you feel yourself moving once again through the web of dimensions...and returning to where you started.

You are back...to this time, this place, and to a quiet room where a candle flame burns on a small altar.... And when you feel that you have completely returned, you may open your eyes.

Journey Two

(Because I live very close to the sea, this is the journey I use most frequently.)

Settling before your altar, you light the candle at the center. Become aware of the Directions that surround you—East, place of Air; South, place of Fire; West, place of Water; North, place of Earth, and Center, place of all beginnings and endings, and of the Void…. Let your awareness of these directions carry your love and respect to them, and the beings that dwell therein. Then return your attention to the candle. As you gaze at this center flame, breathing slowly in and out, you find that you are becoming more relaxed, calm and serene with each breath. When you are completely relaxed and settled, close your eyes, seeing the candle with your inner vision. As you look upon it, you feel yourself moving through the web of dimensions… and notice that the flame you are seeing with your inner vision is growing larger and brighter till finally it coalesces into a column of flame, a pillar of fire.

You walk toward the column of flame, and pause to tune into it and pay your respects to this bright flame of life… Then you turn toward the

Western Gate, and walk toward it. It is an archway, decorated with many shells: mother-of-pearl, nautilus and spiral shells... When you reach it, you step through it to the other side, and find you are standing on a walkway that runs right along the edge of the sand.... and beyond that is the Sea.

You spend a few moments here, becoming aware of the great multitude of beings which dwell here—the fish, the sea mammals, the insects, the seabirds, the seaweeds which drift lazily in the tidal waters, and the creatures which dwell in the tide pools... You feel into the sea itself, and feel the great host of life—both visible and invisible—that makes its home there. You look up into the great sea of space, and then towards the western horizon, where the silvery sliver of a crescent moon is about to sink into the western sea, with the first stars of night twinkling faintly around it in the darkening sky...

You walk into the ocean and stand there for a moment, noticing the pull of the tide on your legs and feet, and the feel of the lapping waves. You walk out further... Then you allow yourself to be carried by the tides, going out further and further still... Finally you dive down into the sea, and swim towards the bottom. Your eyes are open as you swim, and you notice that dolphins and fish are swimming beside you; they seem very curious about you. You swim down and down... and it grows darker and darker, lit only by the phosphorescence of some of the sea creatures, till at length you can barely see around you at all. But still you swim on, going deeper and deeper, down and down, until you reach the ocean floor.

Even in the dimness you can see that there is an opening on the ocean floor, and you swim into it. You find it is like a tunnel, so you dive down into it, swimming deeper and deeper. It levels out, becomes horizontal, and you see a doorway before you. You move through the doorway, and find that you are now walking instead of swimming. You are in a courtyard that contains many pools and streams of water, beyond which is a large temple. Before you stands a priestess in a silver-blue gown. She takes your hand and leads you to the door of the temple, opens it, and ushers you in....

She invites you to step inside and shows you around the temple. The main floor is a large chamber; off to the right a staircase ascends to the second level, where you can see several doorways. To the left you can see a curtained doorway; she tells you that behind the curtain is a staircase that descends down into a chamber within the earth. Straight ahead of you there is another doorway. The priestess opens it and leads you into a long rectangular stone room, with many niches in it. Some of the niches contain items, such as candles, lanterns, icons, seashells, seaweed, and rocks, but many are empty…

There is another room beyond this one and now the priestess leads you through a doorway and into that room… As soon as the door opens you hear a loud sound of rushing water. You see before you what looks to be a huge seashell filled with water; it is fountaining huge gushes of water that rush over the edge and flow down the sides of the shell like ribbons of water. As these touch the ground they become small rivers, and flow off in each of the eight directions…

The room is filled with immense power. The priestess tells you that this is the Inner Court of the element of water, and that this shell-fountain, deep in the heart of the Sea Temple, is the power of the Void as it comes into manifestation as the element of water. You spend a few moments experiencing this power…..

You know it is time for you to leave. The priestess leads you out of the room… through the room with the niches in the wall… and out to the main chamber again. She leads you to the exit, walks with you through the courtyard… She guides you to one of the many pools of water in the courtyard… and as you stand before it, she gives you a sudden push and you fall in.

You find yourself being carried downward into the pool's waters, then thrust sideways and upward… Ahead, you see a tunnel and you begin swimming toward it. You enter it and find yourself swimming upward. Suddenly the tunnel ends and you know you are back in the ocean again… You swim up and up through the ocean's waters, noting the creatures who swim around and beside you. You swim towards the surface, feeling as if there are water currents helping to bear you upward… When you reach the surface you swim to the shore… And finally, reaching the shore, you walk out of the sea and back onto the sand. You see the Western Gateway before you, and walk through it. As you do, the scene around you begins to waver like a mirage, and it dissolves into a mist… You walk into the mist, and after a few steps it begins to clear and you see before you the wavering image of a room that seems familiar… A few more steps and you see that you have returned to the place from which you started.

You are back… to this time, this place, and to a quiet room where a candle flame burns on a small altar… And when you feel that you have completely returned, you may open your eyes.

Dedication Ritual

Holding your stole or shawl in your hands, sit before your altar and center yourself. Orient yourself to the Four Directions and Center. Using one of the visualizations above, go in vision to the Sea Temple and stand at the threshold. Request that a priest or priestess come to meet you, and walk with them into the temple. They will take you to the Inner Court, the central part of the temple where the energy is the strongest. Stand before the huge shell-fountain there and state that you wish to be of service to the Sea Temple. In a prayerful way, ask to be blessed and aided in this endeavor. Dedicate your shawl or stole to the service of the Sea Temple, and, in vision, lay it upon the ground in the temple for several minutes so that it can absorb the temple's energies. While this is happening, pray to the Goddess of the Sea and Stars, sending her your love and devotion. Then simply sit quietly and receptively, open to whatever messages she might send you.

When this feels complete, pick up your shawl or stole from the floor of the temple, offer your thanks, and take leave of the temple, reversing the route you took when entering.

This object is now dedicated, so treat it as such: keep it in a safe place and do not use it for purely mundane purposes.

Suggestions for Work

You should work weekly in the Sea Temple, especially at first, to establish a lunar rhythm. But you should also go into the temple to work whenever you feel guided to do so.

The specific work you do in the Sea Temple is your choice, but at the same time you must allow the work to be guided by the inner beings. Work first with the sea or largest body of water closest to your geographic location. At the beginning you should physically visit this body of water to establish a relationship so that you can more easily call it up in your mind and imagination, and feel its energy, for subsequent workings.

❖ Here are a few suggestions of work that might be done in the Sea Temple:

❖ Work with your local waterways to improve their health. Do physical clean-up if that's what is needed, but do inner work with them first and ask what they need and if there's anything specific they want you to do on either outer or magical inner levels.

❖ Healing the Coral—Scientists are telling us that the world's coral reefs are imperiled; some are dying. Much of this comes from the waters being overheated, which causes the coral to lose oxygen, become bleached, infected with a fungus, and die. Coral is vital to the health of the coastal ocean waters; and loss of healthy coral imperils all oceanic life nearby. Go in vision to the Sea Temple and, asking for helpers, allow them to take you to a coral reef that is in need of help. Ask what you can do, and let them guide you.

- ❖ Transmuting Waste—With the help of your spirit helpers, work on deconstructing and transmuting the waste (nuclear, chemical, oil, etc) that has been dumped in the oceans in the last 100+ years. Pay strict attention to how (and if) they want you to do it, as they know much more than you do about how to go about this.

Chapter Seventeen - The Themes of the Sea Temple

In this chapter we will elaborate further on the Sea Temple themes listed in Chapter Fifteen. In addition we will provide some vision journeys to help you get an experiential sense of the some of the themes.

The Virgin Mother

She who gives birth to the Cosmos
As well as each Age that comes around.
Mari,
The Binah force
Mother of Form
The Great Void from which all arose.

All begins with the Great Void who is the Cosmic Mother, the womb from which all else arises. She is the Mother of Form, the Virgin Mother who gives birth to the Cosmos. With Form comes Time: she also births each of the Astrological Ages.

I call this Cosmic Mother Mari (Mary). She is the darkness of the sea of space and her "child" is the light—referred to in many cultures and spiritual traditions as the Son of Light or the Child of Light.

As stated in *Chapter One*, science refers to a unitary field, generated at the moment of the Big Bang, that connects and unites all matter. Physicist Max Planck, the originator of what we now call Quantum Theory, referred to this unitary field as "the force by which all matter originates and exists." Matter exists, he said, "only by virtue of a force which brings the particle of an atom to vibration and holds this most minute solar system of the atom together." He felt that behind this force was a conscious, intelligent mind, which he referred to as *the matrix of all matter*.[1]

It should be noted here that the root of the word *matrix* is the Latin *mater* or *matris*, which means mother, and sometimes, womb.

From a spiritual perspective, this conscious field itself is Mari—the Mother of Form—and the matrix/mind behind it is Mari in the androgynous but birth-giving aspect of the Great Void. What would later become physical form was birthed by the Mother at the moment of the Big Bang. Mari is the force field of energy whose all-pervasive web gives pattern and structure to the universe. The field is like a vessel that holds all material form, containing, connecting and uniting all parts of the universe. By magical workers this matrix is perceived as both Mother—the container that holds Life—and the very Web of Life itself. [2] Because it is an all-encompassing and interwoven field, it is also the bridge that connects our inner realities with the outer realities, the ones beyond our immediate self.

In his book, *The Divine Matrix*, author Gregg Braden[3] suggests that feelings—particularly non-judgmental feelings—are the key to working with this field, this matrix. The field is the conduit that carries feelings–which are really various vibrations and qualities of energy—from one place to another, from one being to another, on the web. When we are filled with feelings they can be broadcasted and radiated outward.

Fertility

Because Mari, the Great Void, is fertile with the possibility of all things, fertility is also a theme of the Sea Temple. When that first fluctuation or "movement within the Void" occurred, life burst forth from her. It follows that for life to continue, there must be fertility—which is the natural capacity to conceive life.

It has been said that we are all made from stardust and when you think about it, it is quite literally true. We tend to think of our lives here on earth as isolated from the faraway stars overhead, but in truth, we are in constant interaction with the energies (and molecules!) of the sun and stars. These interact with the earth in a complex way—over a cycle of larger time spans than we can imagine—one that, over time, helps the planet sustain life. Seen from a human perspective, the cycle looks to be full of ups and downs, proliferations and die-offs. All of these are part of a balancing act that is much too large for us to really comprehend. But it works—we're still here!

Below is an inner journey to help you feel the reality of the ever fertile Great Void of the Universe and your relationship to it: The experience of deep space—the Great Void, the cauldron that seethes with the potentialities of emerging life—and the experience of life and form manifesting from it.

JOURNEY –The Great Void and the Mysteries of Life Manifesting

> ***Preparation:*** *Set up a small altar with a candle in the middle. Seat yourself before it, making sure you are comfortable. Close your eyes and breathe deeply for a while, allowing your body and mind to slow down and be at rest. With every inhalation of breath, breathe in relaxation, and with every exhalation, breathe out the cares and concerns of the day...till you are focused only on the now.... As your mind slows down you find yourself becoming more receptive, and as you read or hear the words below, you find yourself following them easily, and traveling where they lead you.....*

You find you are standing by the sea at sunset, watching the full moon rise. As the moon rises, the last rosy rays of the sun fade from the horizon and the sky fades from azure...to turquoise...to cobalt...and finally to a deep midnight blue.... A few stars appear, undimmed by the light of the full moon.... In particular, you notice Venus...hanging in the sky near the bright lunar sphere.

The moon's light sparkles on the sea and seems to create a bright pathway which stretches from where you stand, to the horizon...and from the horizon...into space. You set foot upon this pathway and begin to walk. Your eyes on the far horizon, you walk on the moonlit path...across the sparkling waves...further and further out....finally stepping out of the sea and into the sky..... You continue to walk, walking upward into the sky... your feet drawn to the moonlight path as if by magnets....

You walk and walk... climbing upward on the moonbeam path... till finally... you are very close to the moon. You pause for a moment, enraptured by its brilliance and beauty... Then you notice that the path does not end at the moon, but diffuses outward, going through, to the sides, and beyond the moon... You continue walking, though now it feels less like walking and more like flowing... And you find that the further you walk or flow into the sky, the more you feel yourself stretching beyond your small earthly self and its limitations, your current persona... and into your larger, eternal divine cosmic self.....

The path is more dimly lit now; no longer a path of moonbeams, it is illuminated only by starlight... Finally even the starlight grows dim...but you find you no longer need it to find your way. You continue to walk, deeper and deeper into ever-darkening vast reaches of space... sure of your way now... because something deep inside you and far beyond your conscious mind remembers, and tugs you onward....

Finally you come to a place of complete utter darkness and stillness. You turn slowly and notice that you are surrounded by this darkness on every side. And then you realize that there is no such thing as "every side," because there is nothing here, nothing at all—no stars, no stardust, and no you..... You are not physical; you are consciousness...... that is all.... And yet it is everything.... And with the "eyes" of this consciousness you are acutely aware of the gigantic dark void in which you seem to exist...yet you are part of it..... You are it... and it is you...... All thinking ceases... all time ceases… and you simply ARE......

Slowly.... you become aware of a movement... it seems to sweep through the dark void… and as it does so, you become aware of yourself as something separate from the all, but still part of it..... You hear a sound—as of a sigh, or a breath slowly exhaled... then slowly inhaled.... You become aware of other things too—other consciousnesses, other potentials, seething all around you.... It is as if the darkness has been ignited—sparked into movement, consciousness, self awareness—by the movement of an invisible dark flame.... You hear the breath again...... Its slow rhythm is like a steady pulse.... You feel more movement, as things are kindled into life all around you.... You feel them moving, shifting, darting off into what has suddenly become different directions.... You put your attention on one of these moving things, and let your awareness follow it out a bit...and as you do so you see it begin to sparkle like a tiny flame.... You follow it further and it begins to flow...to twist and turn... and finally... it seems to condense.... and come into a form....

Suddenly you become aware that you, too, are moving—this outward movement is happening to you, too.... You see that you have become incandescent, and as you move you leave a trail of light where once there had been only darkness.... Your sense of yourself as a separate self grows as you speed through space....

Then suddenly you feel a shift—your movement changes and you are flowing, floating.... You begin to feel as if something delicate and malleable has begun to envelope you, limiting your previous limitless expanse.... This sensation grows as you continue to whirl through space... and you are aware of it happening to the other tiny sparks that flow along beside you as well... and you are aware that the great darkness is now filled with specks of light of many sizes—a veritable cloud of stardust.... But the further you go the more separate you feel from the other sparks and from the dark void source from which you all sprang.... You feel a sense of agitation at this, and turn your attention back to the source......and become aware that it is still there, surrounding and supporting you on every side as you shift and transform.... You are not separate from it, and yet you are—a seeming paradox.... All around you the tiny specks of light are forming into stars, highlighted against the darkness which surrounds you....

All this while you are still moving.... shifting.... continuing to speed through space... while at the same time you feel soft liquid-like layers developing around you... gently surrounding and enclosing you, though you inner spark still grows brightly... You look around and see this is happening to the other sparks as well.... Finally you feel yourself contract again.... and come into a distinct form—that of a large sparkling star.

You feel a sense of immense joy as this happens.… and you are simultaneously aware that the star is made up of not just you, but that the consciousnesses of many of the specks of light have joined to form it.... It is at this point that you become aware of something else—the sound of singing, the sound of many voices raised together in jubilant concert, singing the joy of their beingness.... You realize you are singing too. It is involuntary… it simply emerges from you without effort.... It is the sound, the song, of who you are....

Then suddenly, you and many fiery flowing others find yourselves whirling more rapidly through space.... Once again you find yourself combining with several others… and coming into a new form… a new shape… a new being.... The singing continues but the song is different.... Confused for a moment, you focus your attention on the singing star from which you came.... You see it is not far away, and that you are still connected to it by threads of golden energy...... Reassured, you join the new song with great joy....

Again more changes occur.… The glowing shape you are part of swirls, and begins to condense. You are part of the swirling and condensing but you are also watching it.... You feel something new now... a heaviness that grows as the glowing shape you are part of becomes more dense and finally solidifies into a form.... But although you have density and form, your form is still pliant and malleable.... and as you move, it easily flows, and shifts, expanding and contracting, streaming fluidly along with your movements....

But now you become aware of something else. You are no longer *in* the sky… you are somewhere else and the sky is above you..… and you feel different.... You watch as forks of lighting streak through the sky… followed by crashes of thunder that cause you to vibrate intensely.... You become aware of heat... and then moisture as a great sea rapidly forms...... Everything shifts now, as changes come in very rapid sequence. Land emerges from the sea—a gigantic land mass that, as you watch, begins to split apart into several segments that drift on the sea.... On the land and in the sea, mountains rise… and fall… then rise again… The land masses continue to drift in the sea… sometimes colliding and merging with other land masses… then breaking apart again… only to repeat the sequence.... Steam, smoke and golden streams of fire issue forth from some of the mountains, creating new land within the sea......

The sea rises up and covers some of the land… then recedes.… leaving its firstborn in its wake. You are part of the ocean… yet you are among its firstborn as well.... You ooze… you slither… you crawl.… you swing in trees… you forage for food… you walk…. You seek shelter in caves… you build dwellings among the trees…. You build huts of reed… shelters of branches… dwellings of clay, of stick, and of stone….

Things change again and suddenly you feel like you are flying forward in time… day following night… season following season… over and over and over again… the landscape changing rapidly around you…. Then… this slows… and slows some more…. At length it stops… and you find yourself standing on the sea, walking towards the shore on a path of moonlight…

You reach the shore…. you stand there for a few moments, turning to look back at the path of moonlight….. Then you turn inland and begin to walk. A mist suddenly rises up and swirls around you… you walk through it and find that you emerge into a room in which a candle burns… Slowly… you become aware of yourself…. your body…. your breathing…. aware of *this* life… *this* time… *this* place…. and the candle that burns before you… With your inner vision, you focus on the candle… You take a deep breath and let it out slowly…. You are back….. And when you feel ready you may open your eyes.

The Rhythms of the Tides and the Cycles of Change

Beginning, middle and end.
The Ages,
The Seasons of the Year,
The Seasons of Life,
The Moon's cycles.
The inner tides of our feelings, emotions,
Our physical liquids of blood, lymph, and hormones.
The inner body tides of organ and cellular renewal,
Past, present, and future,
Ancestors and the Bloodline.
We and our descendants,
The inner tides that draw towards birth, death, and rebirth.

With form comes time, and with time comes change. Forms are born; they grow, mature, wane, decay, and then they die. The material that composed the form is then recycled by the universe, and over time becomes part of new forms.

There is an inherent rhythm to this process, a rhythm that is best illustrated by the sea tides, which—governed by the moon—ebb and flow, bringing things in when they flow in to shore, and sweeping things away when they ebb out again. That is the nature of form and time.

Thus, the World of Form, the cycle of life, is about beginning, middle, and end—and then beginning again. All of the physical universe is subject to the laws and rhythms of time, form, and change. That is why that we find not just the sea and earthly tides in the Sea Temple, but also the astrological ages, the solar seasons of the year, the moon's cycles, and the seasons of our own lives. We also find in the Sea Temple our own inner tides of feelings, emotions, and hormonal flow, as well as the flow of blood and other liquids in our body.

Even the organs and tissues of our bodies have their own flowing cycles and rhythms—renewing and regenerating themselves on a cellular level at regular intervals of time.[4]

In addition to being the beautiful "light of the night," the moon, in actuality, is directly connected to form and its cycles of change. By virtue of its gravitational pull it rules the oceanic tides, and the tides of our cellular fluids as well.

The moon is an appropriate image for the Sea Temple because the moon really *is* our mother in a very physical way. If it weren't for the moon and its gravitational pull that helps maintain earth's axial tilt, we would have no seasons, no oceanic tides, and the conditions which permitted the evolution and growth of life would not exist. [5] In this way, the earth and the moon are like a dyadic unit, one that functions, in conjunction with the sun, to create and sustain earthly life.

Here is a short vision journey to experience the moon's and all life's ebb and flow.

JOURNEY - Being with the Moon

> ***Preparation:*** *Set up a small altar with a candle in the middle. Seat yourself before it, making sure you are comfortable. Close your eyes and breathe deeply for a while, allowing your body and mind to slow down and become at rest. With every inhalation of breath, breathe in relaxation, and with every exhalation of breath, breathe out the cares and concerns of the day, till you are focused only on the now.... As your mind slows down you find yourself becoming more receptive, and as you read or hear the words below, you find yourself following them easily, and traveling where they lead you....*

> You are standing on a seashore, watching the tide come in.... The full moon dominates the sky above you. You stand there for a long while, watching the waves flow in and out, and the moon move toward the western horizon, till finally the tide recedes and becomes low once

more.... Suddenly time seems to speed up and you are watching this process more rapidly.... You watch the tide move quickly in and out, again and again—high tide, low tide, neap tide—as the moon travels across the sky from new to full to dark to new again, and the seasons change.... You watch as the tides bring things in—branches, seashells, pebbles, seaweeds, sea foam—then washes them out again as it recedes.....over and over.... You watch as it wears down sea cliffs and rocks......and dissolves them.....

Now time slows down....and as you watch the tides roll in and out, the sun rise and set, and the moon expand and contract, you become aware that your senses and feelings are matching the changing cycles of the moon and tides. You feel your energies and inner being expand and contract with the changing moon. When the moon is full you feel expansive: your energies increase and flow outward...your arms are open and outstretched as if to embrace the world.... As the moon contracts you feel yourself drawing ever more inward... and when it goes dark... you feel fully withdrawn: slow... quiet... thoughtful... reflective... very inward.

Time slows yet again....until it reaches a more normal pace.....and as the waves become smaller and pull back from the shore as the low tide comes in, you feel it is time to leave. You turn and walk away from the shore... and as your footsteps take you away from the sea, you notice a mist has arisen before you.... You step into it and feel the cold moisture swirl around you.... You quicken your pace, and as you walk you find that every footstep brings you more and more into everyday consciousness. The mist thins and you step out of it to find yourself where you began this journey....sitting in a room where a candle burns.... You allow yourself time to settle in, and when you feel ready you may open your eyes.

Emotions – Energy in Motion

It is difficult to precisely define the word *emotion* because there is no precise standard definition for the word. Its root is the Latin *motere*, meaning "to move," with the prefix *e* indicating that the motion is "away from." I like to think of emotions as "energy in motion."

Emotions are physical and mental responses that occur within an entity as a result of some form of input or stimulation, either within the entity or external to it. We react with emotional responses not just to things that happen in the physical world, but to our own thoughts and perceptions. Much of the time these emotional reactions are involuntary, but we can sometimes consciously instigate them, and generally speaking, we can bring them under our control.

We can change our emotions by changing our perceptions, world-view, and intentions. To a certain extent this happens automatically as we grow up—for instance, we learn more and no longer fear the things that frightened us as children.

But in fact, emotions are energetic frequencies which move and affect things. They can build, change, and destroy realities. These frequencies can be set into patterns, known as energy fields. Emotions occur in us as individuals, of course, but also are present in groups of individuals, giving rise to what is known as the "group mind." The power of group minds is such that they can also effect change, but on a much larger scale than individual minds. Emotions are powerful; their ability to rise and fall, move and change, are related to the element of Water, and thus, esoterically, to the tides, waves, and depths of the sea.

As the research of Dr Candace Pert has shown, the mind-body-spirit connection is very real, and has a basis in the body's actual chemistry. The molecules that make up the human body, are held together by electromagnetic and electrochemical forces which bond together to create the form and structure. Dr. Pert's research showed that chemicals called neurotransmitters and neuropeptides act as messengers between cells, carrying emotional energies throughout the body—from cell to cell, organ to organ, system to system, to the brain and back again.

The peptides attach themselves to cell receptor sites, thus changing the cells' electrical setpoint and modulation. As a result of the electrical charges of our cells, we, quite literally, vibrate, and the vibration causes the cells to broadcast our emotional frequencies outward—to others. This is why we are affected by the moods of others, and they are affected by our moods. [6]

Emotional Frequencies are a Form of Non-Verbal Communication

We unconsciously both send and receive these vibrations of emotional frequencies; however, we can make the choice to become more conscious about that fact. When we become conscious about emotional frequencies, we can teach ourselves to not simply "react" to people and situations, or to get caught in the emotional waves of another, but to tune in, check things out, and choose the frequency we wish to broadcast. For instance, slow deep breathing has the effect of calming us down, giving us time to get hold of ourselves. When we calm ourselves this way, our mind stops racing and we are given space to make that choice to handle our emotions in a different way. Mothers often do this instinctively when their children get hurt. While the mother is undoubtedly upset and the injury must be dealt with, mothers often handle things calmly, and with a smile, so that the child will not overreact.

We change our emotions by means both physical and mental. On the mental level we can do this by making a choice about the thoughts on which we choose to keep our minds focused. In addition we can learn to develop an awareness of our emotional state at any given time by doing periodic check-ins with ourselves, especially at times when we feel agitated. This allows us to make the necessary adjustments before we slip deeper into an unwanted and unhelpful emotional state. On the physical level we aid this mental process by changing our locations and surroundings to support the new mental/emotional state we are trying to achieve. This can be something as simple as deep breathing, taking a walk or drive, turning on uplifting music, lighting a candle and some incense, focusing our attention on something beautiful instead of on the inner turmoil.

Please understand that what I'm suggesting is not mere distraction, though that, too, can sometimes be helpful. Nor is it the denying of true feelings. What I'm suggesting is that we learn to map our own emotional landscape for the pitfalls that send us over the edge into energy states that do not help the situation at hand and that may well deplete us, and be prepared to catch ourselves before we tumble into an emotional pit.

Because we can change our emotions, and manage our emotional reactions, we can changes our lives and affect the world around us.

Here is a journey working that I use to help me manage such situations.

JOURNEY - Becoming Serene

> ***Preparation:*** *Set up a small altar with a candle in the middle. Seat yourself before it, making sure you are comfortable. Close your eyes and breathe deeply for a while, allowing your body and mind to slow down and become at rest. With every inhalation of breath, breathe in relaxation, and with every exhalation, breathe out the cares and concerns of the day, till you are focused only on the now.... As your mind slows down you find yourself becoming more receptive, and as you read or hear the words below, you find yourself following them easily, and traveling where they lead you.....*

> You find yourself standing on the seashore at twilight. The moon rides low on the horizon; it is about to set.... You see a campfire on the beach, and walk towards it.... As you approach you see a woman sitting on the sand, tending the fire. She is wearing a dark robe; its hood hides her face from your view. As you come closer she looks up from her task, and you see that she is of a mature age...with wise and compassionate eyes. She smiles at you and gestures for you to come join her by the fire....You sit down beside her and there is silence for a while between the two of you...the only sound is that of the waves and the hiss of the fire...... Finally, she puts her hand on your hand and asks you why you have come.... You tell her that you are very emotional...you say that you need

help calming down so that you may deal with what has upset you. You ask her if she will help you....

Removing her hand from yours, she tells you to lie down upon the sand and you do so. Then she reaches into the leather bag that sits beside her and pulls out a white feather. She begins to hum softly as she raises the feather to the sky. She reaches out to the four directions in turn with the feather and begins to chant. She takes the feather and—ever so slowly—begins to use it as a comb on your auric field, combing it as if she were combing your hair—slowly and gently untangling the knots and smoothing the fibers of your auric field as she goes. You close your eyes as you lay there, feeling the emotions begin to untangle and your thoughts clearing as she proceeds to comb you from head to toe..… As she does this you begin to feel better… your mind slows down… your stress drains away… your strong emotions subside… and a sense of peace begins to wash over you… filling your heart and mind….

At length she stops humming… and you realized she has finished.... You sit up… and see she is smiling at you.... You thank her… and rise to your feet.... Reaching into your pocket you find a gift for her and put it into her hand.... She smiles again as her hand closes over the gift. You bid her farewell...and turning around... walk back across the sand.... After several steps, the scene before you begins to shimmer and shift as a mist rises and envelops you..… You step into the mist and walk a few more steps.... and then the mist slowly dissolves into a view of the room from which you started.... You see your body there, resting comfortably.... You walk to it… settle back into it... and take a deep breath… letting it out slowly..... You are back.… to the here... and the now… and when you feel ready you may open your eyes.

The Power of the Emotion of Love

Love is a very overused word in our society. We "love" everything from our nifty new clothes to our nearest and dearest, from chocolate ice cream, to God.

But I believe that love is something more than a feeling of deep liking or caring. I believe love to be the magnetic power of both attraction and desire—and thus, the very glue that holds the universe together. We are attracted to someone, and we desire to connect in some way with them. That sets up one half of a magnetic flow, that, if it elicits a corresponding flow in the object of our affections, serves to pull the two together. Just as chemical bonding occurs when the electro-magnetic charges of atoms cause them to attract other atoms to themselves to exchange electrons and come into balance by forming ionic or covalent bonds, so too, I think, do the emotional frequencies of attraction and desire exert a similar electro-magnetic effect on life's subtle energetic levels.

The difference is, with regard to humans, our capacity to expand that magnetic attraction into something beyond strictly the electro-chemical arena and bring our higher human capabilities of caring, selflessness, and compassion into the picture.

This is why love is found in the West and in the Sea Temple. At its most basic level, love is the raw power of attraction and bonding. As it expresses on this plane, the human plane, it expresses as desire, attraction, love, caring, empathy, compassion, and all those other fine emotions.

Empathy is the ability to feel into emotional states, and especially the suffering, of another. Compassion is an expansion of consciousness and feeling that encompasses others beyond the self in a way that enables us to identify with them by feeling their pain and emotion—by suffering *with* them. This opens our heart and creates a desire in us to help alleviate their suffering. It is the ability to put oneself truly in the shoes of another. Empathy and compassion often go hand in hand.

Empathy and compassion elicit responses in us. We care; we want to help—to ease the suffering, to make positive changes.

JOURNEY - To Open the Heart

> *Preparation: Set up a small altar with a candle in the middle. Seat yourself before it, making sure you are comfortable. Close your eyes and breathe deeply for a while, allowing your body and mind to slow down and become at rest. With every inhalation of breath, breathe in relaxation, and with every exhalation, breathe out the cares and concerns of the day, till you are focused only on the now.... As your mind slows down you find yourself becoming more receptive, and as you read or hear the words below, you find yourself following them easily, and traveling where they lead you.....*

> Become aware of the Four Directions that surround you—East, South, West, and North. East, place of Air.... South, place of Fire.... West, place of Water.... North, place of Earth... and the Center, place of all beginnings and endings and of the Void that contains all things. Let your awareness of these directions carry your love and respect to them, and the beings that dwell therein.

> With your inner vision see the candle that burns on your altar... As you look upon it, you feel yourself moving through the web of dimensions.... and the flame grows larger and brighter... till it finally coalesces into a column of flame... a pillar of fire....

You find that you are in a large open space and the pillar of flame is in the center. There are many beings present around the flame, in communion with it. This is the inner realm Convocation of Light—an expression of the enlightened collective consciousness of the planet's adepts of wisdom.

You are drawn to the pillar of flame and walk closer to it. This flame is the Hearthfire of the Cosmos, the flame of life and being as it burns in the many worlds.

You gaze into the Hearthfire for a few moments, communing with it....Then you turn and see that there are four arched gateways which lead from the open space and the center flame, going off into the four directions of East, South, West and North. The Eastern gateway is white with gold spirals. The Southern gateway is the many hues of fire, with flames that seem to flicker and spark as you watch. The Western gateway is blue-green, and decorated with many seashells. The Northern gateway is black stone, inset with rocks, crystals, and bones, and although it is black it seems to emanate a soft glow.

Through each of these gateways you can see a temple. You look at each of them in turn but feel drawn to the Western gateway, so you turn your steps in that direction. You step through the gateway and walk into the courtyard of the Sea Temple, and see that it is filled with pools, springs, and fountains of water.... You walk up to the door of the temple and knock on it. The door is opened by a priestess who is clad in a silver-blue gown. She steps out the door, takes your hand and leads you to a path that runs along one side of the temple… The two of you walk along this path; it turns and goes behind the temple… then slopes gently downward toward the sea..…

As you approach the sea you hear the sounds of the pounding surf...but as you get closer you hear other sounds.... They grow louder as you approach what looks to be the edge of a cliff that looks down over the sea.... There is a wooden bench there, and the priestess sits down on the bench and motions for you to do the same. You sit on the bench...inhale the sea air...and close your eyes for a moment.

The priestess turns toward you and puts her hands over your eyes...then, after a moment, removes them. Instantly the sounds you've been hearing grow louder and more distinct. They are the sounds of weeping and wailing…. You open your eyes to see who is weeping...and visions begin to flash before your open eyes. You see scenes of turmoil… war… disease… death… and of people mourning and weeping....

Looking closely at these people you notice that it is you yourself, your immediate family, and your ancestors who are undergoing these disturbing events.... You are startled and upset by this, and suddenly there is great pain in your heart and mind.... Your body, too, feels pain.... you become weak and shaky.... You look at your hands, arms, and legs, and see that you are injured and bleeding.... Your belly feels empty and hurts from the pain of hunger....

You begin to weep.... Your body hurts... your heart feels as if it will break. ... Your wails increase... and your eyes close in sorrow....

After a while you become aware that people have arrived to help you. These helpers treat and bandage your wounds.... They give you food and drink.....they embrace you...and hold you till your tears have stopped.... You feel their sincere love as they care for you......and your pain is assuaged.......

Suddenly you hear more cries and wailing.... The sound strikes at your ears and troubles your mind so that you feel a pang in your heart.... You feel your heart chakra expand and enlarge..... it opens... and you can feel the sorrow of all these people and creatures... and you begin to cry once more.... As you do so the vision changes and you realize that those who helped you earlier have their own crosses and sorrows to bear, their own tragedies.

In sympathy you move toward them and reach out to help..... binding their wounds as they bound yours... giving them food and drink... holding them while they sob..... As you hold them you feel their pain as your auras merge with theirs... and blend into one.... You reach into their aura... and, with great intention... you absorb as much of their pain as you can..... weeping as you do so..... and channel the energy of their pain into the earth.... You continue to do this... until their sobbing slowly ceases... and you can see they are feeling better.... You move back a few inches... and your auras separate.... They speak their thanks to you... and you speak your thanks to them.... They walk away... moving off to join a great throng of people who seem to be walking slowly toward the sea..... .

You sit down on the bench and watch them go.... The priestess beside you has borne silent witness to all of this.... She stands up now and takes your hand, pulling you up, and leads you away from the sea and back up the path to the temple. When you reach the Temple Courtyard she bids you farewell. You turn and walk through the Courtyard... out the gateway... and back toward the Hearthfire Flame in the center of the Convocation.... You pause before it for a moment.... then step into the flame… and feel yourself once again passing through the web of dimensions… returning to this time… this place…. and this room…. You are back…. and when you feel ready you can open your eyes.

The Mother of Destruction and Regeneration

The nature of physical form is inherently temporary, as it progresses through the stages of life toward its inevitable end. All form comes to its end: human lives, planetary lives, even the lives of stars and galaxies will eventually come to their conclusions. But the end is only of that particular form. The life force which ensouls the form lives on and, after spending a while in spirit form, will take on another form—again and again and again.

Death makes way for new life. Not only does it create "space" by removing the old, but the time between lives allows for purification, cleansing, rest, and preparation for the new cycle of life.

Just as the Goddess ferries souls from non-form into form in the life passages we call conception and birth, so too does she ferry souls from form into non-form—from life into death. Catholics have instinctively recognized this through the ages, and call upon her, in the prayer known as the "Hail Mary," *now, and at the hour of our death.* And of course, Isis, Hathor, and many other goddesses also had links with the death realm.

Ancestors and the Blood

Since one of the primary themes of Sea Temple work has to do with blood lines and birth, it is not surprising to find that ancestors can be involved in this work as allies.

Some say that ancestral influence or inheritance comes by way of the blood. This is, of course, a metaphorical way of saying that our DNA comes to us via our parents, who pass on to us some of what they have received from their parents—and so on, through countless generations. All of our cells, including those of our blood, contain our DNA, but are not *merely* DNA.

Our unique self is "made" from the DNA and chromosomes passed to us from our parents, and I believe that we inherit both the physical and etheric contents of these. In this sense, the DNA and chromosomes may be considered to be our "blood" because genetic information from our ancestral lines—often called bloodlines—is passed to us in this way.

But this inheritance is added to by our own input—everything from food to life experiences have their influences on us. This inheritance plus our own input is literally "in our cells," and can be passed on to our children. And what are our organs but organized conglomerations/communities of cells, which carry these memories in their DNA? This is why we can access memory and emotion through organs and cells, which are able to be activated by touch therapies such as acupuncture and acupressure, something which I experienced first hand in my acupressure training many years ago.

All of this falls within the province of the Sea Temple.

There is a curious term often used by magical practitioners with regard to the ancestors. This term is the *redemption of the blood*. What does this mysterious term mean? It means nothing more than the process of working with what the ancestors have given us—physical and emotional—sorting through it, transmuting the toxins, dumping what's unneeded or unhealthy, and choosing to carry forward the beneficial, healthy strains. This is done through thought, emotion, and intention; love for the ancestors and compassion for their faults and failings plays a large role. Quite often, ritual is a good tool to use in this kind of work.

Death Rites

In days past, most cultures had specific death rites. These were to help the soul cross over and also to help those left behind establish a new type of relationship with the deceased, as the deceased had now joined the ranks of the ancestors.

Death rites of some sort are important not just for the departing soul, but for the descendants left to deal with what they have inherited—not just physically, but also psychically, spiritually, mentally, and emotionally—from the deceased. The soul of the deceased might possibly need help making the transition into the otherworlds, and the death rites provided this help. But those left behind often needed emotional closure and ways of sifting through their genetic and etheric inheritance. Death rites could be helpful with this aspect, too—in ways often culture-specifically ritualized. The ability to look, in some way, through these hereditary "karmic bundles" allowed one to make a choice to deal with their contents, both positive (talents and abilities) and negative (disease and defects) in an appropriate way. The rituals of the death rites allowed the previous relationship with the deceased person to be formally ended, and a new relationship formed.

In spiritual workings, ancestors often come forward to be allies for their descendants. Some years ago, while doing work in the Sea Temple as part of a working for a person in need of elemental rebalancing, I found that many of this person's ancestors came forth as priests and priestesses, wishing to be of assistance. It was quite interesting to me to note the way in which they directed the proceedings. They simply took charge and directed me as to what I was to do, which turned out to be to facilitate a rebirth of sorts that took the person through the stages of being implanted in the womb, growing in the uterus, being birthed, cleansed, and finally blessed with waters in a sort of non-religious baptism. The ancestors were expressing great love and caring for this person all during the process, as well as a great deal of pride in him and a desire that he be able to manifest the fullness of the gifts they had given him as a genetic inheritance. As I worked with this I could feel their loving renewing energy flowing through me to him, as it worked to straighten out the inner levels of the problems and blockages.

As I watched this unfold, particularly the washing and blessing parts of it, I was reminded that water has memory and that it holds the emotional and mental patterns that are laid into it by intention. I am sure that the "inner waters" with which the ancestors cleansed and blessed this man were infused with the patterns of their love for him.

JOURNEY - To the Cave of the Ancestors

> *Preparation:* Set up a small altar with a candle in the middle. Seat yourself before it, making sure you are comfortable. Close your eyes and breathe deeply for a while, allowing your body and mind to slow down and become at rest. With every inhalation of breath, breathe in relaxation, and with every exhalation, breathe out the cares and concerns of the day, till you are focused only on the now.... As your mind slows down you find yourself becoming more receptive, and as you read or hear the words below, you find yourself following them easily, and traveling where they lead you....

With your inner vision, see the flame of the candle on your altar.... and as you watch, it grows large and becomes a wall of flame.... You step through the wall of flame and find that you are standing on a broad plain beside a river. Spanning the river is a bridge that seems to be made of light. You can hear the sound of the sea in the distance, and know that you are not far from the shore. As you look beyond the bridge you see the sun slowly sinking in the sky, and realize that you must cross the bridge to get to the seashore and thus to the land of the ancestors, so you begin to walk towards the river.

As you approach the bridge you see it is guarded by two fierce looking angelic beings who stand at the entranceway to the bridge. You stop and stand before them. They look at you; they look *into* you—deeply—for a long time...... Then they stand aside and allow you to cross the bridge of light... As you step onto the ground at the other end of the bridge you notice the sound of the sea is much louder. Daylight is slipping into dusk but the glow of the bridge behind you shows you the way forward. Just beyond the bridge a narrow path stretches out in front of you. You step onto the path and begin walking.... As you walk along the twilight deepens and the soft sound of the wind brings with it the tang of the sea air.

Soon you find yourself in semi-darkness as the light from the bridge is left behind. You walk through a thicket of trees and bushes… and passing them, suddenly there is sand under your feet and you glimpse the sea stretched out before you a short distance away…. There is a dock that extends out into the water and at the end of the dock is a small boat. You can see an island not too far offshore. You walk out to the end of the dock and get on board the boat….. To your surprise the boat begins to move out to sea, and as it does so you become aware of a shadowy presence at the helm. He wears a cloak of midnight blue and from under its hood a shock of white hair protrudes.

Once you are aware of him he turns to look at you, and his eyes, though kind, seem to pierce through you…. At length he turns back to watch the sea and guide the boat, glancing at you from time to time till you realize he is waiting for something. Fumbling in your pocket, you pull out a coin and give it to him. Though it passes quickly from your hand to his you realize it is like no coin you've ever seen before.

As the boat speeds along, you gaze across the water and see that you are approaching land—the large island you'd noted before…. The boatman brings the craft to shore and you disembark…. Without a word he turns the boat toward the sea and moves away.

You turn and begin walking inland…the path leads straight to some low hills or mounds. You come to them and pause before the one that seems to call to you…. You notice a small gateway of rock which seems to lead directly into the mound. You enter the mound and see before you a path which leads downward into the earth. You begin to walk it…following its twisting and turning… as it leads you ever deeper into the darkness of the inner earth…. After a while you reach out with your arms and feel your way along…. Eventually you see a dim light in the distance and hear what sounds like the muttering of many voices…. It is impossible to distinguish a single voice from the sound of the many voices you are hearing. You hurry along now, toward the light, toward the voices…and rounding a bend in the path you come upon the entrance to a large cavern.

Looking in, you see a large group of people seated around a fire. They are talking quietly amongst themselves; this is the muttering sound you heard…. They are clad in garments of animal skins, fur and crude homespun cloth, with spirals, lines and dots tattooed upon their faces, legs and arms. But as you watch them it seems that their appearances shift and change…till it seems they are clad in garments of every place and era of history…. Then they shift again…and once again you see them clad in skins and fur. As you watch this interesting phenomena, you realize that this is the Cave of the Ancestors; your own ancestors are among those who sit around this fire....

The muttering and talking ceases for a moment, and several of those in the circle raise their eyes to look at you.... One of them rises and comes over to greet you, inviting you into the cavern.... You are led to the circle and a place is found for you; your companion sits down beside you.... The others who had looked at you previously now move to spots nearby and sit down. You sit there looking at them and they sit looking at you—relatives that you've never met; family, but from many different eras.

The sound begins again—the muttering and humming. Now that you are close you catch snatches of song and conversation, phrases, inflections of tone, different languages, many dialects and accents.... You sit silently for a while, listening....then the ancestor next to you begins to speak directly to you. You turn toward this person and listen carefully...quickly noting this person's gender, appearance, style of dress, and emotional state.... You listen to what they are saying..... After a time there is a pause...and you sense it is time for you to speak. So you do—asking whatever family questions you might have, asking for advice, asking how to deal with family situations, speaking whatever is in your heart to speak.....

Now...another of the ancestors seated close decides to speak to you....and you listen carefully....After a while the conversation ceases...and you sit with them in a companionable silence...noticing that the muttering and humming has ceased, and that the whole assembly sits quietly, gazing into the fire.... After a while, both of the ancestors seated near you turn toward you. One of them takes your hands; the other puts a hand on your forehead and the other hand on the back of your head. They close their eyes.... and you feel energy streaming from their hands into your head and hands.... They breathe out loudly, then begin a very quiet chant, the words of which you cannot understand.... A few minutes later they end their chant...and putting their hands on your heart, they breathe out loudly once again.... You feel the energy they are transmitting to you...and something seems to wake up in your heart chakra....

You know your time here is drawing to a close. You speak again, conveying your thanks to them—for their lives, which have provided you with the gift of your own life.... You ask if there is anything they wish or need you to do for them, and you listen carefully for their reply....

You gaze again into the fire, and as you do so you find yourself taken in by the sight and sound and warmth of the fire. Its crackling sound seems to be a voice speaking to you.... And within its flickering flames you see the faces of those to whom you have just been speaking.... And into those flickering flames, you now feel your energy being pulled...pulled into the fire...merged with the flames...and with the beings within the flames.... You feel your form being transmuted by the flames... then you feel yourself drifting upwards, as if you were the smoke of this fire.... Upward you drift...upward...and upward still.... You reach the spot where the roof of the cavern should be but it is not there...and you continue to drift upward, as if you were smoke.... And as you drift beyond the cavern, you find yourself drifting toward NOW...toward your normal, everyday consciousness and awareness.... You feel your consciousness shifting...and you feel yourself drift back to your own time.....your own place....your own world.....becoming less ethereal and more solid every moment.... You allow this to happen.....and at length you see that you have returned to a peaceful room, where a candle burns before you.... You are back....You settle in....taking a deep breath...and letting it out again....and when you are ready you open your eyes.

Ourselves as Ancestors: The Blood We Pass On to Future Generations

With the prevalence of blood borne diseases such as AIDS, Hepatitis, and so many others, it seems we are living in a time of "blood issues"—an era of contaminated blood. What does this mean in terms of the West Temple and things evolving into the New Age? The purity of the blood is what allows our survival. We give our "blood"—in the form of the genetic material it holds—to our offspring. At the beginning of pregnancy the embryo is embedded in the endometrium, the moon-blood lining of the uterus. During the pregnancy, the baby, cocooned in the amniotic sea of the uterus, grows and is nourished through the placental blood. The health and vitality of this blood is of great importance.

What is happening to us now with all the pollution we encounter? How do all the substances we take in—medicinally, cosmetically, through food, air, and water—affect our blood, our body, and its cells? How does this effect our DNA, and what is passed to future generations? Never in the history of humankind have we lived with as many external chemical influences as we do now.

The changes now being wrought in the natural world by pollution, genetic engineering and the like are significant to the future and to the "new humanity" that is evolving. What will it, and the new world, be like—with premarin-filled rivers and prozac and steroid filled-children? With super-bugs? With compromised immune systems?

And what about the internal mental-emotional pollution, particularly that of fear?

The answers to these questions are unclear at this point, but I feel it is wise for those of childbearing age to err on the side of caution in the care of the blood—taking care to find the purest food and water available, reducing or eliminating exposure to unnecessary chemicals, and cultivating calmness, serenity, and inner peace.

The journey below can be used to clean, energetically, our blood and that of our children. Please be aware that by "blood" I am referring to the energetic level of the blood, tissues, and DNA. Also be aware this must be reinforced by physical means such as a clean and natural diet, clean water, clean air, and repetition of this journey as seems necessary.

In this journey you will be asked to "carry" the person in need of healing into the Sea Temple. [7] This is done, as with all journeying, by use of your faculties of imagination and vision. Think of the person and see them in your mind's eye. Imagine yourself taking their hand or picking them up to take them with you. It often helps to "shrink" them down to a size that you can easily carry, and bring them with you that way. Imagination, envisioning—these are the keys to work in the inner worlds.

JOURNEY - To Cleanse and Transmute the Blood

Preparation: Set up a small altar with a candle in the middle. Light the candle. Seat yourself before it, making sure you are comfortable. Close your eyes and breathe deeply for a while, allowing your body and mind to slow down and become at rest. With every inhalation of breath, breathe in relaxation, and with every exhalation, breathe out the cares and concerns of the day, till you are focused only on the now.... As your mind slows down you find yourself becoming more receptive, and as you read or hear the words below, you find yourself following them easily, and traveling where they lead you....

Focusing your intention and using your inner vision, locate the person on whom you will be working. Pick them up, or take their hand, and bring them to your altar....

Become aware of the Four Directions that surround you—East, South, West, and North—then return your attention to the candle. As you gaze at this center flame... breathing slowly in and out...you find that you are becoming more relaxed... Calm... and serene... with each breath. When you are completely relaxed and settled... close your eyes and see the candle with your inner vision.... As you look upon it, you feel yourself and the person you are holding moving through the web of dimensions. ... As this happens, the candle flame grows larger... and brighter... till finally... it coalesces into a tall column of flame, a pillar of fire.

You are in a large open space, and the pillar of flame is in the center. There are many beings present around the flame. You feel drawn to the pillar of flame and walk closer to it.... This is the Hearthfire of the Cosmos, the flame of life and being as it burns in the many worlds.

You gaze into the Hearthfire for a few moments, communing wordlessly with it.... Then you turn and observe the four arched gateways that go off into the four directions of East, South, West, and North... You feel drawn to the West, so you move toward the blue-green Western gateway that is decorated with many seashells... and you walk through it into the courtyard of the Sea Temple.

As you look at the pools, springs, and fountains in the courtyard, you feel a strong urge to stop here. You stop for a moment... still holding the person you've brought along. You look around, and then one of the pools of water—fed by a spring—seems to pull you in its direction. You walk to the pool, kneel down, and place the person you've been carrying into it.... Gently you cup the water in your hands and pour it over them... again... and again... As you do so, you begin to pray for them.... Instantly you are aware that you are being overshadowed by a large spirit being.... You feel this spirit's energy move into you and through you and into your hands. You feel it seeing through your eyes... and speaking the prayers with your mouth.... You place your hands upon the person. The spirit begins to work through your hands...you feel the energy pouring out of them and into the person before you. For a long while, this spirit of healing works through you... bathing and soothing the person in the pool.... Then the spirit slowly withdraws....

You feel now that you are to take the person inside the temple. You pick them up and walk to the temple entrance and knock. A priestess opens the door and lets you in.... She leads you across the room to where several priests and priestesses stand. You ask them to help you with the work that needs to be done on this person.... They agree to help. They move into a circle around you...and one of them brings a pad on which to lay the person. You lay the person down on the pad...and join the circle of priests and priestesses.

One by one, priests and priestesses move close to the side of the person till they have surrounded him or her.... The remaining priests and priestesses join hands and move in closer.... The priests and priestesses nearest the person kneel down... and begin to comb the person's aura with their fingers. Their fingers move close to the body... into the body... gently probing, then outward—in and out the fingers weave... over and over... as they dig in... remove unnecessary energies... untangle knots...

smooth and straighten the aura's fibers...... Their fingertips seem almost like sieves, as they sift through blood and tissue, straining out and removing impurities.....

They finish this part... and you notice that they've begun placing things inside the body... specifically, inside the bone marrow.... You can't tell what it is they are placing, but the things are tiny, seed-like, and seem to glow with a rosy-golden light....

Finally... they are finished. They pause for a few moments...... Then they lift their arms upward, seeming to gather in energy from above.... They lower their arms and place their hands upon the person's body... and you see ribbon-like streams of colorful, glowing water flow forth from their fingertips... The ribbons of water are immediately absorbed by the body... and once inside, take on a life of their own... moving throughout the body... flowing into and along the body's blood and lymph channels, and the body's energy meridians... circulating throughout the body......

When they are finished, the priests and priestesses rise and walk away.... One remains, however, and she instructs you to pick up the person and follow her... She leads you through another doorway and into another room.... As soon as the door opens you hear a loud sound of rushing water and see before you the huge seashell filled with water, which continually fountains forth the immensely powerful, rejuvenative waters of the Sea Temple....

The priestess instructs you to place the person in the seashell of water, and you do so.... Then you climb in yourself so that you, too, can experience the revitalization it brings....

After a while, you feel it is time to leave.... You step out of the shell... then turn and pick up the person.... The priestess leads you from the Inner Court... through the chamber of priests and priestesses... and out into the courtyard... She bids you farewell and you thank her and the powers of the Sea Temple for providing their assistance.... You carry the person out of the Gateway... and to the Hearthfire... where you pause for a moment and offer a prayer of thanksgiving...... Then you step through the flames to the other side...... and find yourself moving back through the web of dimensions..... coming back to this time... this world... this place... to a room where a candle burns on an altar.... You take the person back to their body and place them securely within it..... then come back to the altar..... You spend a few moments in quiet meditation..... and when you feel you have completely returned.... you may open your eyes.

In Summary

In the watery world of the Sea Temple, the emotional choice is between love and fear.

At the moment it seems that there is a lot in the naturally occurring cycle of destruction that is fear-inducing to us as humans. Since the natural forces of destruction and disintegration seem well under way on their own, I consider the work of the Sea Temple at this time to be the work of mediating the new forces and energies that are trying to come in, while invoking the Great Mother to protect and care for her children.

It is easy to become overwhelmed with the influences of the destructive forces, and to think that they are the only things that exist. But we must remember that they are only one piece of the tapestry that is being woven. The mediation of the Mother energy is needed. Things need to be preserved, cared for, nurtured, and nourished. The world needs to be *"re-enchanted"*—by art, song, dance, poetry, healings, ritual, and right action. These will counterbalance the destructive forces and lead to an eventual rebalancing. This will bring things into harmony, allowing in the new seeds—because nothing can be successfully conceived and healthfully gestated in conditions of utter chaos and destruction. Therefore, the work of the Sea Temple also includes "Mother Work"—taking care of people and creatures, clearing and cultivating a serene inner landscape, and reestablishing right relationship with our kin—the plants, animals, elementals, faeries, and the natural environment.

In the next chapter we will have a look at more ways of working with the Sea Temple and its inner-realm priest/esshood.

Notes:

1) "Das Wesen der Materie" (The Nature of Matter), speech at Florence, Italy, 1944; from Archiv zur Geschichte der Max-Planck-Gesellschaft, Abt. Va, Rep. 11 Planck, Nr. 1797

2) Deeper consideration of the Web of Life spun by the Goddess takes us into the complicated realm of what is called Sacred Geometry, where we learn about original "roundness" or Sphere from which all other shapes emerge — another version of the primal Cosmic Egg, perhaps?

3) Braden, Gregg, *The Divine Matrix*; Hay House, Inc, Carlsbad, CA, 2007

4) Chopra, Deepak, *Quantum Healing*; Bantam Books, NY, 1989

5) The high lunar tides filled Earth's early oceans with the chemicals necessary for life to evolve under the influence of the Sun's radiation. www.astrosociety.org/edu/publications/tnl/33/moon2.html

6) Pert, Candace, *Molecules of Emotion*; Simon & Schuster, Touchstone Edition, NY, 1999

7) Before you do healing work on someone you must ask their permission. In cases of children or those physically or mentally unable to give permission, ask permission of the person's higher self before proceeding. Listen for an answer—often a feeling of yes or no will come to you. If you don't get an answer proceed with the healing, but be aware that if you seem to run into a lot of obstacles and barriers, that might be the person's higher self refusing permission.

Chapter Eighteen - More Vision Journeys for Sea Temple Work

As beings on this earth we are spirit and substance, our consciousness bridging heaven and earth. As such, we literally do function as bridges between the invisible and visible worlds, bringing things—ideas, energies, spirits—from the spirit world into the physical world of substance, and allowing things from the physical world—ideas, energies, spirits, prayers—to cross back to the spirit world.

We are linked to the Divine Source every instant but we are not always conscious of this. By becoming conscious of it, and working with spirit in a conscious way, we become priests and priestesses—living bridges who consciously mediate the energies from one realm to another in ways directed by the Divine Source itself. This is the Priest/esshood.

The purpose of this book has been to provide you with information and tools to be used in your priest/ess work, and specifically, in your work of bridging the Age of Pisces and the Age of Aquarius. Many years ago when I was talking with friends about this work, one of them referred to it as "midwiving," and I thought that was a very good analogy and understanding of what the work actually is. A midwife assists at birth, providing what help is necessary and continually checking both mother and child to see that both are doing well and that things are progressing as they should. A midwife does not force things, yank the baby out when she's tired of waiting, or assume greater powers than that which her training has provided her. A midwife assists, soothes, encourages and empowers the mother, because the mother is the one doing the work.

So too, as priests, priestesses, bridges, midwives, we assist the Divine Mother in giving birth to the new age by listening to what she needs and trying to smooth and prepare the way, doing what we are guided to do. This job is not limited to what we do in our spiritual work; it extends into everyday life with how we think, live, love, and act—the choices we make.

With that in mind, here are a few more tools for your work as a midwife, a bridge between the worlds and the ages.

Since the basic format of the vision journeys to enter and explore the Sea Temple given throughout these chapters gets you into the temple and connected with some of the beings there, they may be used as jumping off places from which to do further work in the temple.

I hope you find these tools useful.

I. JOURNEYS

Journey — To Meet the Sea Queen

> *Preparation: Set up a small altar with a candle in the middle. Seat yourself before it, making sure you are comfortable. Light your candle. Close your eyes and breathe deeply for a while, allowing your body and mind to slow down and be at rest. With every inhalation of breath, breathe in relaxation, and with every exhalation, breathe out the cares and concerns of the day, till you are focused only on the now.... As your mind slows down you find yourself becoming more receptive, and as you read or hear the words below, you find yourself following them easily, and traveling where they lead you.....*

Be aware of the Directions—the East, place of Air, the South, place of Fire, the West, place of Water, and the North, place of Earth, and the Center, place of all beginnings and endings and of the Void, which contains all things. Let your awareness of these directions carry your love and respect to them, and the beings that dwell therein.

With your inner vision, you see the candle on your altar grow and expand into a wall of flame, and you step through it to the other side, and into the Convocation of Light.

You see the Great Hearthfire that burns brightly in the center and the gateways in each of the directions.... You turn toward the Western Gate, and walk toward it. It is an archway, decorated with many seashells: mother-of-pearl, nautilus, scallop, and spiral shells. When you reach it, you step through it to the other side, and find you are standing on a walkway that runs right along the edge of the sand....and beyond the sand is the Sea.

You spend a few moments here, becoming aware of the great multitude of beings that dwell here—the fish, the sea mammals, the insects, the seabirds, the seaweeds which drift lazily in the tidal waters, and the creatures that dwell in the tidepools. You feel into the sea itself, and feel the great host of life—both visible and invisible—that makes its home there. You look up into the great sea of space, and then towards the western horizon, where the silvery sliver of a crescent moon is about to sink into the western sea, with the first stars of night twinkling faintly around it in the darkening sky.

You walk into the ocean and stand there for a moment, noticing the pull of the tide on your legs and feet, and the feel of the lapping waves. You walk out further.... Then you allow yourself to be carried by the tides, going out further and further still. Finally you dive down into the sea, and swim towards the bottom. Your eyes are open as you swim, and you notice that dolphins and fish are swimming beside you, and seem very curious about you. You swim down and down...and it grows darker and darker, lit only by the phosphorescence of an occasional sea creature, till at length you can barely see around you at all. But still you swim on, going deeper and deeper, down until you reach the ocean floor.

In the dimness you can see that there is an opening on the ocean floor, and you swim into it. You find it is like a tunnel, so you dive down into it, swimming deeper and deeper. As the slant of the tunnel becomes more steep, you find yourself moving more rapidly, being carried down by a cascade of water into a swirling watery vortex. As you fall into this you can no longer see your surroundings, but are sucked downward, swirling down and down till the narrowing vortex suddenly widens out, the water flow decreases and slows, and the remaining water empties itself into a pool within a dimly lit cavern. You flow in with the water and find yourself being dumped into the pool.

The water seems warmer here, and steam rises from the pool you are in. You look around and notice the cave walls, the rocks, the shells, and the many creatures gathered on the rocks around the pool. They seem to be watching you. Colorful seaweeds of many varieties drape around the rocks and creatures in the cave.

You notice a woman sitting on one of the larger rocks in the pool; she is watching you. She, too, is draped with seaweed, her gown seems to be made of it as well. Her skin has the suggestion of scales and iridescence upon it, and her hair seems to glimmer as if reflecting moonlight. Her eyes are like deep pools of blue-green water. This is the Sea Queen, and she is watching you with great curiosity.

She beckons you closer. You stand up in the shallow pool, and move closer to her. She looks upon you with wonder. You look at her… She has a strange, elemental feel to her. She speaks to you… and you listen… You reach into your heart, and pull out a gift for her…… something that represents your humanness. And she reaches into the folds of her seaweed-like gown and produces a gift for you. She speaks....and asks that next time you come to visit, you bring her something from the land as a gift.

You ask the Sea Queen if there is anything you can do to help the sea, and to help in the work of the Sea Temple. She looks into your heart... and then she begins to speak to you. You listen....

She finishes, and you know it is time for you to leave. She points across the cave to an opening in the rock wall, and you walk through it. Immediately you fall into a deep pool of water. You start swimming and see a tunnel going off to one side. You swim into it, finding yourself swimming upward. The tunnel ends and you swim back out into the ocean. You swim up and up through the ocean's dim waters, again noting the creatures who swim around and beside you. You swim towards the surface and there are water currents helping to bear you upward. When you reach the surface you swim to the shore. And finally, reaching the shore, you walk out of the sea and back onto the sand.

You turn back to the sea, and make an offering to the Sea from your heart.

Then you gather driftwood that is lying nearby, and lay a fire on shore. Reaching into yourself, you pull out a bit of your own inner flame, and use this to light the fire. Do this as a love offering to the Sea Mother, the Maris Stella, the Star of the Sea. You watch it as it ignites and blazes up. You know the tide will come and take your fire offering to the Sea Mother..... You spend a moment thinking about the creativity inherent in fire and water.....

You arise now, walk across the sand, and back toward the walkway. As you approach the walkway the scenery fades and changes, and you find yourself stepping back into this room, this place, this time... You spend a few moments settling back into your body and coming back to your normal state of consciousness. You are back. When you feel ready you may open your eyes.

Journey — To the Primal Waters of the Sea Temple

Preparation: Set up a small altar with a candle in the middle. Seat yourself before it, making sure you are comfortable. Close your eyes and breathe deeply for a while, allowing your body and mind to slow down and be at rest. With every inhalation of breath, breathe in relaxation, and with every exhalation, breathe out the cares and concerns of the day, till you are focused only on the now.... As your mind slows down you find yourself becoming more receptive, and as you read or hear the words below, you find yourself following them easily, and traveling where they lead you.....

Be aware of the Directions—the East, place of Air, the South, place of Fire, the West, place of Water, and the North, place of Earth, and the Center, place of all beginnings and endings and of the Void, which contains all things. Let your awareness of these directions carry your love and respect to them, and the beings that dwell therein…

You gaze into the candle flame for a few moments and it turns into a curtain of flame… You step through and find you are standing beside a small campfire on the beach. Nearby is a river, its grassy banks turning to sand as it approaches the sea. The roar of the sea is loud and you can smell salt in the air. You see piles of driftwood, scatterings of seashells, and tangles of seaweed on the sand…

You walk down to the shoreline and stand there, looking out into the twilight sky. The sun is sinking and the moon is rising, and Venus is close by the moon… Standing there, letting your energy flow into the sea, you become aware of its vast powers, and of the Sea Temple that is just under its waves…

You walk out into the surf… and stand for a moment, feeling the waves upon your legs… Then you walk our further, going deeper and deeper till the water comes up to your chest… Suddenly there is a drop off and the water has become much deeper. You dive down into water and swim down and further out, toward the seafloor far below you. You swim and swim, deeper and deeper, the sea creatures all around you… At first the glimmer of the newly risen moon accompanies you, but at length you are too deep for even the moonlight to reach, and your way is lit by the phosphorescent sea creatures who swim beside you…

Finally you come to the sea floor, and notice an opening. You swim into it and find it is a wide tunnel that slants downward, and is lit with a phosphorescent glow. You are greeted by merpeople, who tell you this tunnel leads to the deepest level of the sea temple; they lead you into its depths… Although you are deep in the sea, beneath the ocean floor, it doesn't seem that way now as it is brighter than the ocean depths and you can easily see what's around you as you swim through the halls and corridors of this sunken temple… The merpeople are the priests and priestesses of this temple, and they are leading you deep to its inner sanctum.

You pass through a doorway and into the deepest recess of this temple, the deepest place of the inner court. Before you is a huge seashell filled with water, which fountains forth and rushes over the edge, flowing down the sides of the shell like ribbons of water... As these touch the ground they become small rivers, and flow off in each of the eight directions. This shell-fountain, deep in the heart of the Sea Temple, is the power of the Void as it comes into manifestation as the element of water.

You reach down and touch one of these rivers, placing your hand in it. The sensation is so cooling, refreshing, and invigorating, that you climb up the nearby rocks and jump into the huge shell of water.

The experience is one of pure bliss. As you submerge yourself in the shell-fountain, the rushing sound of the water dies away and you feel as if you have gone back to the womb. You float in silence, still and peaceful, a sense of nourishment and well-being pervading you... Your mind becomes quiet and content... You know that you are IN the water, but you also become aware of the water within you, and feel that the shell-fountain's water is permeating you... as if you were a teabag. The water flows in you, through you, and you begin to lose your boundaries of self, and become one with the water... You float like this for a few minutes...

After a bit you begin to come back to yourself... You feel refreshed, clean, blessed. Your sense of selfhood awakens, and you feel renewed, rejuvenated, purified, reborn. It feels like the first day of the world, when all was possible... These primal waters have not only cleansed you, but have filled you with their energy—their primal energy—and with the power of the Void as it flows into manifestation as the element of water.

You allow yourself to flow over the edge of the shell and down the waterfall into one of the rivers. You step out of the river, full of the watery power of the Void and all it contains by way of purification, renewal, rejuvenation, and new life.

The priestess is waiting for you, and leads you from the inner sanctum. She leads you back through the Sea Temple to the place where you entered. Thanking her, and thanking the powers of the temple, you swim away, and upward to the surface of the ocean...

You emerge from the sea, and walk ashore, dripping. As you reach the shore you give way to an impulse that arises within you. You turn back towards the sea and standing on the tide-line, you stretch out your hands and watch as drops of water flow from them into the ocean... The water that flows from your hands seems lit from within; it glows and shimmers as it falls down in drops and touches the sea. And where it touches the sea, the seawater absorbs it, and begins to sparkle… The sparkle of renewal spreads rapidly through the waters at the sea's edge, and goes beyond, stretching out into the sea, and deep into the sea, till the sea seems to be made of sparkles of liquid light.

You realize that you have carried the primal, raw, and regenerative elemental power of water up from the depths of the Sea Temple, and have blessed the ocean with it. You have carried the primal energy from the depths to the surface, and the power of the inner words to the outer.

You turn and walk onto the sand, once again stretching your hands out to allow the primal healing waters to drip from them onto the sandy ground, and you feel the power of cleansing and regeneration flowing through you and out of you, and into the water, and then into the ground…

As you continue walking, you realize that the water is not just dripping from your hands, but from your hair, and your clothing. All of it drips to the ground, healing, cleansing, renewing as it is absorbed by the thirsty earth as you make your way through the sand to where the campfire burns.

You glance over at the river, then realize you are to bless this river as well. So you walk to the river and extend your hands over it, wringing your wet hair over it and allowing the drops fall into it. Just as had happened with the sea water, the river water begins to sparkle where your drops have touched it. You watch as the sparkling drops spread through the river as it flows toward the sea…

You become aware that there is another current of flow in the river as you see some of the sparkling drops begin flowing upriver and inland.

You continue sprinkling the blessed waters from hands, clothes, and hair as you walk back to the campfire… You pause at the fire's edge and feel the sacred waters within you. They seem to be concentrated in the area of your heart and your womb, but you know that you can summon them forth to flow from your hands whenever you need to. And you will need to, as what has just happened has given you the task of cleansing, blessing, and renewing with the power of the primal waters of the Sea Temple.

The campfire turns into a curtain of flame… and you step into it… You step through to the other side and you find yourself back in the room from which you started this journey—a quiet room in which a candle burns…. Take a deep breath…and allow yourself to come back to your normal waking conscious state.... and when you are ready you may open your eyes.

This gift of water given in this journey may be used in other journeys, but also in ceremonies in your waking world. Simply close your eyes, think about the sacred primal water within you, feel how that feels, then reach with your imagination and inner vision into your womb or heart, scoop out some of the water, and sprinkle it where you feel it is needed for healing and regeneration. In particular, it is good to do it at physical places such as rivers, oceans, and the land - especially damaged and/or ecologically imperiled places.

The journey that follows was given to me in two parts: one part came in a very vivid dream in 1992; the other part came in a sort of "waking dream" in 2011.

Journey – To the Chapel of the Stars

Preparation: Close your eyes and breathe deeply for a while, allowing your body and mind to slow down and be at rest. With every inhalation of breath, breathe in relaxation, and with every exhalation, breathe out the cares and concerns of the day, till you are focused only on the now.... As your mind slows down you find yourself becoming more receptive, and as you read or hear the words below, you find yourself following them easily, and traveling where they lead you....

Become aware now of the Four Directions that surround you—East, South, West, and North—and focus your attention for a moment on each of them in turn.... In your mind's eye, see the candle that burns at the center of your altar.... Focus on its flame.... As you gaze at this flame, you feel your own inner flame, the spark of divinity within you, awaken in response.... You watch as the candle's flame begins to grow. As you continue to breathe slowly and deeply, you watch it growing in size, strength, and brilliance...and you feel your inner flame growing stronger and brighter as well, and your awareness increasing along with it.

With your inner vision, you watch the candle flame increase in size till it becomes a wall of fire, a curtain of flame. You step through the curtain of flame and find yourself in a very different kind of place. You are standing at the edge of a wood, looking into a clearing, in the midst of which sits a small stone building. It is a cold wintery night, and overhead the stars shine brightly in the dark clear sky. The moon has set but the stars are bright and provide illumination. You walk toward the building in the clearing, and as you get closer you can see it is a small chapel, with three wooden stairs that lead up to a porch and a wooden door. You reach the porch, and spend a few moments looking at the carvings on the wooden door.... Then you climb the stairs, push the door open, and enter the chapel, closing the door behind you.

To your surprise, the chapel has no roof ... Starlight gleams down, giving a dim illumination to the interior. You see a floor of roughly cut flagstone, with a spiral carved into one of the larger stones just beyond where you stand. You see a several icons on the chapel walls, several rows of wooden benches that start just beyond the spiral, and at the front of the chapel, a stone altar.

You gaze at the carved spiral on the floor, and it comes to you suddenly that you must walk this spiral. You feel incredulous about this because the spiral is so small, you know your feet will not fit within the measure of its lines. But the impulse to walk it is strong, so you step gingerly onto it, feeling large and clumsy, with your foot just touching the opening of the spiral. As you step into it further, the urge to walk intensifies, so you take another step, then another, and another.... As you walk, you become aware that your consciousness is changing, deepening.... Taking the next step you notice that walking the spiral is not as difficult as you thought it would be. You take another step, wondering if you have grown smaller or the spiral larger. With the next step, you know that it doesn't matter... and that somehow, you are doing what is necessary to do.

You have an awareness, now, of those nameless others who have walked this spiral path before you. In your mind you hear a voice say, "Many have walked this path before you and many will walk it after you." As you continue watching your feet move along the spiraling line, the room around you seems to disappear, and the spiraling path you are walking seems to grow larger. A thought comes to you of the soul's spiraling path into and out of incarnation.... You continue walking, focusing your attention on each step as you take it. With each step, your consciousness expands, and your awareness of your surroundings dissolves... only the path remains, and your feet, treading it.... The spiral grows smaller... tighter... smaller... and tighter, as you spiral inward, step by step....

At length you reach the center of the spiral, and look up. You find that you are within a vast, starry expanse. Directly in front of you the brighter stars seem to form the outline of an oval shape, larger at the bottom than the top. As you gaze at it, noting the dimmer stars twinkling within it, you are aware that "It" is a presence, a feminine presence, and most definitely alive—in fact, pulsating with Life. You realize that She is very lovingly aware of you. Her size and power are awe inspiring; you feel blessing and beneficence radiating from Her. You know that you are in the presence of the Source of all creation. You pause for a few moments to simply BE in the presence of this enormous Being....

As you gaze at her, you notice that there is a particularly bright star gleaming in her center, the area of her heart and womb.... Suddenly it bursts forth brilliantly, shooting out many bright sparks. A large spark shoots toward you, enters you, floods through your being, filling you with its light and enlivening power, and comes to rest in your heart center.... Other sparks shower through the sky and down toward the earth... you sense that they are filling the planet with their divine light, coming to rest in the body of the earth—in the mountains, the plains, the deserts, the rivers, and the oceans... and in all beings, including humans.

As this happens you become aware of a sound... it is the sound of many voices singing a wordless but harmonious melody. The melodious voices stir your soul, open your heart, and expand your being; you feel full of love—love for life, love for all of the wondrous creation, love for all that is.... You spend some time experiencing this....

After a while... you know that it is time for you to return, and that you must set your feet once again on the spiraling path and travel outward, returning back the way you have come.

You pause and give thanks for the love and blessings you have been given. With the star spark glowing within you, you turn, and looking down at your feet, you begin walking clockwise...out of the spiral ... step after step.... As you walk, the path broadens ...you feel your consciousness begin to shift... Beneath your feet you see once again the flagstone floor of the chapel... and the carved lines of the spiral....A few more steps... and you step out of the carved spiral... and become aware once more of the chapel in which you are standing....

As you stand there, you feel that something else is required of you....You walk up the center aisle to the altar... and reaching into yourself, you take a spark from the glowing star spark within your heart. You place it upon the stone altar with a prayer.... The spark blazes up for a moment, then sinks into the stone... becoming one with it....

You feel now that it is time to leave. You turn and walk down the center aisle to the back of the chapel. You step over the threshold, out into the night, closing the wooden door behind you. You walk down the wooden steps and out into the clearing. After a few more steps you pause... looking upward at the sky... feeling the vast consciousness there. The stars twinkle in the dark sky... and as you gaze upon them, your vision shifts, and you see that the stars outline the form of a woman swaddled in a long hooded cloak. Her womb is glowing, and she holds a child in her arms..... As you perceive this image, you feel her presence and her motherly love....

Then your vision shifts again, and although you still feel her presence, you see only a starlit sky.... You begin walking across the clearing, and just past the tree line, you see a fire burning in the distance.... You walk toward the fire, and find that each step you take brings you more and more into your normal waking awareness. You reach the fire, step through the flames, and find that you have come back to this time... this place... and into a room where a candle burns.... You are back.... Settle into your body, and when you feel ready you may open your eyes.

* * *

The following vision journey was one I received one night as I was dozing. It came through unbidden, full force, woke me up, and demanded to be written down immediately and included in this book. So here it is....

Journey — To Meet the Mother Who Births the New Age

Preparation: Set up a small altar with a candle in the middle. Seat yourself before it, making sure you are comfortable. Close your eyes and breathe deeply for a while, allowing your body and mind to slow down and be at rest. With every inhalation of breath, breathe in relaxation, and with every exhalation, breathe out the cares and concerns of the day, till you are focused only on the now.... As your mind slows down you find yourself becoming more receptive, and as you read or hear the words below, you find yourself following them easily, and traveling where they lead you.....

As you sit thinking about what you have read so far in this book, a question arises in your mind, and soon becomes a wish.... You wish to receive more information about how you can be of service to the Goddess and the world in this time of the transition of the ages.

With this wish firmly in your mind, you set up your altar; you do a grounding exercise, and light your candle.

Sit quietly, breathing deeply and slowly.... Allow yourself to calm down and let the cares of the day flow away.... After a few minutes you feel relaxed..... but not completely; there is something that is preventing you from being completely relaxed and is, indeed, making you feel a bit restless. You tune in and feel for what it is. In a few moments you sense that it is an inner call...You are being called to enter the Convocation and meet with the Goddess in each of the Four Temples.

So now... become aware of the Four Directions that surround you—East, South, West, and North—then return your attention to the candle. As you gaze at this center flame, breathing slowly in and out, and with your intention firmly in mind, the restless feeling slips away and you become more relaxed and serene with each breath... When you are completely relaxed and settled, close your eyes, seeing the candle with your inner vision... As you look upon it, you feel yourself moving through the web of dimensions, and the flame you are seeing with your inner vision is growing larger and brighter, till finally it coalesces into a column of flame, a pillar of fire...

You find that you are in a large open space; the pillar of flame is in the center. There are many beings present around the flame. You are drawn toward the flame and walk closer to it. This is the Hearthfire of the Cosmos, the flame of life and being as it burns in the many worlds.

You gaze into the Hearthfire for a few moments, communing with it.... Then you ask that you be given what is necessary for you to serve as priest/ess or midwife of the transition of the Ages.

You turn and notice the four arched gateways which lead from the open space and the center flame, going off into the four directions of East, South, West and North. The Eastern gateway is white with gold spirals. The Southern gateway is of the many hues of fire, with flames that seem to flicker and spark as you watch. The Western gateway is blue-green, and decorated with many seashells. The Northern gateway is black stone, inset with rocks, crystals, and bones, and although it is black it seems to emanate a soft glow. Through each of these gateways you can see a temple. You look at each of them in turn but feel drawn to the Eastern gateway, so turn your steps in that direction. You step through the gateway and walk into the courtyard of the Temple of the East.

A priest and priestess come out to greet you, and they take you into the temple. You pass through the outer rooms and into the innermost part of the temple. As you enter the chamber you see that a great whirlwind spirals up from the ground and down from the heavens in the chamber... You feel its strong pull but stand at a respectful distance and commune with it—the power of Air..... When you are finished you leave... You walk out through the other chambers of the temple... out the temple door... and into the courtyard.

You see a beautiful young woman coming toward you. This is the Goddess of Air—and all that the element of air governs. She approaches you and takes your hand.... She leans close to you.... then surprises you by blowing directly into your mouth. You feel filled with a wild, restless, and very alive energy... it seems to whirl within you, refreshing and enlivening you. After this the young woman turns and walks back into the temple. You watch her go...and then you begin walking toward the gateway.

You step through the gateway and out of the courtyard of the Temple of the East, and walk over to the gateway of the Temple of the South, the Fire Temple. You step over the threshold and into the courtyard and as you do you see a priest and priestess step out of the temple door and walk toward you. They greet you, and take you into the temple. You pass through the outer chambers, and into the inner court of the Temple of Fire.... You see that there is a pit of glowing fire on the floor in this chamber, and as you watch, it rises up.... exploding upward into a volcano that spews out a column of fire.... This fire rises up and touches, then passes through the chamber's ceiling.... It rises into the sky, higher than you can see.... Fiery sparks begin to rain down from above, infusing you with the power of the element of fire....

When this stops, you leave the inner court. You walk through the temple, passing through the other chambers....and you step out into the courtyard. You find a beautiful woman with pale red hair awaiting you there. This is the Goddess of Fire—and all that the element of fire governs. She speaks to you.... then she reaches into her heart and takes out a small tongue of flame. She puts it into your chest, where your heart is. You feel it leap up and join with your own inner flame... revitalizing you. Then she walks back into the temple, and you leave.

You step through the gateway and walk toward the Temple of the West, the Sea Temple, and step over the threshold and into its courtyard. A priest and priestess emerge from the temple and greet you. They take you into the Sea Temple, passing through its outer chambers and into the inner court. Stepping over the threshold into the inner court, you see an enormous seashell filled and overflowing with water; water fountains upward and out of it.... The water splashes you and refreshes you.... The priest and priestess lead you over to the edge of the shell fountain. The priestess picks up a silver cup that sits nearby and, filling it with water from the shell fountain, she speaks a few words in a language you do not understand and pours the water over your head in the manner of a baptism. Instantly you feel cleansed, enlivened, and a sense of exhilarated renewal sweeps through you.

When this feels done you leave this chamber and walk out of the temple and into the courtyard. There is a beautiful woman with silver hair awaiting you. This is the Goddess of the Sea—and all that the element of water governs. She is holding a lovely chalice in her hands. It is filled with water and she puts it to your lips and bids you take a sip.... It tastes a bit salty, but you feel very refreshed from just that one sip. Then she hands the chalice to you and leaves, walking back into the Sea Temple, and you leave.

You walk now toward the Temple of the North, the Earth Temple. A priest and priestess come out to greet you. They take you into the Earth Temple, passing through the other chambers until you come to the inner court. You see that there is an enormous stone in this chamber; it seems to glow from within.... Power is pouring from the stone.... You move towards it and place your hands upon it... You feel its power flowing into you.....filling you, restructuring you... recharging you… and regenerating you… on a very deep level..... When this feels done you move away from the stone. You turn and leave the inner court, and walk out of the temple and into the courtyard. You see a beautiful older woman coming toward you. This is the Goddess of Earth—and all that the element of earth governs. As she comes closer you see that she is holding a stone that is about the size of the palm of your hand.... She stops before you, looks into you deeply, then places the stone into your hand. She blesses you.. and leaves, walking back into the Temple of the North.

With the chalice of water in one hand and the stone in the other, and the fire and air within your body, you now walk out of the courtyard and to the area where the Cosmic Hearthfire burns.... As you stand there you feel an urge to offer these to the hearthfire. You lay the stone as close to the hearthfire's base as you can.... You feel impelled to pour the water over the stone so you tip the chalice and watch as the water flows over and into it.... Then you reach into your heart and take out a tongue of flame and place it on the stone, which begins to glow as it gets hot.... Finally, you lean over the damp but glowing stone and breathe on it. It immediately begins to glow a brilliant red-orange, with streaks of blue and green at its outer edges....

You feel an urge to pick the stone up and place it directly within the Cosmic Hearthfire... so you do this... The hearthfire immediately flares up... growing more brilliant and taller by the moment.... Looking down, you see energy flowing up from the Underworld...you can feel it as it enters the base of the flame pillar and moves upward. At the same time you feel the energy from above flowing down into the flaming pillar. You watch as these energies meet and merge, and burn together as one....

Gradually the flames in the center of the pillar begin to coalesce into the shape of a woman. She stands within the pillar of flame and looks out at you. There is a crown of stars upon her head. Her face is pale, almost white. Her hair is golden and made of flames. The gown which covers her rounded belly is the color of flame... but as you watch you see the gown changing color....turning a dark red that soon gives way to deep brown....then it changes again, lightening gradually into a springlike green.... this green pales into a light yellow...then into white...which turns into pale blue...and then darkens into an azure sky blue. The azure darkening into cobalt blue... then into midnight blue...then into indigo...to magenta...and then into a deep red...and finally, lightening into a flame color again. As you watch, this cycle repeats over and over. The woman's pale skin changes color as well—its pale hue darkening to pink...and then into a light brown...a dark brown...a rich ebony...then lightens again, and this, too, repeats.....

She reaches out from the flame and touches you, and communicates mentally to you... This is the Mother of the New Age, the Sea-Star Goddess who births the Child who is the New Age. She is coming into existence.... and she carries this child within her belly right now. She lets you know that you may come and work with her when you feel so inspired...but also, to listen for her call...and to come to her when she calls you.

Then she fades back into the pillar of flame, which becomes a great roaring flame... and finally settles back down into the steady, serene flame of the Cosmic Hearthfire that it was when you first saw it.

Giving thanks for this experience, you turn to leave... and passing thru the web of dimensions... you feel yourself returning to this time... this place.... You find yourself in a room... where a candle burns before you. ... You bring yourself back to normal waking consciousness... Take a deep breath... and let it out. And when you feel ready you can open your eyes.

* * *

You may use this journey any time you feel called to work with the Aquarian goddess who is now manifesting to give birth to the new age. Listen for her call. She will come to you like a breath on the wind, or a flicker of flame in the dry grass. She is inspiration;

that is her specialty. Listen for her and do as she bids you. There is no instruction booklet for this. You just have to listen....[1]

II. MOVEMENT MEDITATION

Toward the end of my work on this book I was given a dream about a manner of working in the Sea Temple. The words that came to me a few days before the dream were "Receptivity is the Key to working in the Sea Temple." The images in the dream were about receptivity.

Receptivity is the key to the Sea Temple and this moving meditation is one that can allow you to become receptive to, and serve as a vehicle for, the stellar influences that are moving toward and into the planet at this time of the changing of the Ages.

Based on this dream and others I've had over the years, I have created what I call simply a Movement Meditation. It is an advanced grounding/connecting technique that allows you to connect with both heaven and earth, combine the energies in the inner court of your heart, and send them out into the world. It can be done either sitting on the ground or standing. It can be done anytime, but doing it at night outside at Beltane and on Samhain—the Gates of Life and Death—while facing the Galactic Center (if possible) might just be the best times of all.

Star Grounding Movement Meditation

> Close your eyes, and allow yourself to become still and quiet, and your breathing to become slow and regular. Take a deep breath, and as you do, focus on your spine. Feel it as if it were a tree—straight and tall—or an axis that connects you to both upper and lower worlds.
>
> From there, move your attention to your root chakra, then down to your feet. You feel roots beginning to grow from the soles of your feet and from your root chakra. Keep your attention on these roots and as you exhale allow the exhalation to carry your roots down into the Earth. Allow your consciousness to accompany the roots as they go down... You feel them extending down into the earth, passing through layers of soil, rock and sand... going down deeper and deeper... till they come to the center of the earth, the fiery heart of the Earth with its iron crystal core. Anchor your roots here.
>
> As you inhale, feel enlivening energy from Earth's Heart moving into your roots and traveling upward.... Once again, your awareness and attention follow the energies as they flow, ever upward, through the layers of Earth. Allow the energy to flow upward through your roots, and into your body, starting with your feet, then moving into your legs, torso, chest, arms and head.... Feel yourself to be filled with this energy. With

every breath you take, more Earth-heart energy fills your body. And with every exhaled breath, you feel the departure of energies that are no longer useful to you. You feel this energy from your roots as it runs upward through your chakras. Keep your attention on it, and feel the energy spiraling up your chakras from root to crown… You feel it especially in your heart. It fills and stays in your heart, yet also moves upward into your head, out your crown chakra, and spirals upward into the sky.

Feel it, follow it, as it spirals upward, passing through the atmosphere, and going higher.…. The spiraling energy cord passes to and through the moon, to and through the Sun. It spirals beyond the solar system, continuing now into the great vast depths of space… and inward along the curving spiral of the galaxy, toward the very center of the galaxy. Feel the burst of energy as you open to, connect with, and enter into this great Source. Spend some time being with this, feeling, noticing, filling, receiving, communing…..

Now you become aware that the energy has begun to flow downward… flowing to you, through you… spiraling down now on the arm of the galaxy. Your awareness follows this energy, and you feel it flow downward, past the stars, through the Sun, the Moon, toward the Earth… downward… You raise your arms to the sky to receive these energies, cupping your arms to form a chalice with your body as the stem and your roots as the base. The galactic, solar, and lunar energies travel down the cord and into you, into the chalice of your cupped arms and your body, filling you with the golden light of the sun, the silver light of the moon, and the blazing, creative energies of the galactic center… These energies fill you to the brim as they pass through your body, your chakras, and especially your heart. As they pass through your heart chakra, notice how they combine with the vital green Earth energy already there. They travel downward to your feet, pass downward into the earth, traveling down your roots and into the earth's fiery heart.

Receive these energies as long as you are able, allowing them to fill the chalice, while simultaneously the chalice flows, via your body, head, heart, abdomen, legs, feet, roots—down into the earth upon which you stand....

Now move your arms down and turn your palms toward the earth, and feel the energies flow from your palms and into the earth below. Feel the energies flow through your roots into the layers of the earth, and down to the earth's molten fiery heart, and from there into its crystalline core.

You can feel how the energy spirals both upward and downward at the same time. Feel the Sky-Earth energy exchange happening *through* you as you simultaneously feed Earth energy to the Sky, and Sky energy to the Earth. You are a conduit, therefore this energy runs through you, leaving a plentiful residue to feed you as well. You can feel how you are related to both Earth and Sky.

You spend time allowing this to occur..... then allow your consciousness to travel up through your roots and back into your body. Once again you feel yourself, and especially your heart and soul, to be full of the enlivening green-gold energies of earth and sky. You are aware that your body is filled with both earth and sky energies, and that they have been mixed within your heart, the seat of your humanity.

Extend your arms out to the side, holding them out from your body and parallel to the ground, legs slightly apart, so that your body forms a star shape. From the chalice of your loving heart, shower the sky energies into the earth. Then lift your arms to the sky and radiate the earth energies up to the sky. Now extend your arms in front of you and turn to the East, South, West, and North in turn, sending these energies out into the world with your love.

When you are done, move your arms to your sides, and bring yourself back to normal waking consciousness. Give thanks for being allowed to be a priest/ess. And when you are ready you may open your eyes.

III. BALANCE AND PEACE

The changing of the ages has been a rough transition so far and will probably continue to be, so it is good to pray for peace and balance during these times. It is especially good to practice these in our own lives, and to send our prayers for peace and balance for those in power, who are in the positions of making decisions that affect our country and the world. Below is a simple ritual for doing this.

After attuning to the directions, light a candle in the center and focus on it.

Bring yourself into a state of peacefulness, pull in energies of all the elements and directions and let them circulate through you till you feel a sense of inner balance.

Think about the power of love—the force of desire and attraction that holds the world together, that pulls lovers together, that links mother and child—and breathe it into yourself.

Picture the planet in your mind, and then, filled with this sense of peace, love, and balance flowing within you, breathe it outward as you speak these words into the candle flame:

Peace unto heaven and down to the earth;
Peace to this planet, peace to all beings;
Peace to all creatures great and small.
Deep peace I breathe to you all;
Deep peace from the Author of Peace to you.

Peace of the Mother of the World to you.
Peace of the Father of the World to you.
Peace of the Child of Light to you.
Deep peace.

Let there be peace to the stars and the planets,
Let there be peace to the sun and the moon,
Let there be peace to the lands and the seas.
Let there be peace to the elements and directions.
Deep peace.

In the name of the Three who are One, peace...
And in the name of the One Source of all life, peace!
Deep peace!
   —inspired by the Peace Prayer by Fiona Macleod

Notes

1) In vision, I have recently seen this goddess both sitting within the pillar of flame holding her baby and sometimes stepping out of the pillar with the baby. She is here; the new age now begins.....

BIBLIOGRAPHY

A

Apuleius, *The Golden Ass*; William Heineman, London, MCMXV

Armstrong, Herbert A & Garstang, John, *De Dea Syria*, Introduction, p 1; Constable & Co, LTD, London, 1913

Ashcroft Nowicki, Dolores; *The Forgotten Mage*; The Aquarian Press Ltd, Thorson's Publishing Group, 1986

B

Barker, Margaret; *Temple Themes in Christian Worship*; T & T Clark, Int., London & NY

Bayley, Harold; *The Lost Language of Symbolism*; Dover Publications, Inc., NY, 2006; Williams & Norgate, London, 1912

Braden, Gregg; *The Divine Matrix*; Hay House, Inc, Carlsbad, CA, 2007

Breck, John, *The Spirit of Truth*; St Vladimir's Seminary Press, Crestwood, NY, 1991

Budge, E. A. Wallis, *The Gods of the Egyptians*; Gilbert & Rivington, London, 1903

The Holy Bible, King James Version

C

Carmichael, Alexander, *Carmina Gadelica, Volumes 1-5;* Oliver and Boyd, London & Edinburgh, 1928

Cayce, Edgar Evans. *Edgar Cayce on Atlantis*; A.R.E. Inc, Virginia Beach, VA, 1968

Chopra, Deepak, *Quantum Healing*; Bantam Books, NY, 1989

E

Ellis, Peter Berresford; *The Druids*; Wm B Eerdman's Publishing, MI, 1995

F

Fortune, Dion; *The Sea Priestess;* Samuel Weiser, Inc., NY, NY, 1972

G

Geoffrey of Monmouth, *Vita Merlini, & History of the Kings of Britain*; Latin text by Geoffrey of Monmouth, translated by John Jay Parry [1889-1954], University of Illinois, Urbana, IL. 1925

Graves, Robert, The Greek Myths, Volumes 1 & 2; Penguin Books, Canada, 1955

H

Hall, Manly P.; *The Secret Teachings of All Ages;* CV, The Philosophical Research Society, Inc., Los Angeles, CA, 1988

Hartley, Christine, *The Western Mystery Tradition*; The Aquarian Press, Thorsen's Publishing Group, Wellingborough, North Hamptonshire; 1986

BIBLIOGRAPHY

J

Jackson, Nigel A., *Call of the Horned Piper*; Capall Bann Publishing, Freshfields, Chieveley, Berkshire; p 18; 1995

Jenkins, John Major; "The How and Why of the Mayan End Date in 2012 A.D." The Mountain Astrologer, Dec. 1994

____, *Maya Cosmogenesis 2012*; Bear & Company Publishing, Santa Fe, NM, 1998

K

Knight, Gareth; *Practical Guide to Qabalistic Symbolism*; Red Wheel/Weiser LLC, Boston, MA, 2001

L

LePage, Victoria, *Mysteries of the Bride Chamber*; Inner Traditions, Rochester, VT, 2007

M

Macleod, Fiona (William Sharp), *Winged Destiny: Studies in the Spiritual History of the Gael*; Chapman and Hall, Ltd., London, 1904

MacKillop, James, *Oxford Dictionary of Celtic Mythology*; Oxford University Press, 1998

Malory, Sir Thomas, *Le Morte D'Arthur*; New York, University Books, 1961

Markale, Jean, *Cathedral of the Black Madonna: The Druids and the Mysteries of Chartres*; Inner Traditions, Rochester, VT, 1988

McArthur, Margie; *Wisdom of the Elements*; Crossing Press, Freedom, CA, 1998

Mead, G.R.S., *The Wedding Song of Wisdom*, p 52; The Theosophical Publishing Society, London & Benares, 1908

Mini, John; *The Aztec Virgin: The Secret Mystical Tradition of Our Lady of Guadalupe*; Trans-Hyperborean Institute of Science, Sausalito, CA, 2000

P

Patai, Raphael, *Man and Temple in Ancient Jewish Myth and Ritual*; KTAV Publishing House, Inc., NY, 1947

_____, *The Hebrew Goddess*, Avon Books, NY, 1967, 1978

Planke, Max; "Das Wesen der Materie" (The Nature of Matter), speech at Florence, Italy, 1944 (from Archiv zur Geschichte der Max-Planck-Gesellschaft, Abt. Va, Rep. 11 Planck, Nr. 1797)

Pert, Candace, *Molecules of Emotion*; Simon & Schuster, Touchstone Edition, NY, 1999

R

Robinson, James M., *The Nag Hammidi Library*, The Gospel of Thomas; Harper & Row Publishers, 1981

____, *The Nag Hammidi Library*, The Gospel of Philip; Harper & Row Publishers, 1981

S

Spence, Lewis, *Ancient Egyptian Myths and Legends*; George G. Harrap & Co, London, 1915

Starbird, Margaret, *Goddess in the Gospels*; Bear & Company Publishing, Santa Fe, NM, 1998

Stewart, R. J.; *The Prophetic Vision of Merlin*; Arkana, Routledge & Kegan Paul, London, 1986

T

Teubal, Sabina, *Sarah the Priestess: The First Matriarch of Genesis*; Swallow Press, Athens, OH, Chicago, London; 1984

W

Wilde, Lady Jane Francesca, *Ancient Legends, Mystic Charms & Superstitions of Ireland*; Ward & Downey, London, 1887

Wolkstein and Kramer, *Inanna Queen of Heaven and Earth*; Harper & Row Publishers, NY, Cambridge, Philadelphia, San Francisco, London, Mexico City, Sao Paolo, Sydney; 1983

Wikipedia

en.wikipedia.org/wiki/Ogdoad

en.wikipedia.org/wiki/Bata_(goddess)

en.wikipedia.org/wiki/Mehet-weret

en.wikipedia.org/wiki/Neith

en.wikipedia.org/wiki/Morgan_le_Fay

en.wikipedia.org/wiki/Canaan

Websites

astrosociety.org/edu/publications/tnl/33/moon2.html

www.billcasselman.com/place_names_of_the_world/arabic_place_names_one.htm

www.crystalinks.com/isis.html

www.etymonline.com/index.php?term=Gloucester

www.holymary.info/didshesayguadalupe.html

lexicorient.com/e.o/carthage.htm

www.margaretstarbird.net

www.news.ku.edu/1997/97N/AprNews/Apr17/ralston.html

physicsworld.com/cws/article/news/2011/jul/25/was-the-universe-born-spinning

www.sacred-texts.com/neu/grimm/ht11.htm

www.rochester.edu/pr/Review/V60N1/feature5.html

www.thekeep.org/~kunoichi/kunoichi/themestream/mehetweret.html

www.trumpetuniverse.org/universalaxis.html

APPENDICES

Appendix A

The information below is taken from my blog and is about the relationship between Asherah, Wisdom, Shekhinah, the Holy Spirit, and Mary:

www.musingsonthedivine.blogspot.com

The Divine Presence – Ruach HaKodesh, Shekhinah, and the Sabbath Bride

musingsonthedivine.blogspot.com/2012/03/divine-presence-ruach-hakodesh.html

March 29, 2012

According to the Bible, the Presence of God, which was also referred to as the Spirit of God, dwelt with the Hebrew people and manifested itself in several ways over time. The first way noted was as the divine breath, the *Ruach HaKodesh*, which hovered over the waters of the primeval deep, the Tehom, (a word related to and with the same meaning as the name of the primal Babylonian mother goddess Tiamat). The Spirit of God moved over the face of the waters, and creation began.

In the *Book of Exodus* the Presence of God manifested to Moses as the Burning Bush. During the Exodus itself the Spirit of God manifested as a Pillar of Cloud by day and a Pillar of Fire by night—to guide the people along their way.

In the Tabernacle (or *Mishkan*) used for worship during the Exodus, the Divine Presence manifested as a brilliant light which had a burning and sometimes destructive power. Sometimes the Divine Presence would manifest as a cloud above the Tabernacle.

When the Temple was built, the Divine Presence resided in the temple's most sacred precinct, the Holy of Holies, a chamber so sacred that it could only be entered by the High Priest on the High Holy Days of Rosh Hashana as he went in to make the sacrifice of Atonement; this sacrifice absolved the sins of the nation and allowed it to move forward into the new year.

When the Presence manifested in the Holy of Holies, amidst the clouds of fragrant incense, the Presence showed itself as the bright shining "glory" of God; it appeared to the priests and was sometimes evident on their faces after they left the sacred enclosure. Moses was said to have shone with God's glory when the people saw him after he'd come down from the mountain after receiving the Ten Commandments.

In the New Testament stories, the Presence/Spirit of God manifested itself as the dove (symbol of the Goddess in ancient times) that hovered over Jesus during his baptism by John in the Jordan River, as well as the Voice that declared him "beloved son" at that time, the tongues of fire that appeared over the heads of the apostles at the first Pentecost, and the wind that heralded their appearance.

And so it was said that the Presence of God dwelt with the people. The Hebrew word used for this is *shakan*, which means "to dwell with, or dwell within." This is a feminine word—just as *Ruach HaKodesh*, or Holy Spirit, is a feminine gendered word.

This indicates that the Presence of God was seen to be a feminine presence. At first, the goddess Asherah may well have been the Presence that dwelt in the Sanctuary since she was worshipped as Yahweh's consort and bride in Jerusalem's Solomonic Temple for over two-thirds of its time of existence. But in later years, the Spirit of God who dwelt in the Temple began to be referred to as the *Shekhinah*, from the Hebrew *shakan*.

In Israel's darkest hours, such as their defeat at the hands of the Babylonians, the Romans, and finally, the destruction of the Jerusalem temple, it was thought that God's Presence—the Shekhinah—had left them, and that the reason for this was because the people had in some way broken their covenant with God, perhaps by worshipping pagan deities or some other form of disobedience or disrespect. When this happened it was felt that the bonds between the realms of heaven and earth had been torn apart, and that only when these bonds were repaired would the Presence of God, the Shekhinah, return to her people. The 6th century B.C. prophet Ezekiel had visions of both her departure and return.

The 1st century CE destruction of the Jerusalem temple by the Romans was particularly devastating for the people. The Shekhinah's sanctuary, the Holy of Holies, no longer existed. She had no residence, no place to be. The people were dispersed, and felt that the Spirit of God had left them.

The temple's sacred treasures, such as the menorah—the seven-branched golden oil lamp made in the form of a stylized, flowering almond tree—were carried off to Rome. The menorah's blossom-shaped lamps represented God—the Life Force—in the form of Light, while its stem and branches represented the Tree of Life...a worthy representation of both the Divine Spirit's presence and its manifestation in the physical plane.

The defeat of Israel and the temple's destruction resulted in a loss of national identity and a feeling of being deserted by God. This caused many people to flee into exile.

Later, Talmudic tradition began to teach that God's Presence/Spirit, the motherly Shekhinah, had dwelt not only within the Holy of Holies but within the very life of the world itself. She did not desert her children; her love for them was so great that she went into exile with them.

Because there was no longer a temple in which to worship God, the religion centered ever more around observance of the Sabbath (referred to as *Shabbat*), a remembrance of the seventh day of creation—which God had decreed must be a day of rest to commemorate his own rest after six days of creating the world. The Shabbat was considered a sacred and blessed day, a day of delight.

Traditions grew up around Shabbat: blessings recited over the candles to usher in Shabbat, eating of the Challah, chanting the Kiddush blessing over the wine, the sacred duty of married couples' lovemaking, and the chanting of the Havdalah ceremony the next evening as Shabbat ended.

Over time, and unsurprisingly, the sacred occasion of Shabbat became personified as the Shabbat bride or queen. This is remembered every Friday night when the candles are lit by the woman of the house and many Jews welcome in Shabbat by singing or playing a traditional song that refers to the Shabbat as a bride. When Shabbat ends the following evening as the first three stars appear in the sky after sunset (often Venus was among them), the Shabbat queen is bid farewell in the Havdalah ceremony, which involves song, wine, fragrant spices, and a candle which is extinguished in the wine.

One cannot help but think that these ceremonies reflect a dim memory of a time when the Hebrew goddess was known, loved, and regarded as the bride and consort of God the Father...as well as the Queen of Heaven.

* * *

The Bread of Heaven

musingsonthedivine.blogspot.com/2011/09/bread-of-heaven.html

Sept 9, 2011

"Seest thou not what they do in the cities of Judah and in the streets of Jerusalem? The children gather wood, and the fathers kindle the fire, and the women knead their dough, to make cakes to the queen of heaven, and to pour out drink offerings unto other gods, that they may provoke me to anger."

—Jeremiah 7:17–18

But the people defended their worship of her, saying,

"But we will certainly do whatsoever thing goeth forth out of our own mouth, to burn incense unto the queen of heaven, and to pour out drink offerings unto her, as we have done, we, and our fathers, our kings, and our princes, in the cities of Judah, and in the streets of Jerusalem, for then we had plenty of victuals and were well and saw no evil..."

—Jeremiah 44:17

The Temple of Solomon, the first of the Hebrew temples, was designed to be a model of the cosmos. The two most sacred precincts of the temple were called the Holy Place and the Holy of Holies. These two precincts were separated by a special curtain that represented the boundary between the material and immaterial parts of the universe. It was woven of colors that represented the four elements of the natural world—air, fire, water, and earth. The Holy of Holies was the most sacred spot in the whole temple. It represented the timeless, immaterial center of the universe, and was the place where the Presence of God, who was also called the *Shekhinah* and the Holy Spirit of God, dwelt.

The word Shekhinah is from the root *shachan/sakan*, meaning "to dwell within," with the additional implication that the dweller was a royal presence.

The Holy Place contained the sacred objects and implements necessary to the rituals of the temple, including the weekly offering of shewbread, or "Presence Bread" which sat upon a special golden table. The Presence Bread was called the *most holy food*, most holy meaning that it had the ability to *impart* holiness to those who ate it. Twelve loaves of this special bread were baked fresh weekly. They sat on the table for the week, from Sabbath to Sabbath, becoming sanctified with the holiness and Presence of God in the Holy of Holies. On the Sabbath, an invocation of the Presence of God's Holy Spirit into the bread was performed and the holy bread was eaten by the temple priests.

This weekly ritual of the sacred bread was, according to author Margaret Barker, not so much an offering to God as a ritual of thanksgiving to God for the gift of the divine presence.[1] The priests were "consuming" God's spirit, God's presence, and thereby partaking, in some small way, of the nature & divinity of God. This ritual was very like what later became the Catholic celebration of Holy Communion.

The priests performed this weekly ritual because they felt God had commanded it. The bread itself was considered an eternal covenant between the Hebrews and their God; the divine injunction for the priests to eat the Presence Bread was considered an eternal statute.[2] In other words, it was an important and mandatory part of the temple ritual.

> *Wisdom has prepared her meat and mixed her wine;*
> *She has also set her table.*
> *She has sent out her maiden,*
> *And she calls from the highest places of the city,*
> *"Let all who are simple come to my house!"*
> *To those who have no sense she says,*
> *"Come, eat my food and drink the wine I have mixed.*
> *Forsake the foolish and live; go in the way of understanding."*
> — Proverbs 9:2-6

The divine presence that resided in the Holy of Holies, variously termed the Shekhinah, the Ruach HaKodesh or Holy Spirit of God, was a feminine presence. We know this because the words referring to it—Ruach and Shekhinah—are feminine-gendered words. The Divine Presence was also equated with the feminine Biblical figure of Wisdom, God's first creation and his helper in the creation of the rest of the universe.[3]

All of this tells us quite clearly that the Spirit of God, God's very presence in our world, was considered feminine. So the Divine Presence being ritually consumed by the priests of the temple each Sabbath was that of the feminine aspect of the divine,

Wisdom, who, "set out her table" and called in "the simple" who wished to walk in the way of understanding.[4] It was Wisdom, the Goddess who was known in early Hebrew tradition as the Divine Mother Asherah, consort of El, and later, of Yahweh.

It was Asherah, the Divine Mother, who dwelt in the Holy of Holies. It was to the wise Asherah, or her daughter/later self, Anath, that the people condemned by Jeremiah were baking their cakes and offering their incense and libations.

Later, when strict monotheism became the order of the day, Asherah's feminine nature was veiled under the more neutral description of "God's Presence," and "the Spirit of God," or the "Holy Spirit."

In erasing the presence of the feminine aspect of the divine, reformers, re-writers, and later, translators have argued that Wisdom was not a Being but an abstract principle—an aspect of the One God. But evidence that the ancient Hebrew religion did indeed include the presence of the Goddess is found in the form of the Yahweh-Asherah shrines discovered by archaeologists, the countless small female statuettes that have been unearthed, references to the sacred poles known as "asherahs," as well as the constant indignation of the monotheistic reformers and prophets (such as Jeremiah) concerning the people's veneration of the Queen of Heaven.

In the temple, both blood and bread offerings were made. Margaret Barker tells us that the bread offerings were considered the most important.[5] So important, in fact, that the Sabbath bread ritual survived the destruction of the temple and became the challah bread that is blessed and consumed in every Jewish home during the weekly Sabbath meal.

The bread offering also survived as part of the Catholic mass in the form of the Holy Eucharist, or Holy Communion. The word "eucharist" means thanksgiving; the term "holy communion" implies a communing with the divine. In the Mass, just as in the Jerusalem Temple, the bread is offered to God and the Divine Presence of the Holy Spirit is invoked (by use of the Epiclesis prayer).[6][7] The bread is consecrated by the power of the Holy Spirit, infused with the Divine Presence, and then is consumed by the priest as a means of communing with the Divine. He then distributes it to the people so that they, too, may share in this communion with the Divine.

Several passages in the Gospels equate Jesus with Wisdom, and many of the early Christian writings do so as well. And while Jesus was indeed a wise being, it was thus that the feminine aspect of Wisdom became conflated with the masculine figure of Jesus. The temple ritual of the sacred bread became one in which the Divine Presence was consumed as *his* body and blood [8], and the concept of Wisdom as an honored feminine being, as the Divine Presence to whom offerings were made, was lost.

Notes:

(1) Barker, Margaret, *Temple Themes in Christian Worship*; T&T Clark, Int., London & New York; pp 209-210

(2) __ , p 211

(3) — , pp 209-210

(4) Proverbs 9: 2-6

(5) Barker, Margaret, *Temple Themes in Christian Worship*; T&T Clark, Int., London & New York; p 210

(6) The Epiclesis is the invocation, or calling down, of the Holy Spirit to consecrate the bread and wine of the Eucharist.

(7) The Roman church has changed this, but it is still done in many of the Eastern churches.

(8) Technically, the wine represents his blood. Wine was used in certain temple rituals and may have been representative of the covenant between God and his people.

Appendix B - Images of Some of the Goddesses Mentioned in the Book

Babylonian/Sumerian

Inanna

inanna.virtualave.net/inanna.html

www.lost-history.com/apocrypha4.html

Ishtar

www.biblelandpictures.com/gallery/gallery.asp?action=viewimage&categoryid=62&text=&imageid=14217&box=&shownew=

http://www.bible-history.com/ibh/Assyrian+Stone+Reliefs/Stela/Symbol+of+the+Goddess+Ishtar

Egyptian

Bata

ancientegyptonline.co.uk/bat.html

Hathor

www.allposters.com/-sp/Statue-of-the-Egyptian-Goddess-Hathor-Posters_i8275717_.htm

en.wikipedia.org/wiki/Hathor

www.museoegizio.it/pages/goddess_hathor_en.jsp

ancientegyptonline.co.uk/hathor.html

Isis

isisoasis.org/docs/giftshoppages/isis-w-open-wings.htm

www.colorado.edu/classics/clas2610/Graphics/Isis.jpg

Mehet-Weret

www.thekeep.org/~kunoichi/kunoichi/themestream/mehetweret.html#.UMkhYnfhdyM

Nuit/Nut

ancientegyptonline.co.uk/nut.html

Neith

ancientegyptonline.co.uk/neith.html

The Levant

Asherah

tumblr.hrmtc.com/post/32314480698/aenorlemusaeisdead-asherah-circa-750-bc

www.bridgemanart.com/asset/397803/Bronze-Age-2000-600-BC/Figurine-of-Asherah-Canaanite-999-600-BC-clay?

www.britannica.com/EBchecked/media/4304/Asherah-detail-from-an-ivory-box-from-Minat-al-Bayda

Anath

cowofgold.wikispaces.com/Anat

matrifocus.com/SAM03/spotlight.htm

Atargatis

galeri.uludagsozluk.com/r/atargatis-131869/

Other

Tanit

www.lessing-photo.com/dispimg.asp?i=11010746+&cr=1&cl=1/thegoddesshouse.blogspot.com/2011/05/tanit-great-goddess-of-carthage.html

Kybele

www.allposters.com/-sp/Kybele-Mother-Goddess-Sculpture-Found-at-Catalhoyuk-Posters_i8637082_.htm

Hera

www.citelighter.com/history/history/knowledgecards/hera

Our Lady of Pontmain

ourladystears.blogspot.com/2007/11/our-lady-of-hope-part-ii.html

Appendix C - Other Images

Torus

www.optcorp.com/edu/articleDetailEDU.aspx?aid=720

Kabbalistic Tree of Life

www.greatdreams.com/Qabalah/hod.htm

Cube Unfolded

www.math.union.edu/~dpvc/talks/2001-04-28.hrumc/cube-unfolded.html

Hand of Miriam/Fatima

www.etsy.com/listing/108471544/sale-2-pcs-antiqued-sterling-silver

traditionscustoms.com/folk-beliefs/hamsa-your-protection-evil

Appendix D - Upperworld, Middleworld, Underworld

Here is an explanation of the terms Upperworld, Middleworld and Underworld, as given in my book, Faery Healing: the Lore and the Legacy, New Brighton Books, 2003, pp 224-225.

Our world may be looked at from two very basic and complementary perspectives -- the horizontal and the vertical. The horizontal world view encompasses that which is all around us---the circle of the world, the four primary directions of right, left, front back, also referred to as East, West, North, South. The vertical world view brings in the perspectives of Up and Down. All of these perspectives exist relative to us, human beings, standing in an upright position, upon the surface of the earth.

Both of these perspectives are valuable, but it is the vertical one which I wish to focus on at the moment....

The vertical perspective has been recognized and worked with in many spiritual traditions. In Christianity, we find it in the ideas of Heaven, Earth, and Hell. In many of the old pagan traditions, we find it in the form of the concept of the World Tree, whose roots are in the Underworld, whose trunk is in this, the Middle or Surface World, and whose branches and leaves are in the Upperworld.

One can readily see how this perspective easily applies to a standing human being, whose feet touch the ground, and with gravity help, seem to root the body into it; whose body, like a tree trunk stands upright on the land, and whose head, like the treetop, extends into in the air, or upperworld, the brain complex thought processes taking it even higher. This very useful perspective gives us a way of accessing the Three Worlds of Upperworld, Middleworld, and Underworld, just as the horizontal perspective of the Four Directions allows us access into the world of the Elements and Elemental Beings.

The Middleworld (sometimes called Middle Earth) is the spiritual dimension of this everyday world of humans, animals, plants, and stones, while the Upperworld is the realm of the Old Gods, the angelic beings and the star powers. The Underworld, as we have previously emphasized, is the realm of the star powers within the earth, the Dark Goddess and God, and all the rich deep powers of both destruction and creation.

Index

A–
Abyss - 4, 5, 6, 7, 29, 30, 56, 62, 80, 92, 146
Aditi - 4, 5, 22, 31
Ana - 6, 28, 30, 62, 78, 92
Anna - 33, 35, 36, 37, 54, 76-79
Anat/Anath - 40, 41, 46, 48-50, 52-56, 59, 105, 221
Angel/angelic - 2, 3, 49, 58, 66, 75, 76, 79, 81-83, 94, 106, 107, 109, 133, 182, 221
Anu - 6, 24-26, 41, 42, 44, 57, 71, 83, 101
Apparition - 86-91, 93-95, 97, 100, 126, 132
Apuleius - 44, 46
Aries - 64-66, 144, 145
Asherah - 48-58, 84, 100, 107, 109, 112, 122, 124, 212, 213, 216
Atargatis - 46, 55, 56
Athena - 40, 68
Aquarius - 25, 64, 69-71, 114, 115, 117-122, 124, 126, 127, 133, 154, 190
Aquarian - 107, 116, 118-120, 123, 126, 152, 204

B–
Babylonian - 3, 5, 6, 49, 54-56, 58, 59, 93, 103, 130, 132, 212, 213
Binah - 36, 59, 119, 126, 128, 166
Black hole - 7, 60, 63, 71
Black Madonna - 83, 88, 103, 109, 111, 158
Boann - 23-25
Boyne - 23, 24, 26,
Brigid/Brighid - 16, 24-26, 90, 93, 122, 123, 139, 140
Bull - 19, 20, 25, 29, 42, 43, 67, 147

C–
Caduceus - 51, 60, 151
Canaan/Canaanite - 48-50, 52-55, 58, 59, 100, 103, 105, 111, 143, 145, 147
Cancer - 43, 64, 67, 84

Cauldron - 7, 11, 24, 32, 33, 102, 111, 167
Chaos - 2, 4, 6, 42, 43, 127
Chokmah - 36, 37, 59, 126, 128
Christ/Christian - 25, 43, 44, 51, 57, 58, 65, 66, 74, 76, 81, 83, 87, 90, 92, 103, 107, 110, 116, 117, 120, 121, 122, 126, 128, 134, 140, 143, 216, 217, 221
Cow goddess - 16, 19-21, 23-26, 40, 42, 62

D–
Dana/Danu - 6, 16, 26, 28-31, 62, 78, 79, 92
Dark Goddess - 6, 7, 8, 12, 78, 90, 109, 141, 150, 158, 221
Dove - 42, 52, 53, 56, 97, 100, 124, 130, 212

E–
El/Elat - 49, 50, 122
Elohim - 5, 6, 12,

F–
Fortune, Dion - 36, 62, 75, 102, 105, 106, 111, 150
Foundation Stone - 80, 146

G–
Galactic Center - 61, 63, 71, 84, 205, 206
Gemini - 29, 42, 61, 64, 67, 68

H–
Hathor - 21, 38-43, 49, 52-54, 75, 83, 84, 100, 180
Holy Spirit - 12, 36, 52, 57, 58, 76, 99, 100, 111, 120, 128, 212-215, 217
Horus - 21, 38, 39, 41-43, 93, 100, 111

I–
Inanna - 41, 46, 49, 50, 54, 55, 58, 59, 84, 87, 102, 105, 122, 128
Ishtar - 46, 49, 50, 54-56, 58, 59, 103, 105
Isis - 6, 8, 21, 36, 39, 41-46, 49, 50, 52-54, 59, 62,

67, 83, 84, 94, 100, 108, 109, 111, 180

J–
Jenkins, John Major - 70, 71
Jeremiah - 48-50, 54, 58, 214, 216
Jesus - 50, 52, 53, 57, 58, 65, 66, 74, 76, 78,79, 81-83, 86, 91, 94, 96, 99, 100,106-112, 212, 216

K–
Kaaba - 10, 12
Kabbalah - 10, 36
Kybele/Cybele - 9, 34

L–
Lady of the Serpent - 50, 55
Lady of the West - 38, 52
Limitless Light - 1, 2, 7, 11
Leo - 25, 64, 68, 117, 119, 120-122, 124, 125
Libra - 64, 69, 128, 142-144
Lion - 51-53, 55, 56, 68, 120-125

M–
Ma'at - 40, 57
Mary/Mari - 11, 42, 50, 54, 59, 65, 76-84, 86-92,
94, 96-98, 100, 102, 103, 106-112, 122, 123, 126, 127, 143, 158, 166, 167, 180, 212
Mary Magdalene - 43, 59, 94, 106-112
Mayan - 15, 61, 70, 72
Milky Way - 3, 14-16, 21-24, 38, 41, 61, 62, 71, 84, 87
Miriam - 77-79, 102-105, 108, 111, 112
Modron - 34, 35, 37
Morgan, Morgen - 33-37, 62, 63

N–
Nammu - 5, 46, 54, 56
Neith - 4, 38-41, 46, 54, 105
Ningal - 46, 102
Nuit - 4, 16, 39, 67

P–
Patai, Raphael - 49, 50, 51, 58, 104, 111, 145, 147
Pillar - 39, 50, 52, 53, 57, 66, 86, 89, 100, 124, 159,
161, 178, 186, 187, 201, 204, 208, 212
Pisces - 30, 65, 108, 124, 133, 189
Precession - 24, 64, 69, 70, 133

Q–
Queen of Heaven - 48, 49, 54, 55, 58, 59, 76, 82, 83, 214, 216

R–
Rosh Hashana - 143-147, 211, 212, 214
Ruach - 5, 6, 12, 36, 52, 100, 211

S–
Sagittarius - 15, 61, 64, 69
Sarah - 58, 67, 84, 103, 111
Saturn - 117, 118, 127, 149, 152
Sea Temple - 32, 37, 58, 102, 103, 105, 106, 108, 111, 136, 138, 140- 143, 148-152, 154-161, 163, 164, 166, 167, 172, 177, 178, 180, 181, 186-191, 193-196, 202, 203, 205
Scorpio - 25, 61, 64, 69, 117, 118, 142
Shekhinah - 25,57, 78, 100, 111, 112, 127, 145, 212-215
Sirius - 43, 75, 84, 94
Sophia - 36, 57, 100, 99, 109, 111, 112, 120
Star of the Sea - 43, 50, 75, 76, 79, 82, 84 89, 106, 134, 193
Sumerian - 3, 5, 9, 28, 41, 46, 49, 54, 56, 59, 78, 103, 105, 132
Sun Temple - 106, 139, 140

T–
Taurus - 19, 23-25, 29, 42, 43, 61, 64, 67, 117, 118, 145
Tehom - 6, 56, 59, 80, 146, 212
Theotokos - 81, 82, 92
Tiamat - 6, 56, 59, 111

Tiphareth - 126, 128
Torus/toroidal - 7, 10, 60

U–
Understanding (Binah) - 36, 37, 57, 59, 119, 126, 215, 216

V–
Venus - 12, 29, 46, 49, 54-56, 58, 59, 65, 87, 102, 103, 128, 168, 194, 214
Virgo - 64, 68, 69, 71, 79, 84, 115, 119, 121, 124, 128, 142-144
Void - 5, 7, 10, 11, 15, 22, 31, 40, 56, 60, 63, 77, 83, 88, 89, 92, 104, 137, 138, 145, 151, 155, 158, 160, 161, 163, 166-169, 177, 191, 193-195

W–
Wisdom - 1, 5, 7, 9, 23, 31, 34-37, 51, 52, 56-59, 68, 70, 72, 99, 100, 107, 109, 111, 112, 120, 123, 126-128, 152, 159, 178, 212, 215, 216

Y–
Yahweh - 48, 49, 51, 53, 66, 67, 76, 213, 216
Yesod - 36, 126, 128
Yemaya - 6, 16, 44
Yom Kippur - 80, 143-146

www.ingramcontent.com/pod-product-compliance
Lightning Source LLC
Chambersburg PA
CBHW080459110426
42742CB00017B/2940